HGTV Landscape Makeovers

HOME & GARDEN TELEVISION

50 PROJECTS FOR A PICTURE-PERFECT YARD

Meredith Books® Des Moines, Iowa

Table of Contents

TABLE OF CONTENTS

Good landscaping works wonders. It welcomes you home each day and lets

you relax in a yard that is comfortable and private. When guests arrive, it greets your visitors, showing them where to park, walk, and enter. It's beautiful and practical, providing safe passage, lighting the way, and creating convenient access around your home. Good landscaping ensures your yard works, plays, and lives like you do.

Landscaping is more than plopping shrubs along the foundation of the house or planting a few annuals in rows beside a path. The trees and other plants you select and the way you use them can make a big difference for a relatively small investment of time and money. Landscaping gives children (of any age) a fun, imaginative, and secure place to play even in a limited space. Screening ugly views while enhancing lovely views increases your enjoyment of outdoor living. Developing curb appeal increases your property value.

Outdoor living requires rethinking landscape spaces and turning them into extensions of the home, and HGTV is a leader in showing viewers how to do just that. Using hundreds of photographs and the advice and experience of the landscape architects and designers who appear on HGTV, *HGTV Landscape Makeovers* explains how to assess your outdoor needs and to solve problems in your yard through examples from the channel's programs. Many real yards with typical landscaping problems have been made over on HGTV. *HGTV Landscape Makeovers* revisits some of the most popular so that you can see how they have grown. In addition, it brings you detailed, step-by-step, illustrated instructions for building the projects. It proves that it is possible to become landscape smart, to get to the core issues of dull, drab, or challenging spaces, and to create landscapes for real life within a real budget.

The instructions for each project are adaptable to your needs and specifications. Some projects are simple and require only basic skills; others involve strong construction skills, which you may not have. Use this book to spark ideas for projects you can do or as a guideline on those projects for which you need professional assistance. Include the whole family and have fun planning and creating the landscape that suits your site and makes your wishes come alive.

Welcome to *HGTV Landscape Makeovers* and welcome home as you make your vision of an inviting landscape come true.

CURB APPEAL

Community appeal. Make an impact on your entire neighborhood with simple front-yard changes.

PROJECTS

curb
APPEAL

It's that special quality that pleases the eye and gladdens

the heart. It's charm that warmly welcomes family and friends and makes passersby smile. It's curb appeal.

Does your yard have it? If you have to ask, chances are your yard needs an infusion of style. With an eye to detail, your landscaping should guide guests where to park and walk, stop and enter. Delights along the way, such as color, texture, fragrance, and maybe even a little whimsy, make the journey from roadside to welcome mat enjoyable.

A beguiling front yard turns the otherwise mundane daily trips in and out of the driveway or strolls up the sidewalk into pleasurable experiences. An inviting yard pays off for you in other ways too. Anyone who has ever sold a home knows that curbside charm can be the ticket to getting house hunters to take notice. And a yard offering comfort that complements the house increases the property value.

The smallest of changes can have dramatic impact. A new flower bed near the end of the driveway greets guests. Pots of flowers at the door invite them onto the porch. Details including house numbers that are attractive and easy to read from the street, paths that flow where walkers need to go, and lighting that offers security and direction at night create a pleasant atmosphere. In the pages that follow, the landscaping experts at HGTV offer boundless ideas on how to bring curb appeal to your home.

A BROAD WALK WELCOMES VISITORS TO THIS DOOR WITH OPEN ARMS. A SMALL ROCK GARDEN HOLDS A SLOPE IN PLACE AND ELIMINATES THE NEED FOR MOWING IN AN UNSAFE SITUATION.

show off
personal style makes your home a standout

Your house needs curb appeal and you want to take action.

Congratulations! You've taken the first step. Next is deciding whether to hire a landscape designer or landscape architect to draw plans and do the installation or whether you want to do it yourself. If you want to tackle the project, HGTV designers and home and garden books can help you give your house a stamp of individuality by enhancing its curb appeal.

Even if the rooflines, driveway, and garage of your house are identical to the neighbors', what's in front of your home keeps it from being swallowed up in sameness. While the house will always be the dominant feature, landscaping should provide the context or proper setting for the home. The house and yard should work in harmony, causing passersby to take a second look.

Make sure something is going on in your yard in all seasons. Flowering border plants begin blooming in spring. White flowers create night gardens that shimmer in summer moonlight. Shrubbery with red berries or red branches blaze in the fall and stand out against snow. White-barked trees brighten gray winter skies.

Make easy, attractive access your first consideration. Lead the eye to the front entry by framing the doorway with tall shrubs or large pots. If space permits, a chair or bench becomes another invitation to approach. Pots of colorful flowers, a birdbath, or a light post/address post add highlights.

If a courtyard dresses up your front entry, accessories such as colorful pots holding fragrant plants, a birdbath, a fountain, or a toad house tucked under ferns add touches of charm or humor.

By using similar hues and textures in hardscape elements such as walls, edging, sidewalks, paths, driveway, and house trim, you can blend these elements with one another as watercolors in a painting. Use plants to blend the vertical lines of the house with the horizontal lines of the ground. A grassy green area soothes the eye in summer.

Create a pathway from curb to porch or door using materials such as stepping-stones, concrete, flagstone, gravel, or brick. How much space you have determines whether you choose a winding path or a straight one. If you opt for the latter, soften sharp edges with a curvaceous border.

Color draws attention, so use it where it pulls the eye away from areas you want to de-emphasize, such as garage doors. Although many landscapers think that garden art is best used in the backyard, others note that a well-placed garden bench or a birdhouse atop a pole creates a focal point or bright spot in the front yard.

Have fun creating an appealing space from the curb to the door for yourself and your guests.

SOFTEN THE IMPACT of vertical walls with tall ornamental grasses or lacy shrubs, suggests landscape architect Louise Leff.

THE ROAR OF TRAFFIC FADES AWAY WITH THE RELAXING SOUND OF WATER (RIGHT).

LIGHTS ALONG A FRONT WALK (CENTER RIGHT) ENSURE SAFE PASSAGE FOR GUESTS.

LARGE HOUSE NUMBERS (FAR RIGHT) ADD TO THE DESIGN AS THEY GUIDE VISITORS TO YOUR HOME. THESE ARE STENCILED NUMBERS PAINTED ON A TILE.

PLAIN TO PIZZAZZ

■ **Cookie-cutter or custom design,** every house can be inviting and individual with a well-thought-out landscape plan that shows personality while creating harmonious year-round appeal.

■ **Thorny issue:** Some shrubs, such as barberries, have lovely color and might be tempting for brightening an entry, but scratchy thorns say "stay away." Use them under windows instead, as attractive security features.

■ **Create visual impact** with a trellised vine that surrounds and draws attention to an otherwise bland doorway. Select a flowery vine for accent color or simple greenery to cool a sunny entry.

A SUBURBAN RANCH HOUSE (ABOVE) GAINS STYLISH APPEAL FROM A UNIFIED DESIGN, WHICH COMES FROM THE USE OF SIMILAR-LOOKING MATERIALS IN A FOUNTAIN, URNS, AND STATUARY. A WINDING PATH DEFINES THE ENTRY. SCULPTURAL SPIRAL CONIFERS ADD CHARM.

set the scene with plants

Plantings have a big impact on the appearance of your home. The placement of trees and shrubs works to frame a house, enhancing it just as the right frame enhances a painting. Plantings tie the house to the ground, incorporating it into its environment.

Trees provide scale and proportion. A tall, wide tree behind a low house provides a leafy backdrop. Columnar trees against a tall house draw the eye upward. Clustering three smaller trees on one side of the house with one large tree on the opposite side achieves asymmetrical balance. Accent trees and shrubs soften sharp edges, hide unattractive spots such as utility boxes, and serve to welcome visitors by gently directing them.

Shrubs. The right shrub to spruce up a spot might be a conifer such as a pine, fir, or hemlock. Privet is ideal for creating private space. When setting the stage, think about how you use the area and what will enhance function.

Shrub beds, traditional foundation plantings, add visual impact and hide ugly areas in side yards and along fences and driveways.

Evergreens provide year-round privacy, block wind, and give your landscape life even in the dead of winter. Some deciduous shrubs display razzle-dazzle blossoms in season. Winter appeal comes from shrubs with colorful bare branches, berries, or interesting shapes.

Figuring out what shape a shrub bed will take and how many shrubs you'll need requires planning. Using chalk, string, a garden hose, or spray paint, form the shape of your bed directly on the grass. Curving beds and staggered shrubs create visual interest and look more natural than straight lines. Balance comes from keeping the size of beds in scale with the house and yard. Plant tall shrubs in the back row; medium-size shrubs, about half the size of the tall ones, next; and low-growing shrubs in front.

Know what size mature plants will be and measure the space, allowing room for growth. Planting to the space saves money over time. Pulling out a mass of overgrown shrubs five to ten years down the road can be costly.

Trees. If shrubs are the supporting chorus line of the garden, then the tree is the principal dancer. The right tree—or combination of trees—in the right place can be the star of the show.

Researching a tree is important. Believe the nursery labels when they say how large a tree grows. A basic planting formula is to divide the mature height by 2 to get the planting distance from a house, garage, walkway, or driveway. Plant a tree that grows 30 feet tall, such as a mulberry or magnolia, at least 15 feet away, or a smaller tree such as a Japanese maple at least 10 feet away.

Tall trees that spread provide ample shade. Narrow, columnar, and oval trees are good for framing a house or entryway. Planted close together, they provide a green screen. Open, lacy trees create dappled light and

delightful shadows, while weeping trees provide a measure of romance as well as shade.

A specimen or accent tree—with showy flowers or luscious leaves or a gnarled trunk—becomes a focal point. Plant this showpiece where it calls attention to the front of the house, or place it where a fence or row of evergreens provides a background.

Equally important to form when selecting trees and shrubs for curb appeal is adaptability. Always select plants that will grow in the conditions your yard offers.

FENCING MAKES A TRADITIONAL BACKDROP FOR A COTTAGE GARDEN. WHITE PICKETS ECHO THE POINT OF THE ROOFLINE. AN ARBOR ANCHORS ONE SIDE OF THE HOUSE AND BALANCES A TREE ON THE OPPOSITE END.

FIND YOUR FAVORITES

Be nosy. When styles of landscaping or specific plant material in neighboring yards speak to you, ask about them. The owners may even offer you a cutting. Keeping an eye on what's growing nearby also clues you in on what plants thrive in local growing conditions.

Ask for help. Snap photos of your yard and make lists of your existing plants and trees. Look through gardening books and magazines and take note of the pictures of plants you like. Take these to your favorite nursery. If you are unsure of the names of your plants, take samples for identification. You need to know if what you have and what you want will be the right fit for your space, style, and budget.

SHADE TREES IN THE BACKGROUND AND SMALL ORNAMENTAL TREES AT THE CORNERS COMBINE TO FRAME AND GROUND A HOME (LEFT).

AN ACCENT TREE (BELOW LEFT) ECHOES THE SHAPE OF A WALK, DRAWING THE EYE TO THE ENTRY.

A MIX OF PLANT MATERIALS AT THE FOUNDATION (BELOW) CREATES INTEREST.

finding your landscape style

Stylish allure. So, how do you start achieving that curb appeal you desire? Go across the street and take a long look back, as if seeing your home for the first time. Ask yourself what you like, and what you don't. Check whether you see the front door and windows. Does the place look overgrown or scraggly, barren or blighted, or just plain neglected? Not to worry. With some planning, planting, elbow grease, and sweat equity, you'll have a place that gets attention for all the right reasons.

To make your task easier, measure the space. Note what kind of soil you have and how much sun and shade the yard gets at various times of day. These facts are important in determining plant selection and placement.

Consider how you use the area, and think about the time and energy requirements for replanting annuals, fertilizing, and pruning. Your front yard may need tuning up more than a major overhaul. Maybe some serious pruning of existing plants and the addition of well-selected, well-placed flowers will suffice.

Curb appeal relies more on personal style than hard-and-fast rules, but HGTV landscape designers offer suggestions for pleasing looks.

Foundation plantings do more than hide the base of the house. They define space and create a format for blending and unifying a landscape, making sure design elements create appealing views from inside the home as well as from outside.

Knowing how tall shrubbery will grow or how to prune a bush to control growth are important when plants are in front of windows.

Consider whether you want to diffuse or increase indoor light and whether you want to disguise or enhance a view when selecting window plantings. Remember to leave space between the plants and the house so you can get to the windows to wash them, or to reach sprinkler faucets.

Planting tips. Put colorful annuals about 18 inches in front of shrubs, or place the flowers in pots against darker foliage. Remove plants that aren't quite right for a space or design concept. Transplant them to another spot, or recycle them as gifts to interested friends or neighbors.

Selecting trees. Consider designing your yard around a specimen tree. Or plant a tree in a bed and surround it with shade-loving ground cover. Offset a protruding garage by planting a tree on the opposite end of the house.

Trees provide shade, balance, color, texture, and interest, and choosing the right tree is essential. Arm yourself with tree knowledge. Before buying, learn how the plant will perform not only today but also 10 to 20 years from now. Ask whether the tree's shape will change as it matures. Other important points to know are whether

EYE-POPPING COLOR MAKES THIS DOOR (LEFT) A CLEAR DESTINATION FROM THE FLAGSTONE PATH, AS A FLOWERY ARCH SOFTENS BRICKWORK AND INVITINGLY PERFUMES THE AIR.

WHIMSICAL TOUCHES SUCH AS RECYCLING TROWELS INTO GATE HANDLES (ABOVE) WELCOME VISITORS WITH A FUN STYLE.

the tree will protect the house and yard from summer sun or winter winds for decades or whether it will one day tower over your house, sweep its branches into the neighbor's yard, break up the concrete driveway, or drip sticky sap.

Avoid planting trees that shed fruit, seeds, twigs, and other debris close to sidewalks, driveways, and porches to prevent greeting guests with a mess at the door.

Select trees whose height and canopy width camouflage expanses of roofing but don't intrude on neighbors. If you're using trees to block views or provide privacy, remember that when deciduous trees lose their leaves in the fall they may leave areas exposed in winter.

Check out more ideas from HGTV.com
Find advice on achieving curb appeal at
- www.hgtv.com/landscapemakeoversbook

A JOYOUS PALETTE BLENDS HOUSE AND YARD INTO IMPRESSIONIST ART (ABOVE). THE COLOR IN THE FLOWER BORDER MELDS WITH THE WOOD FRAMING AND TONES OF THE BRICK. LARGE CONTAINERS TAKE THEIR HUE CUE FROM THE DOOR.

THE UPRIGHT FORM OF THIS CLASSIC IVY TOPIARY (LEFT) DRAWS ATTENTION.

front-yard makeover
a blank slate becomes a showpiece

Turning this plain front yard into a well-landscaped welcome center shows how the basic design guidelines in this chapter come together to solve problems and create landscapes that are special.

- Gentle curves define space.
- Small trees frame the house and create privacy.
- Functional details such as paths add easy access.
- Open areas can take accents.
- Plants or hardscape mask problem spots such as pipes.
- Repetition of color, plants, or materials unify design.

Duncan McIntosh, the landscape designer for this makeover, believes design guidelines provide basic rules you can lean on to boost your confidence. "Just remember," he advises, "they're only guidelines, not rules that are carved in stone."

The problems. This big yard had much the same problem as many home landscapes: straight lines, poor access, and nothing to attract attention

or welcome guests. Ugly sprinkler valves were the first thing visitors saw when approaching the front door.

The ranch house was attractive but in need of plantings to visually frame it. An existing corner bed where the driveway and street meet softened the rectangular lines but was too small for the scale of the yard. The expanse of grass had one spot that the home-owner had torn up to fix a leaky pipe.

The plan. Renovations begin with a blank slate, much like a yard in a new housing development. Stripping away nearly half the grass allows space for adding curving gravel paths to improve pedestrian access, plus larger decorative planting beds. (Using a sod cutter to remove turf from planting areas provides sod to repair damaged spots in the lawn.)

Pulling up spent plants from the existing beds makes way for large focal points, such as a water feature, and allows for discovering small spots for accent points. Gentle, curving lines expand the beds while adding a sense of cohesive flow and movement.

A larger flower bed along the driveway frames the lawn. The

LUSTROUS PLANTING POTS ON SHELVES (ABOVE) MASK UGLY IRRIGATION VALVES.

PEOPLE USED TO CUT ACROSS THE GRASS TO REACH THE FRONT DOOR. NOW, A CURVY GRAVEL PATH FROM THE STREET AND ONE FROM THE DRIVE, WHICH RUNS THROUGH A GARDEN, PROVIDE CONVENIENT ACCESS (OPPOSITE).

PLAIN AND SIMPLE LINES OF A RANCH HOUSE (ABOVE) CALL FOR A YARD WITH VISUAL IMPACT AND A WELCOMING APPROACH.

TIPS FOR STREET-SIDE PLANTINGS

Put safety first. Have utility companies mark buried utilities before you dig. Check mature heights of plants to be sure they stay below 2 or 3 feet tall, so the view is clear when you're backing out of the drive.

Amend the soil with compost or other organic materials. Soil near the street is often infertile and compacted.

Choose sturdy perennials and shrubs that can take abuse, standing up to heat reflected from pavement, foot traffic, and car exhaust. In areas with snowy winters, select plants that also are salt-tolerant, such as spirea.

To help plants that are less salt-tolerant, flood the soil with water each spring to flush deicing chemicals. Here are a few sturdy plants to consider:

- **Bush cinquefoil** (*Potentilla fruticosa*) Zones 2–6
- **'Crimson Pygmy' barberry** (*Berberis thunbergii*) Zones 4–8
- **'Elijah Blue' fescue** (*Festuca glauca*) Zones 4–8
- **'Golden Baby' goldenrod** (*Solidago* spp.) Zones 3–9
- **Yarrow** (*Achillea millefolium*) Zones 3–10

fountain, in circles of gravel and cobblestone, aligns with the front window and new path. Small trees on each side of the yard frame the house and create privacy. Twin columns with planters (see how-to on opposite page) mask sprinkler valves but allow easy access.

The appeal. Our makeover provides a welcoming view from the street with an inviting path leading visitors to the front door. The pink gum trees (*Eucalyptus sideroxylon*), hardy in Zones 8–11, planted on both sides of the yard, visually frame the ranch-style house and help create privacy.

In the streetside bed, lavender cotton (*Santolina chamaecyparissus*) greets visitors. An attractive, fragrant evergreen woody perennial hardy in Zones 6–9, it grows only 1 to 2 feet tall and doesn't block the view from the driveway. It stands up to the withering conditions encountered at curbside. For colder climates, consider calendula.

An attractive fountain in front of the large living room window provides an enjoyable focal point viewed from inside or out. Circles of gravel and cobblestone surrounding the fountain help make an even bigger impact by breaking up space, emphasizing shape,

and adding texture. An outer circle planted with horsetail (*Equisetum hyemale*) adds color and dimension. Water-loving horsetail, hardy throughout the United States, makes a natural companion for water features, but its invasive habit needs reining in.

Repeating material and color by coordinating rock elements in the planting bed, the columns made from concrete pavers, the stones around the fountain, and the gravel for the paths ties the landscape together.

Check out more ideas from HGTV.com

For a Top-10 list of curb appeal projects, see

■ www.HGTV.com/landscapemakeoversbook

A CIRCULAR FOUNTAIN WITHIN A ROUND GRAVEL BED (LEFT) ADDS DIMENSION AND TEXTURE.

TREES IN A NEW ISLAND BED OBSCURE VIEWS OF THE NEIGHBORS. THE YARD IS NOW A WELCOMING OASIS WITH GREAT CURB APPEAL (BELOW).

make a plant shelf

tools & materials
SPECIAL TOOLS: Spade, hand tamper for compacting rock, power drill with ½-inch masonry bit, mallet, level, eye protection.

- Gravel
- 8 – 24×24×2-inch concrete pavers for each column
- Mortar
- Rebar, ½-inch diameter
- 2×6 boards for shelves

A simple column of pavers supports a plant shelf and masks sprinkler valves at the front door while allowing easy access to the valves. Substitute flagstone, brick, or broken pieces of concrete for the concrete pavers, if desired.

1 | dig a hole 24 inches square by 6 inches deep. Pour in a 2-inch layer of gravel as a mortar base.

2 | compact the gravel with a tamper until it is level and firm.

3 | drill a hole in the center of each paver to fit ½-inch rebar.

4 | mix the mortar according to package directions. Then spread a 2-inch layer over the gravel. Set a paver on top of the mortar.

5 | center rebar in the paver hole, pounding the steel rod through the mortar into the ground at least 10 inches.

6 | stack pavers by threading them onto the rebar rod, adding mortar between the pavers. Turn each paver 45 degrees to create a star pattern (shown) or, for a more formal look, line the pavers up straight.

Once the stack is at the desired height, drive down the remainder of the rebar rod flush with the top paver. Build a second column to match. Top the columns with boards for use as planter shelves.

BEFORE

AFTER

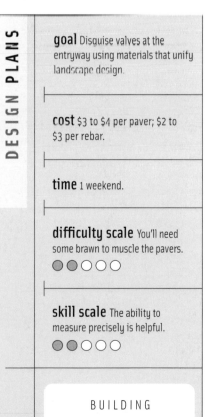

DESIGN PLANS

goal Disguise valves at the entryway using materials that unify landscape design.

cost $3 to $4 per paver; $2 to $3 per rebar.

time 1 weekend.

difficulty scale You'll need some brawn to muscle the pavers.
●●○○○

skill scale The ability to measure precisely is helpful.
●●○○○

BUILDING

cottage garden charm
an intimate arbor offers seclusion in a garden that delights the senses

In most neighborhoods, another green grass lawn is the landscaping equivalent of a ditto mark. But a cottage garden—that's an exclamation point!

This hillside front yard greets guests with an informal cottage garden that creates a natural, relaxed mood. A succession of bountiful blooms brightens the yard with an ever-changing kaleidoscope of color. Fragrant climbing roses will one day cover the lattice trellis, scenting the air while providing privacy for the seating area and a perfect backdrop for this garden.

Update tradition. Although this yard is hidden from the street by a fence and steep slope, the homeowners wanted a garden with

A COLORFUL COTTAGE GARDEN (RIGHT) MAKES CLIMBING THE STONE STEPS TO THE GATE A PLEASURE.

A GLORIOUS COTTAGE GARDEN (FAR RIGHT) COMPLETE WITH A LATTICE ARBOR AND BENCH, IS INVITING AND TIES IN PERFECTLY WITH THE STYLE OF THE HOUSE.

MAINTAINING YOUR COTTAGE GARDEN

Part of the charm of a cottage garden is that it looks natural, as if it maintains itself. Of course, there's more to it than that. To keep your cottage garden from turning into a jungle, maintain mulched paths throughout the garden. Keep an eye out for volunteer tree seedlings, pulling them while they're still small. Allow plants to intermingle, but be ruthless in removing those that spread beyond their bounds. To prolong blooming, keep pruning scissors handy to clip spent flowers.

Cut perennials back to basal foliage when their foliage is no longer attractive. Cut back plants with disease-prone foliage, such as asters and lilies, in autumn. Wait until spring to trim coneflowers, ornamental grasses, tall sedums, and other plants that provide winter interest.

BEFORE

STARTING OVER IS THE WAY TO GO IN AN OVERGROWN YARD (ABOVE) THAT MAKES EVEN THE HOMEOWNERS WANT TO DASH PAST.

cottage garden charm
(continued)

walk-by appeal for guests as they approach the front door.

This garden also helps control water runoff from steep slopes, retaining soil and trapping water before it reaches the house. Front-yard gardens that are more visible create appealing drive-by views and become good conversation starters for meeting the neighbors.

Sensual structure. Cottage gardens seem unstructured, but subtle design guidelines produce a prettier picture.

relax and enjoy the sights and sounds of your peaceful sanctuary?

The family behind this project chose a special spot under a majestic old tree where a timeworn wooden bench sat on a flagstone base. Their plan was to replace the bench with an attractive seating unit that provides intimate seclusion. The result of their labors—complete with lattice walls and trellis top—became another element of a striking setting.

A RUSTIC BENCH under a simple arbor becomes an inviting seating area off the beaten path. Perennials such as cape daisies have a well-behaved wildflower effect as they provide color and interest throughout the year.

In creating your own charming version, begin by laying out winding paths of bark or other soft mulching material for pleasant strolls and easy maintenance of flower beds. A path guides the eye and the feet toward a focal point, such as a seating area or colorful front door.

Plant small trees, flowering shrubs, and ornamental grasses to provide "bones," or structure, even in winter. Sturdy, bushy perennials such as peonies and Russian sage help add dimension to your cottage garden.

Mix random drifts of perennials with blooming shrubs, reseeding annuals, scrambling vines, and fragrant herbs and shrubs such as lilacs and hardy shrub roses that entice the senses.

Build an arbor. You've invested lots of time and effort (not to mention money) in a beautifully landscaped entry garden. It's a cheery welcome to all who enter, and it frames your home with elegance and charm. Why not also reward yourself with a cozy seating area where you can

Degree of permanence. Before you begin, decide whether you want to build a freestanding unit like this one—or sink posts in the ground and create a permanent seating area.

A freestanding design is heavy enough to remain stable if it's sitting on a solid surface, yet it's portable enough to move (with a little help) to another part of your garden.

If you prefer a permanent installation, you'll need to sink the posts deep enough that the arbor is free of freezing and thawing cycles. Local building code officials can advise you on depth.

Whichever option you choose, construction details are nearly the same. The homeowners who built this project used redwood throughout. It's a beautiful wood but pricey. Pressure-treated components are a suitable substitute if you want to save money.

COTTAGE GARDEN TIPS

■ **Allow self-seeding annuals** to weave in and out of perennial plantings to give the garden a cohesive appearance. Some self-seeding plants that do double duty as long-lasting cut flowers include cosmos, globe amaranth, larkspur, love-in-a-mist, poppy, and spider flower. If seedlings sprout where they're not wanted, pull them out or transplant them to another spot.

■ **Plant fragrant herbs** such as scented geraniums and pineapple sage near the path so passersby who brush against the leaves will release the plants' sweet, invigorating scents.

MASSES OF FLOWERS (LEFT AND BELOW LEFT), INCLUDING YELLOW AND PURPLE CAPE DAISIES (*OSTEOSPERMUM*), PINK AND PURPLE ROSE VERBENA, AND ROSES, MIX WITH SHRUBS AND GROUND COVERS FOR A LUSHLY EXUBERANT GARDEN WITH COLOR, TEXTURE, AND DIMENSION.

VINES FOR YOUR ARBOR

Sweetly scented climbing roses provide a perfect backdrop for a cottage garden. In this garden, pink blossoms of 'Cécile Brunner', hardy in Zones 6–9, will adorn the arbor. In colder climates, you can substitute 'William Baffin', a dark pink variety that's hardy in Zones 3–7.

Climbing roses actually are leaners, not climbers. However, their long canes are easily tied to a lattice or wire trellis for support. Clematis vines make excellent companions, intertwining with the roses and extending the bloom season. Unlike a climbing rose, clematis is a clasping vine that climbs a trellis with specialized stems called tendrils. Another choice for a cottage garden: old-fashioned sweet peas (*Lathyrus odoratus*), clasping vines with heavenly fragrance.

'Winifred Coulter' climbing rose and 'Venosa violacea' clematis

build a cozy arbor seat

tools & materials

SPECIAL TOOLS: Circular saw, table saw, pneumatic nail gun, jigsaw, rasp

- 4 – 4×4 posts, 8 feet long
- 1 – 2×4, 10 feet long
- 2 – 2×8 lattice sheets
- 1 – 1×8, 8 feet long
- 5 – 2×6s, 8 feet long
- 10 – 2×4s, 8 feet long
- 2 – 1×4s, 6 feet long
- 1 – 1×4, 8 feet long
- 3 – 1×2s, 8 feet long
- 1 – 1×2, 6 feet long
- 4 – 2×3s, 8 feet long
- 4 beveled post caps
- Deck screws, 3-inch

Construct side panels This arbor measures 5 feet wide, 2½ feet deep, and 7 feet tall. You'll first build two identical side panels, then the seat, then the arbor. Start by cutting the posts from the 4×4s. For a freestanding unit, cut posts 88 inches long. For a permanent unit, add the depth of the posthole to the 88 inches.

1 | notch posts Across all four 4×4s, cut 1½-inch-wide, ⅜-inch-deep notches at two locations: 6 inches and 64 inches from one end (freestanding) or ground level (permanent installation). To notch, score the posts with a circular saw, then chisel out. Smooth with a rasp.

2 | add crosspieces For each side panel, lay two 4×4s side-by-side with notches facing each other. From the 2×4, cut two 24¾-inch-long pieces. Slip these crosspieces into the notches. With a square, ensure that the crosspieces meet the posts at 90-degree angles, then attach them to the posts by driving deck screws at an angle from the crosspieces into the posts.

3 | install lattice panels Shorten a 2×8-foot sheet of lattice to fit between the crosspieces. Then from the 1×8 cut 1-inch-wide stops to hold the lattice in place.

Attach the stops to the inside edges of the crosspieces and posts, nearly flush with the top surfaces

of each. (A pneumatic nail gun makes quick work of this task; however, you can do the job with hammer and nails.)

Turn the side panel over so that the stops are on the ground side. Press the lattice down into the side panel frame and against the stops. Nail in two more stops—one along the top edge and one along the bottom edge of the frame—to lock the lattice in place.

4 | attach brackets It will be easier to attach the arbor support brackets while the side panels are on the ground. Cut four 13½-inch-long pieces from a 2×6, then fashion decorative ends for each bracket with a jigsaw. (Duplicate the design used here or create your own.) Attach the brackets to the front and back of each post, 9½ inches below the top.

5 | build seat frame The frame looks like a short ladder. To make it, cut two 56-inch-long and five 21-inch long pieces from a 2×4. Mark each of the longer boards at the center and 14 inches to each side of the center.

Stand the long boards on edge parallel to each other. Set a shorter piece between them at each marked point. Check that all the pieces are square and evenly spaced. Then screw them together.

6 | attach seat frame How the seat frame is attached depends on whether the unit will be freestanding or permanently installed. For permanent installation, go to Step 8. For a freestanding unit, lay one of the side panels flat on the ground. Mark a line where the bottom of the seat frame will sit—about 15½ inches up from the ground ends of the posts. Stand the seat frame on end over the side panel. Lining it up with the marks, slip it between the two posts of the side panel. Rest it firmly

against the lattice. Make sure the frame is perpendicular to the side panel, then screw it to both posts.

7 | stand up panels Stand the entire L-shape unit upright, temporarily propping up the seat frame. Place the other side panel

against the free end of the seat frame. Level the seat frame, then screw it to the second side panel.

8 | stabilize the frame To make the seat more stable, tap the two remaining 21-inch 2×4s into place at each end of the seat frame. Drive

build a cozy arbor seat

(continued)

screws at an angle through them to the front and back of the frame.

For permanent installation, dig holes for each post, 55 inches apart, side-to-side, and 27½ inches front-to-back. (All measurements are from the center of the holes).

Have someone help you stand the two side panels in their respective holes. Anchor them in position with stakes and braces, making sure they are plumb. Pour concrete in the holes; let it set up overnight.

To attach the seat frame to the posts, measure up from the ground 15½ inches and mark all four posts. Slip the ends of the seat frame inside the two side panels. Level the bottom of the seat frame with the marks. Attach it to the posts. Add the end pieces of the frame.

Now, regardless of the process you used to get to this stage, the remaining steps are identical.

9 | prepare for the backrest

From the 2×4s, cut six 56-inch-long boards for the seat and one 56-inch-long board for the backrest. Also cut three 22-inch-long slats from the 1×4 and thirteen 22-inch-long slats from the 1×2.

Temporarily lay the seat boards in place on the seat frame. Stand a scrap of 1×4 between the back two and with an angle gauge, determine the angle you'd like for the backrest. Also mark on the top of the seat frame where the back side of the base of the backrest will meet the frame.

10 | bevel rear seat boards

Set your table saw blade to the

angle you just measured for the backrest and cut a bevel along the entire edge of two seat boards. These will be the two rear seat boards, which sandwich the bottom edge of the backrest.

11 | build the backrest

Lay one non-beveled board flat on the ground. Arrange the 1×4 and 1×2 slats 1½ inches apart in a random pattern on top and perpendicular to the 2×4. Ensure that the top of each slat is flush with the top of the 2×4, then screw it in place.

12 | attach rear seat board

Cut notches on the beveled edge of each end of one rear seat board. The notches should be deep enough to wrap around the two rear posts yet overlap the back of the seat frame by

A DESTINATION FOR CONTEMPLATION

or private conversation was the guiding principle for Cynthia Egger, who designed this garden.

1 inch. Align this board with the mark you made for the backrest on the seat frame. Then screw it to the seat frame, with the beveled edge facing front.

13 | attach the backrest Stand the backrest upright, slip it between the two back posts and slide it down until the ends of the slats reach the bottom of the seat board you just attached to the frame. Screw the ends of the slats to the front edge of the seat board. Then attach the top of the backrest to the two rear posts by angle-screwing the ends of the 2×4 to the posts.

14 | finish the seat Screw the remaining seat boards to the frame, starting with the other beveled 2×4. Place it next to the bottom of the backrest, with the bevel facing the rear. Notch the front seat board at both ends to fit around the posts and overhang the front of the frame a bit.

Dress up the top of the backrest by cutting a 1×4 into two 51½-inch lengths. Screw them to the backrest.

15 | assemble the trellis Cut four 88-inch-long beams from 2×6s. Jigsaw the same decorative design on the ends as you chose for the support brackets.

Rest one beam across the brackets of the front pair of posts. Screw it to the front faces of the posts. Attach a second beam to the other side of the posts, creating a sandwich. Do the same with the back pair of posts.

16 | finish the arbor Cut seven 48-inch-long slats from 2×3s. Starting on the left, lay the slats at right angles atop the beams. The slats should overhang front and rear beams equally. Space them 6 inches apart, using a scrap of 2×6 as a guide. Screw the seats into place. Top the posts with beveled post caps.

an italian garden
terraces transform a suburban house

This hilltop house, with its creamy stucco siding and terra-cotta tile roof, has continental charm, but its sloping front yard was a mass of unsightly weeds, overgrown evergreen ground cover, and yucca. Cracks marred the concrete driveway. Water pipes and a dryer vent protruded from the front of the house. A stairway up from the sidewalk paused at a landing of crazy paving stones before a second set of steps to the classic arch-window entryway, which was underfurnished.

"It's like a nice outfit with bad shoes," laments the homeowner. "You've gotta have the right accessories." The entire layout, the family agreed, was in serious need of curb appeal.

Designer Laurie Callaway saw several possibilities for creating a landscaped setting favorable to the architecture, including a Spanish or Mexican theme, but Italian was the homeowner's favorite style.

Ripping out the overgrowth and pruning an existing tree reveals abundant garden space. Taming the slope by installing low retaining walls imparts an Etruscan identity from the start. (Check with local building officials about wall-height regulations.) Built of rectangular light-color flagstone blocks in hues similar to Italian travertine, the walls create staggered, gently curved terraces that expand the usable space and provide access to the planting beds.

Tearing out the damaged driveway and pouring a new concrete pad as a replacement became a major priority. A faux-stone treatment blends it into the landscape and design concept.

Terra-cotta tiles replace uneven paving stones on the landing between staircases, picking up the color of the roofing tiles while creating a safe path. A rustic stone bench built in place from the same limestone as the

HOW DO YOU make a house look like it's in the hills of Tuscany? Get artsy with the driveway, add some Italian accessories, and build a terraced hillside.

TERRA-COTTA TILES (RIGHT) **PROVIDE SAFE FOOTING AND TIE IN WITH A FLOWERPOT WATER FEATURE.**

TAMING THE SLOPE WITH RETAINING WALLS (OPPOSITE) **CREATES FLAT AREAS FOR PLANTING AND A PRIVATE OUTDOOR ROOM UNDER THE ARCHED ENTRY WINDOW.**

OVERGROWN EVERGREENS AND WEEDS (ABOVE) RETAIN SOIL BUT DIMINISH CURB APPEAL.

EXUBERANT EXTRAS

Spiral stakes. Wind varying lengths of refrigerator copper pipe (available at home centers) around a broom handle. Create clever finials for the stakes from colorful polymer clay (from craft stores) that's baked and hardened in a home oven. Stick stakes with finials in flowerpots to add a humorous twist.

Know your pots before buying one. Terra-cotta pots made by families of Italian artisans for generations have lovely sculptural accents and

outlast similar pots made elsewhere, explains designer Laurie Callaway. Take pots indoors for the winter in cold areas.

Landscape lighting combines safety with decoration. Conical walkway lamps complement the pointy conifer in this garden.

Accent the mundane by making it a design element. This homeowner chose an oversized hammered metal mailbox for its rustic practicality.

an italian garden

(continued)

retaining walls gives an aged look to a corner of the newly constructed top terrace. Carrying on the design theme, a round flagstone tops a pedestal, creating a handy table near the bench. Repeating textures and colors in this way rises to the challenge of successfully mixing building and gardening materials.

Mediterranean plants fill the new terraces with vibrant color and scale. A conical cypress stands at attention next to the stone bench. An olive tree softens the scene with lacy gray-green leaves. Lavender provides heady scent. Consider adding coreopsis for color and spiky palm grass for texture. Surrounding plants with a pebble mulch continue the color palette and stone texture into the garden design.

Check out more ideas from HGTV.com

For more ways to create Mediterranean appeal in the garden, see

- www.hgtv.com/landscapemakeoversbook

PURPLE GERANIUMS (*GERANIUM INCANUM*) ALONG THE TOP OF A WALL (ABOVE RIGHT) HAS A COOLING EFFECT, WHILE SPIKY NEW ZEALAND FLAX ADDS HEIGHT AND TEXTURE.

CUSHIONS ON A STONE BENCH (BELOW RIGHT) PICK UP COLOR FROM A TERRA-COTTA FOUNTAIN AS A FLAGSTONE TABLE AND RIVER-ROCK MULCH CONTINUE THE DESIGN THEME.

MEDITERRANEAN GARDENS FOR WHEREVER YOU LIVE

- **Vibrant warmth** comes from bright sunshine colors. Gazania, windflower, Italian lily, calendula, and grayleaf cranesbill shine brightly.
- **Cool contrast** from white heron's-bill, lilac salvia, and silvery gray lamb's-ears gives respite from hot hues.
- **Fragrance** whisks you on a trip to Tuscany. Sweet-scented globe candytuft, lavender, and clary sage are aromatic delights.
- **Texture and height** come from spiky variegated broadleaf sedge, silky foxtail millet, or feathery fountain grass.
- **Recreate Mediterranean** allure in cooler climates with vibrant coreopsis, blanketflower, black-eyed Susan, hairy primroses, marigolds, and asters. Use lavender for contrast and scent. White asphodel "candles" offer height, texture, and fun.

imitation stone driveway

tools & materials

SPECIAL TOOLS: Power paint sprayer; concrete trowel; framing square; sponges

- Liquid bond coat
- Narrow vinyl tape
- Concrete resurfacer
- Concrete paint, 4 neutral colors
- Concrete sealer

1 | create pattern Apply an adhesive bonding coat to new or clean, level, unbroken concrete. Use narrow tape and a small framing square to create a mock stone pattern.

2 | apply topcoat Pour on the self-leveling concrete resurfacer.

3 | raise details Scrape the wet topcoat with the edge of a trowel to bring the limestone texture to the surface.

4 | pull, paint, and seal Pull up the tape while the surface is still damp to create simulated mortar lines. Let the surface dry 24 hours. Remove the residue left from pulling up the tape with a stiff brush or scraper. Spray the clean, dry surface with base color. Sponge-paint individual squares with coordinating colors to create the look of stone. Vary color combinations for a natural effect. Allow the paint to dry. Apply a concrete sealer.

DESIGN PLANS

goals Create the look of stone without the expense.

cost Approximately $25 per 40-pound bag, which covers 40 square feet at $1/2$ inch thick.

time 2 weekends.

difficulty scale Taping the stone pattern is tedious.
●●●○○

skill scale Concrete work takes patience and timing.
●●●○○

DECORATING

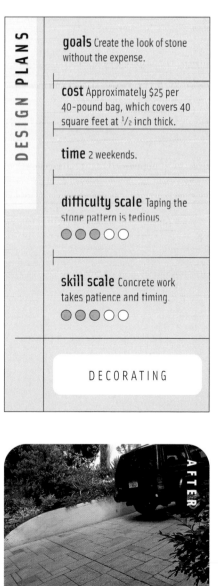

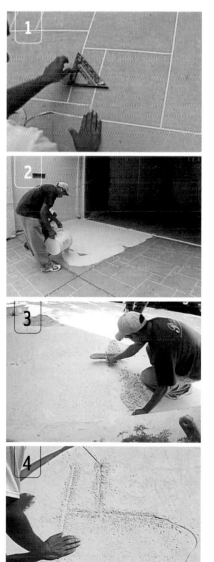

2 PRIVACY

Creating privacy. Having a place to relax outdoors without worldly intrusion is possible wherever you live.

PRIVACY

When you close your front door, you feel as though

you are shutting out the workaday world and entering an inner sanctum of privacy where you can relax. This feeling should extend into your outdoor living spaces. The garden should provide a calming retreat where you can unwind without uninvited intrusions. But all too often, as you settle in on the chaise in your backyard, you see a neighbor waving to you over the hedge. You look up to admire the cloud formations only to see a child watching from a second-story bedroom window in the house behind you. If you are a city resident, it's easy to feel as if you live under a microscope when windows overlook balconies or rooftop gardens. Renters appreciate ways of creating instant privacy that can be packed up to move with them.

Although individuals have differing degrees of tolerance for interruptions, most care about privacy. It's important to create spaces that are private and intimate without being isolated from the rest of the world. That's where HGTV landscape design ideas help.

Privacy comes from using hedge plantings to filter out vehicle and pedestrian traffic and noise. Fences block views as they also bar neighborhood dogs or, in some areas, deer from the yard, and keep small children and pets at home. Arbors, pergolas, and even oversized umbrellas shield overhead views and provide areas of shade. Within a walled courtyard, the mail or the morning paper can be retrieved—or read outdoors—while you're still in a bathrobe.

Now that's luxury.

A MIX OF MATERIALS PROVIDES PRIVACY WITH STYLE. A SOLID FENCE GIVES THIS YARD COMPLETE PRIVACY AS VINES, TREES, AND SHRUBS DRESS UP AND SOFTEN IT. STAGGERED DECK LEVELS CREATE A SENSE OF UNCONFINED MOVEMENT AND COMMUNITY.

be a private eye
check out the privacy of your yard from all the angles

Peace of mind comes from getting a handle on the degree of privacy that suits your personality. Be your own private eye. Look at your yard from every angle. Take notes. Consider your needs from inside the house as well. Does your kitchen window overlook the siding of the neighboring house or into a window? Window boxes or hanging plants improve the view and screen your window from onlookers. If you need privacy at a window, consider evergreens that won't leave you exposed in winter.

Sit awhile in various locations around your yard. You need both open and intimate spaces. A solid backyard fence provides complete privacy, but sometimes all that's needed is a privacy screen for a backyard spa and sunbathing area or a partial screen to hide or define a fountain and seating area. Where you want only to screen some views, panels of lattice, lacy bushes, or tall ornamental grasses may do the job.

Is street noise a bother? Trees or shrubbery add insulation from noise and create windbreaks. Add soothing sounds such as splashing water, wind chimes, or the rustle of potted fountain grasses to further enhance private spaces and muffle noise from

neighbors' yards or street traffic. Whether you choose a wall, a hedge, a trio of trees, a fence, a trellis, an arbor or pergola, a gazebo, a patio cover, a mound of shrubbery, a lattice screen, a canvas curtain, or any combination to create privacy, the result should make you feel at home. The more comfortable you feel in your yard, the more you'll embrace all the outdoors has to offer.

Making plans. Decide on the purpose, location, materials, height, installation, and maintenance of structures or plantings. Seek input from family members on how they want to use the yard, and think about how landscaping will make these plans possible. Talk with the neighbors. They might agree to share in the cost of an attractive mutual privacy solution.

Fences, walls, or hedges fill many needs. They define property lines, provide security, create privacy, set spaces apart for different uses, conceal unattractive areas, support plants, and buffer wind, noise, and views.

Before installing anything adjacent to a neighboring lot, have property

COMPLETE PRIVACY IS ENSURED WHEN TALL EVERGREENS AND SOLID BOARD FENCING (ABOVE) PREVENT PEEKING INTO OR OUT OF A DINING AREA.

SEMICOMPLETE PRIVACY COMES FROM AN OPEN-WEAVE FENCE (OPPOSITE) THAT ALLOWS AIR CIRCULATION. THE PERGOLA SHIELDS VIEWS OF A SITTING AREA FROM OVERHEAD WINDOWS.

FRIENDLY PRIVACY COMES FROM A TRELLIS-STYLE FENCE (RIGHT) THAT CREATES PRIVATE SPACE WITHOUT NEIGHBORS FEELING SHUT OUT.

creating privacy
(continued)

lines confirmed by a professional surveyor. Become familiar with local ordinances and easements. Most communities have requirements on height and placement and may require permits.

Determine the level of privacy you want to achieve. Privacy can be complete or partial, no-nonsense or friendly. Complete privacy blocks views from all directions, including from above. But privacy need not be total to be effective. Partial privacy might mean screening a specific area while leaving the larger space open, or blurring views in from the street with masses of tall plants and a picket fence or lattice trellis. Friendly privacy clearly designates limits without being intimidating. No-nonsense privacy strictly controls access.

The level of privacy you need and the style that suits the location help determine the choice of materials. Materials include wood, plastic, concrete block, bamboo, brick, stone, corrugated fiberglass, glass block, wrought iron, and chain link fencing.

A formal fence might be wrought iron; an informal one might be split-rail, lattice, bamboo, or woven wood. Traditional styles include picket or stockade fences. For functional fencing, chain link is the most

A LATTICE SCREEN WITH A ROUND WINDOW FOR A HANGING PLANT (LEFT) DEFINES A GARDEN SPOT.

GLASS BLOCKS (BELOW), SCATTERED TO ALLOW AIRFLOW, LET IN LIGHT YET CREATE A PRIVACY WALL THAT INVITES USE OF A TABLE.

common. Determine whether wood (treated or untreated), metal, or plastic will be easiest to maintain and most attractive over time.

Mixing styles creates different moods for different parts of the garden, or solves different problems. A combination fence that's solid at the base and topped with an open design creates privacy yet allows in light and air.

Designers consider 6 feet the standard height for walls or fences because that is above eye level for most people. If in doubt, go higher, because structures that stop at eye-level make many people feel uncomfortable.

Creating spaces. One discovery as you create private spaces within a landscape is the number of choices you have when you shop at garden centers and hardware and home improvement stores. Because outdoor living is a high priority for many people, manufacturers are busy creating products and materials that make good privacy solutions, whether you do it yourself or hire a builder. Pergolas, arbors, and trellises of wood, plastic, and metal come ready-made.

Screens, which are used within the yard as an alternative to fencing, can

FABRIC CURTAINS (ABOVE LEFT) ADJUST TO CONTROL LIGHT AND SHELTER VIEWS, TURNING A PORCH INTO A USEFUL OUTDOOR ROOM.

FOLDING SCREENS (ABOVE RIGHT) ARE EASILY MOVED AS NECESSARY TO ENHANCE PRIVACY.

HANGING LATTICE PANELS (RIGHT) AIRILY SHADE A PATIO AND PROVIDE VISUAL INTEREST.

CONTAINER GARDENS on balconies give urban dwellers a sense of pastoral privacy. A strong open frame supporting hanging baskets blocks views and allows air flow. Faux-stone plastic pots look real but cut down on the weight and create movable gardens.

be solid or open, stationary or portable. Painted bright colors, they can be a focal point in a garden. Recycled gates, old doors hinged together, and sections of fencing can be used as screens while providing architectural interest. Lattice panels can be made to slide behind each other much like Japanese shoji screens, or they can hang from rafters, allowing full or partial coverage. Curtains of weather-resistant fabrics can be opened or closed.

Conceal uninviting areas, such as dog runs, rabbit hutches, trash cans, potting areas, pool and garden equipment storage, and even air conditioning and heating units, by using the same materials as your privacy screening.

If you have more than one private space to work on, such as a spa, a dining and entertainment area, and a play yard, break the projects into bite-size pieces rather than tackling them all at once—easing both your budget and your mind.

Planting privacy. Structures such as fences, screens, lattice baffles, and trellises are built first, then receive a softening touch from plantings. Vines climbing along fences, up trellises, and across arbors provide visual interest and variety to any space.

Trees and shrubbery pair with fences and screens along property lines, providing a measure of privacy while giving a more comfortable look and feel to your space. A combination of evergreen and deciduous varieties

helps achieve your goal of privacy year-round.

A living fence can be a solid hedgerow or an airy lattice covered in vines. Tall trees with wide canopies screen views from overhead and provide shade. Vine-covered trellises offer a quick and inexpensive way to prove shade and privacy.

When planting for privacy near a pool or spa, avoid plants that may be messy, draw bees, or have thorns. Consider plants that will not shed into the water, causing added maintenance.

Selecting plantings means more than choosing between mature trees and shrubs or young ones. Assess your needs and your patience. Consider which trees grow quickly and which are more sedate. Fast-growers provide shade faster but tend to be less hardy and might need replacing in a matter of years, while slower growers tend to reward many generations with their long-term beauty. Young shrub canes resemble a bundle of sticks, and filling out a row often takes several seasons. Larger shrubs require more initial digging but provide privacy sooner.

Plant groupings of shrubbery to shield or conceal less-than-lovely areas. Shrubs used for screening should be planted in beds half as wide as they are tall at maturity. Staggered rows of shrubs offer more density and privacy than those planted in a straight line.

BY VARYING PLANTER HEIGHTS AND GIVING SOME POTTED VINES POLES TO CLIMB, CONTAINER GARDENS CAN PROVIDE INTERCHANGEABLE WAYS OF BLOCKING VIEWS.

PRIVACY ON THE DOUBLE

Create private space with plants that grow quickly. Ideas include 'Chiollipo' Japanese euonymus (*Euonymus japonicus*), a shrub that grows 12 feet tall and 6 feet wide, has green-and-cream variegated foliage, and does well in afternoon shade (hardy to Zone 5). Or try sweetautumn clematis (*Clematis terniflora*), a vine that grows 15 feet tall and 15 feet wide and has white flowers (hardy in Zones 5–8).

Boxwood, holly, and yew can take formal or informal shape as hedges for low borders or living privacy walls. Prickly holly also serves as a security barrier. **Envy ivy-covered** university walls? Chances are the vine is a Virginia creeper, which rapidly climbs 50 feet or more, depending on support height. Grow this vigorous vine on a sturdy frame away from buildings because its adhesive climbers can damage mortar or siding.

A DECK AMONG THE TREES (FAR LEFT) GAINS PRIVACY FROM THE LEAFY CANOPY.

A DENSE HEDGE BEHIND LOW-GROWING SHRUBS (LEFT) MAKES A PRIVATE SPOT FOR A BENCH.

PLACE SHRUBS WHERE YOU WANT TO BLOCK VIEWS (BELOW). LEAVE GAPS IN THE PLANTING TO CREATE VIEWS.

creating privacy
(continued)

Air play. If you're longing for tall fences and trees and shrubs but your outdoor space is small, consider the need for air circulation. If your structures are too dense, you may feel as though you're suffocating, especially on hot summer nights. Lacy-leafed trees and open lattice provide airy screens and dappled light.

Lattice screens seem to cry out for vines, yet a thick cover blocks breezes and sunshine as would a solid wall.

Some vines are evergreen, some are annual, and some are perennial. Vines make good screens, and they are attractive grown on fences, arbors, and trellises. Popular vines include annual morning glory, English ivy, jasmine, honeysuckle, Virginia creeper, grape,

trumpet vine, bougainvillea, and wisteria. Likewise, varieties of climbing roses make for charming arbors.

Hedges. Shrubbery and vines mask the hard planes of a fence, give the illusion of a living wall, and direct the eye to other features of your yard, such as flower beds, a garden bench, or a specimen shrub or tree.

Shrubs that create hedges can be evergreen or deciduous, dense or airy,

MOUNDS OF WHISPERY GRASSES (LEFT) OR A SIMPLE WATER FOUNTAIN OF BAMBOO CANES IN A WOODEN RAIN BARREL (BELOW) MUTE STREET NOISE AND NEIGHBORS' CHAT WITH DELICATE, RELAXING NATURAL SOUNDS.

and short, medium, or tall. Know how big plants will grow before planting and leave enough room for their mature growth. Most hedges need to be trimmed regularly, depending on the look you want.

Many old standbys for creating privacy and defining spaces may take years to grow. For the short term, consider growing vines on net trellises along the front of young hedgerows. Remove the vines and trellis when the shrubbery matures. The same principle can be used for trees. If a tree that you want is slow-growing, plant faster-growing smaller trees and shrubs to fill in the space until the larger varieties mature.

Mixing it up by staggering and layering evergreen and deciduous plants ensures seasonal privacy and ensures against pest or disease problems (you can pull out sick plants without leaving a huge gap). Evergreen and deciduous trees and shrubs may be planted together to offer variety and interest all year.

Varying heights adds interest to the areas within the border. Boxwood is an evergreen often used for formal hedges, while cotoneaster is a popular deciduous shrub.

Block a view by planting a medium to tall tree with interesting features, such as a slow-growing lacebark pine (*Pinus bungeana*), in the sight line. Cypress and other tall evergreens, planted either in the ground or in large containers, make good screens, with or without fences behind them.

Plants in containers travel with you if you relocate, ready to define spaces, screen views, and provide familiar privacy for a new place.

Create spaces that are inviting and not only will you feel at home, but your guests will. When it comes to carving specific privacy niches outdoors or creating an entire private yard, the sky's the limit. Seeing family and friends enjoy your yard is part of the payoff of your work.

Check out more ideas from HGTV.com
Learn more about plants for privacy at
■ www.hgtv.com/landscapemakeoversbook

TALL PERENNIALS that grow up to 8 feet high provide partial privacy. Try butterfly bush, which screens views and attracts butterflies.

CURTAINS MADE FROM FIBERGLASS SCREEN FABRIC (ABOVE) BLUR PASSERSBY'S VIEWS OF PEOPLE ON THE PORCH WITHOUT BLOCKING BREEZES TO THE PORCH.

WILLOW WITHIES (LEFT)—LONG, SLENDER BRANCHES—FORM A UNIQUE DIVIDER BETWEEN A DECK AND A BUSY STREET.

a japanese fence
an airy divider creates small-space privacy

Enter a gate and cast off worldly cares in a Japanese garden. Here, the elements of earth, water, fire, and air converge in creating a private, peaceful place.

Earth. Rocks are points of reverence in Japanese culture, from legends that say they are beings with spirits. Rocks also represent landscapes in miniature, paying homage to mountain vistas. Rocks can be used to surround pools and planting beds or as pathways and stepping-stones. They provide a sensibility of timeless strength.

ALTHOUGH SHIELDED FROM THE NEIGHBORS, THIS YARD (ABOVE) OFFERS NO QUIET NOOKS IN WHICH TO RELAX OR HIDE AWAY.

Water. Water signifies purity and pays tribute to streams and lakes, making these features blend naturally into the landscape. Pools reflect the sky. Simple *kakei* bamboo spouts take the place of fountains.

Fire. Lighting represents the element of fire. Scattering lanterns among the foliage provides a soft glow that won't disturb the neighbors.

Air. Airiness allows the flow of positive energy. Bamboo gates and fences define private spaces but let breezes and *qi*, or chee, waft through.

Perhaps all you need is a privacy hedge but you can't spare the space for a traditional row of fat boxwoods or privets. Landscape designer Yoshi Kuraishi solves this problem with a slim bamboo fence. Much more friendly and welcoming than a solid barrier, a bamboo fence suits this home's Japanese garden.

When the trellislike bamboo fence is finished, install plants along its length to create a living hedge. Kuraishi likes to use camellia 'Setsugekka' (*Camellia sasanqua*), an adaptable, easily trained evergreen

BAMBOO CANES CAN BE USED LIKE LUMBER TO MAKE ARBORS (UPPER LEFT), FENCES, AND SLIM SCREENS (BELOW).

PLANTINGS AND BAMBOO FEATURES (OPPOSITE) NOW DEFINE PRIVATE AREAS.

PLANTS FOR PRIVACY

If you can spare the space for a thicker privacy fence, you can choose from many kinds of shrubs and grasses. Bamboo, for example, makes a tall fence that will look right at home in a Japanese garden. The rhizomes of many bamboos have a tendency to spread aggressively, but they're easy to corral if you plan ahead. Rent a trencher to dig a 30-inch-deep trench, then line it with sheet metal or a plastic rhizome barrier (often available from bamboo nurseries) before planting.

Bamboo offers plenty of privacy, often growing 20 to 30 feet tall in just four or five years. In cold climates, choose yellow-groove (*Phyllostachys aureosulcata*) or canebrake bamboo (*Arundinaria gigantea*). Both remain evergreen to minus 20°F (Zone 5). In colder areas, these bamboos will die down to the ground in winter but quickly grow again in spring to renew your privacy screen.

'Capitata' Japanese yew (*Taxus cuspidata*), another appropriate choice for a privacy hedge in a Japanese garden, is an upright evergreen with soft dark green needles. Easy to maintain with pruning as a 10-foot-tall hedge, this yew thrives in Zones 4–7.

golden bamboo

shrub with semidouble white blossoms and large ruffled petals—hardy in Zones 7–8. Climbing roses would make good substitutes in colder areas. They offer dense growth, with thick, upright canes that can be easily tied to the rails for privacy. Disease-resistant varieties include 'White Dawn', hardy to Zone 5, and exceptionally hardy 'William Baffin', a deep pink climber reliable to Zone 3.

Tripods and arbors. Height helps in creating privacy. Kuraishi uses bamboo tripods as stakes to train Japanese cypress, separating tight branches into an airy shape. Clusters of white flowers cascading from 'Longissima Alba' Japanese wisteria (*Wisteria floribunda*) along a sturdy arbor scent the spring air and screen views from overhead. This vine is hardy in Zones 5–9. In colder areas, create this look with an American alternative, Kentucky wisteria (*W. macrostachya*). Unlike Japanese wisteria, which blooms on wood formed the previous season, Kentucky wisteria's light lilac or lilac-purple flowers bloom on the current season's growth so are less likely to be damaged by a cold snap.

Two exceptionally hardy varieties of Kentucky wisteria, 'Aunt Dee' and 'Blue Moon', have proved hardy as far north as Minneapolis (Zone 4).

A WISTERIA-DRAPED TRELLIS SHADES AND COOLS A STEPPING-STONE PATHWAY, CREATING A TRANQUIL PRIVATE SPOT.

BAMBOO FUN FACTS

■ **Bamboo** flowers every 70 to 120 years. Wind pollination ensures that each cane of the same type blooms at the same time over a huge region in a kind of "plant telepathy." Once it flowers, bamboo dies.

■ **Umbrella bamboo,** a clumping variety, is the favorite food of the giant panda.

BAMBOO TIPS

■ To keep bamboo from splitting, always drill before nailing.
■ Bamboo naturally tapers at one end. For the strongest structures, here's how to put this taper to the best use. When building trellises, line up the bamboo poles so that the small ends alternate with the thick ends. To build fences, place vertical poles with the small ends up and horizontal poles with the thick and thin ends alternating.

building the fence

tools & materials

SPECIAL TOOLS: Propane torch, Japanese or fine-tooth carpentry saw

- Round pine posts, 2½-inches×5 feet
- Cement premix
- Bamboo rails, 1- to 2¼-inch diameter
- String, length of fence
- Galvanized nails, 3-inch
- Heavy-duty, rot-proof black twine

You'll need two end posts plus enough posts to space 6 feet apart along the fence line. Plan on using about 15 canes of 16-foot-long bamboo for every 20 feet of fence. Use only the straightest lengths of bamboo.

1 | age posts Pass the flame from the propane torch across the surface of the posts, then lightly scrub the charring with a wire brush. Dig holes 18 inches deep with a posthole digger for the end posts. Insert posts; brace them, then fill the holes with concrete. Let dry overnight. Quick-drying concrete will save time.

2 | level posts Run a guide between end posts, 4 inches below the tops. String a second lower line at the backs. Install the remaining posts with the fronts touching the lower guide and the tops centered under the top guide.

Mark the position for each bamboo rail on each post. Place the rails at 6, 17, and 25 inches from the ground.

3 | install top rails Cut the wide end of a bamboo rail at a 45-degree angle, sawing it just below a joint. With cut side toward the post, attach the rail by driving a nail through a predrilled hole in the bamboo. Take care to not smash the bamboo as you hammer. For an authentic look, hammer nailheads into squares to resemble handmade Japanese nails.

To extend the rail, slip the wide end of the next length of bamboo over the narrow end of the previous length. Predrill and nail the lengths to each post. Cut the final length of bamboo at a 45-degree angle and attach it to the end post. Repeat for the other two rows.

attach bamboo poles Cut the vertical poles from the widest end of the bamboo just above a joint to prevent water from pooling in the pole. Poles should be slightly taller then posts. Starting at one end post, use a mallet to pound the poles into the ground every 6 inches. Alternate posts front and back of the rails.

4 | tie the joints Lash bamboo rails together with jute at each point of intersection. Traditional Japanese knot-tying (shown) requires specialized training, but neatly tying off the jute rope gives a reasonably authentic appearance.

AFTER

DESIGN PLANS

goal Define private area in a small space with a slender Japanese-style fence.

cost $5 to $10 per post; $5 to $7 per 6-foot bamboo rail; plants for living fence.

time 1 to 2 weekends, depending on fence length.

difficulty scale Predrilling and knot-tying take patience.
●●●○○

skill scale Basic digging, drilling, and nailing skills.
●●○○○

BUILDING

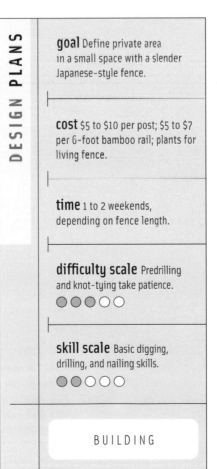

natural privacy in a japanese garden
honor tradition while improving views

Tradition calls for honoring nature in a Japanese garden. In the traditional garden shown here, low berms, stone paths, and boulders mimic a mountain landscape while a screen of bamboo and reed mat shields visitors in the garden from the view of the carport.

Landscape designer Yoshi Kuraishi added trees and shrubs native to Japan, such as Japanese maple (*Acer palmatum*), hardy in Zones 5–8, depending on variety. Some of the other plants used in this California landscape include
- **Dwarf pomegranate** (*Punica granatum*), Zones 8–10
- **Heavenly bamboo** (*Nandina domestica*), Zones 6–9
- **Weeping cherry** (*Prunus serrulata pendula*), Zones 5–8

For maximum privacy year-round in the north, select drought-tolerant evergreens. Good candidates include yew, arborvitae, and juniper. The varieties often languish in poorly drained clay soil on flat ground, especially if there's frequent watering from an automated sprinkler, but they will flourish on berms.

Dense, drought-tolerant shrubs such as lilac and cotoneaster also will thrive on a berm and help provide year-round interest.

Building a berm. Berms are easy to build. Pile soil in a graceful mound with wavy, irregular edges that look natural. To keep the berm from washing away in the first heavy rain, compact the soil by firmly tamping it or renting a roller or compactor for the job. (If you have clay soil, which compacts easily, tamp the soil gently.) For stability, add 3 feet of width for every foot of height. For example, a 2-foot-high berm should be 6 feet wide. A 4-foot-high berm should be 12 feet wide. It's possible to build a berm of any height, provided there's enough space to meet the width requirement.

PROPORTION IS KEY in selecting and arranging plants for a Japanese garden, says designer Yoshi Kuraishi. The goal is to mirror nature.

A BARE CONCRETE PATIO AND EMPTY FLOWER BED (ABOVE) OFFER A BARREN VIEW.

A BAMBOO FENCE (ABOVE RIGHT) CREATES A LIGHT BACKDROP FOR TREES AND SHRUBS. GRAVEL MULCH UNIFIES PLANTING BEDS AND SOFTENS THE LINES OF THE PATIO.

SELECT PLANTS FOR YOUR PRIVATE JAPANESE GARDEN THAT CREATE FOCAL POINTS OR ENHANCE OTHER FEATURES. GROUND COVERS, SUCH AS SPREADING COTONEASTER (RIGHT) AND CREEPING JUNIPER (CENTER RIGHT) SOFTEN HARDSCAPE ELEMENTS SUCH AS BOULDERS AND SIDEWALKS.

Spreading cotoneaster

'Blue Rug' creeping juniper

Japanese maple

A RED-LEAF JAPANESE MAPLE
(LEFT) IS A VIBRANT
ATTENTION-GETTER.

For the most natural appearance, keep proportions that mirror nature. The berms in this yard are piled in graceful shapes about the size of a child's wagon, mounded 12 to 24 inches high.

Trees and shrubs planted on these mounds increase both privacy and visual interest in what might otherwise be a flat, boring yard. Drought-tolerant prairie grasses such as Indian grass, prairie dropseed, big or little bluestem, and switchgrass are a magnificent sight summer through winter, though you'll have to sacrifice some privacy for a short time each spring when it's necessary to cut ornamental grasses to the ground before new growth begins.

Placing plants that require good drainage on top of the berm, with those needing more moisture at its base, allows for a mix of greenery that pleases the eye, ensures privacy, and honors nature.

A STONE BASIN, BAMBOO, AND WATER COMBINE IN A TRADITIONAL JAPANESE *TSUKUBAI* (BELOW). TUCKED AMONG THE PLANTS, IT MAKES A SERENE FEATURE THAT CREATES TRANQUILITY WITH THE SOUND OF TRICKLING WATER.

japanese fountain

tools & materials
SPECIAL TOOLS: Fine-tooth saw
- Round, preformed pond liner
- Recirculating pump, 200-gph and tubing
- Bamboo canes, 2½–inch diameter; 1½–inch diameter; ½–inch diameter
- Stone basin, 2-feet tall
- Plastic grate, 16-square-inch (the grid used in fluorescent lighting fixtures)
- Bricks and cobbles

Tsukubai, stone basins, were designed by Japanese tea-masters to create the mood for the ritual tea ceremony. Water flows from *kakei*, bamboo spouts. Wear rubber gloves when working with bamboo, which is sharp and can splinter.

Prepare the site Draw a template of the preformed liner on a piece of cardboard (trace around the liner lip). Position the template where you intend to place the fountain. The location should be near a GFCI outlet. Mark the outline of the template on the ground, then dig the reservoir. The hole should be 2 inches wider and 2 inches deeper than the liner.

Conform your digging to the shape of the liner, measuring depth, width, and level frequently. After digging the hole, look for sharp objects or stones on the bottom. Then fill the bottom with an inch of moist sand. Use a short board to screed the sand. Tamp to firm the sand.

Set the liner in the hole. Check its level, then fill it with a couple of inches of water to stabilize it and begin backfilling around the sides. Tamp the soil as you work. Keep the water below the backfill level to prevent the liner from bulging out.

Place the pump in the reservoir between bricks. Run the electrical cord over the lip of the liner. (Running a drip irrigation line into the tub at this point, if desired, will help keep the reservoir filled with water.)

Prepare for the bamboo spout by digging a 3½-inch diameter hole 18 inches behind the basin and 1-foot deep for the bamboo upright.

1 | make the upright
Using the hacksaw, cut the 2½-inch diameter bamboo to a 40-inch length. Drill a 1½-inch-diameter hole through the front of one end for the spout. At the base of the bamboo, drill another hole slightly larger in diameter than the tubing, 15 inches from the end. Hollow out the upright by pushing a rebar rod through it.

2 | drill for pin
Drill a ½-inch hole on each side of the larger hole for the bamboo pin.

3 | prepare spout
Cut 1½-inch-diameter cane to 20-inches long. Angle one end for the spout. At the other end, drill a ½ inch hole on each side to line up with the pinholes in the upright. Notch the spout at the pinhole end for the tubing. Hollow out the spout.

4–5 | insert tubing
Feed tubing into the bamboo upright from the bottom, running it through the spout hole and into the spout.

6–7 | insert the spout
Hold the spout in place with a ½-inch-diameter bamboo pin. Set the upright into the posthole. Check that it is plumb then backfill to secure. Attach the tubing to the pump.

install grate
Set the grate over the reservoir. Place the stone basin on the grate under the spout. Fill the basin and the reservoir and test the water flow. Water should pour from the spout into the basin and overflow the sides. Adjust the flow on the pump as needed. Cover the grate with the cobbles so the overflowing water disappears through the pebbles and into the reservoir.

DESIGN PLANS

goal Fulfill Japanese garden design precepts by using the elements of stone and water to create a serene fountain.

cost Varies depending on size of basin, pump, and plants. Bamboo is about $30.

time 1 weekend.

difficulty scale Drilling sharp, round bamboo can be awkward and takes patience.
●●●○○

skill scale Experienced cutting, digging, and drilling skills.
●●●○○

DECORATING

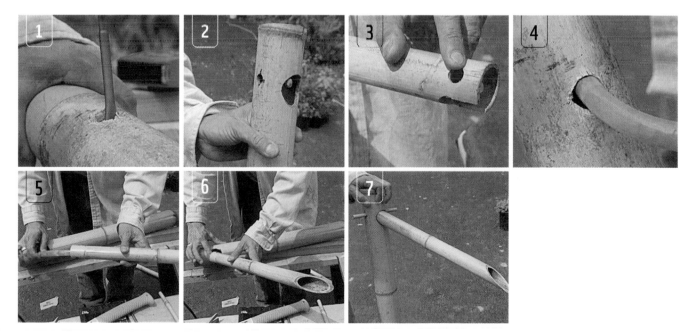

forming a berm

tools & materials
SPECIAL TOOLS: Shovel, hoe, tamper

Simple mounds of soil add visual interest to a flat landscape. Graceful waves and curves imitate hillsides.

1 | toss the soil When planting shrubs, toss the extra soil from the holes into piles about 24 inches high. Scrape that soil and soil in the bed into berms that are three times as wide as they are high.

2 | break up clods of dirt. Tamp or use a roller or compactor on the berm to firm the soil. Firming the soil keeps it from sinking or washing away.

3 | place boulders and large stones near berms, completing the picture of an imitation mountainside. Plants become a forest in miniature.

DESIGN PLANS

goal Build a mound to raise growing plants.

cost No cost. Use soil left over from planting shrubs.

time 1 weekend.

difficulty scale Shifting dirt can be heavy work.
● ● ○ ○ ○

skill scale Simple digging and firming of soil.
● ● ○ ○ ○

GARDENING

BERM TIPS

■ If your landscape project calls for planting trees and shrubs in other parts of the yard, save the soil you remove when preparing planting holes for use when constructing your berms.

■ If you're building berms from sandy soil, which is quick to drain, add up to one-third the volume of compost or other organic matter. The addition makes the soil spongy, helping it soak up soil moisture your plants will need during dry spells.

installing a screen

tools & materials
SPECIAL TOOLS: Propane torch

- 2 – 8-foot×3½-inch-diameter round pressure-treated pine posts
- 2 – 6-foot-long reed mats
- Concrete
- Bamboo poles
- Copper wire, 14-gauge

Shield garden views with an "aged" traditional screen. Scorch the surface of the pine posts by lightly passing a propane torch across the surface, giving wood an aged appearance. Lightly scrub the charred wood with a wire brush.

1 | install posts and rails Dig postholes 6 feet apart and 18 inches deep. Set the posts in the postholes. Brace them and fill the holes with concrete. Allow the concrete to set for several hours.

DESIGN PLANS

goal Build a privacy screen suited to a Japanese garden.

cost $5 to $10 per post; $15 to $20 per 6-foot reed mat.

time 1 weekend.

difficulty scale The hardest part will be ensuring the posts are straight.
● ● ○ ○ ○

skill scale Basic carpentry skills and patience are needed.
● ● ○ ○ ○

BUILDING

Cut six bamboo poles to 6-foot lengths. Angle the cut ends so they will tightly abut the round support posts. Pre-drill the bamboo before nailing. Hammer the nailheads to make them square, resembling handmade Japanese nails (see page 43).

Starting on the side facing away from the garden, nail three bamboo rails horizontally to the posts. Nail one near the top, one near the bottom, and one in the center, spacing them evenly. Drive the nails at a diagonal through the node or joint of the bamboo, which is stronger.

2 | Add reed mat On the garden side, roll one mat from post to post across the bamboo rails.

3 | attach the first mat Cut several lengths of 14-gauge copper wire 2 inches longer than the diameter of the bamboo rails. Push both ends of the short wires through the reed mat. Loop and twist them around the bamboo at the back of the fence (similar to twisting a wire twist-tie).

4 | add the second mat Roll another reed mat across the first one. (Double layering helps to reduce the transparency of the thin mats for added privacy). Attach the second mat with more lengths of the copper wire.

5 | sandwich the mats Attach the remaining set of bamboo rails, this time on the side of the fence that will face the garden. Attach the center bamboo rail first, then nail the top and bottom rails.

PLANTING TIPS

- Plan the spaces between plants, trees, and shrubs as carefully as selecting the plants for flow and balance.
- Use large trees for texture at the highest ground level. Use shrubs to fill in the middle, and flowering ground cover to provide color below.
- Use color subtly. Japanese gardens rely heavily on foliage—especially trees that turn color in the fall or spring-blooming trees—with small pockets of flowers such as chrysanthemums and azaleas.

masking sound
create the soothing sound of serenity with mellow bamboo wind chimes

Quiet solitude provides respite from the hubbub of the outside world. Yet peace is often elusive as traffic noise encroaches or aircraft fly overhead.

No mute button controls this background noise, but there are ways of masking discordant sounds with gentle, relaxing ones. Trickling water is one popular method. Add to that the rhythmic notes of a wind chime crafted of bamboo and beads for a natural look and tones of quiet repose.

Bamboo comes in a wide range of colors, from pale creams to dark russet browns. Its diameter may be as narrow as one-quarter inch or as wide as a foot or more across. A collection of diameters up to 2 inches makes pleasant chimes.

The sound of a chime piece depends on several factors, including diameter, shape, and joints. Narrow pieces clatter, while wider ones have more resonance. Solid joints create deeper tones. Beveling the ends makes lighter notes and gives an artistic touch.

String a few wires with beads alone and hang them from another narrow cane for a complementary chime to hang near your bamboo creation. Other ideas for making musical windchimes include stringing old keys on pieces of fishing line. Suspend them from a short rod and hear them clink together. Varying lengths of copper pipe make delightful chimes, and they will age to a soft verdigris. Take old cutlery out of the drawer and hang it where it can clatter in the breeze and muffle noise. The artistic possibilities are boundless, but the benefit is a soothing, relaxing melody that diminishes the din.

DANGLING CHIMES OF BAMBOO AND BEADS IN COLORS REMINISCENT OF AUTUMN LEAVES SWAY IN THE BREEZE (LEFT) AND SHINE WITH THE JEWEL-LIKE GLIMMER OF SUNLIT GLASS.

BOREAL BAMBOO. Although commonly thought of as a tropical grass, some bamboo varieties can be found at cold altitudes of the Himalayas, making them appropriate for northern climates.

bamboo wind chimes

tools & materials

SPECIAL TOOLS: Fine-tooth saw (power or handsaw), power drill with ¼-inch bit, wire snips, masking tape

- Bamboo, variety of colors and diameters
- Glass beads
- Colored jeweler's wire, 22 or 24 gauge
- Embroidery needle

Introduce a calming sound to your yard with these homemade bamboo wind chimes.

1 | cut bamboo If using a power saw, apply masking tape at cut site; cutting through tape avoids splitting bamboo. If using a traditional bonsai handsaw, use one that cuts on the pull stroke only. Cut a 12-inch crossbar from a narrow cane. Cut various size chimes from different pieces of bamboo, mixing widths and colors. Try beveling one edge for a different look and sound.

2 | lay out pieces Arrange chimes in a pleasing pattern, alternating widths and colors.

3 | drill for anchor Drill through one end of each chime for the attaching wire. Drill through each end of the crossbar for the hanging wire. (Using a bundle of newspapers as a protective cover for the work surface is a convenient substitute for scrap wood.)

4 | insert wire Pick a wire color that complements the chimes. For each chime, thread wire through holes with an embroidery needle so that 4 inches extend from one side. Twist this end around the longer end of wire to hold the chime. Straighten and center the wire above the chime. String beads on the wire. Wrap the wire securely around the crossbar then cut off the excess with wire snips.

For the hanger, cut a 24-inch length of each color of wire used. Twist wires together, leaving a single strand on each end to insert in crossbar holes and wrap tightly around bar. Hang your wind chimes outdoors from a tree branch or shepherd's hook; or indoors in a window where it receives a breeze and the beads can sparkle in the sunlight.

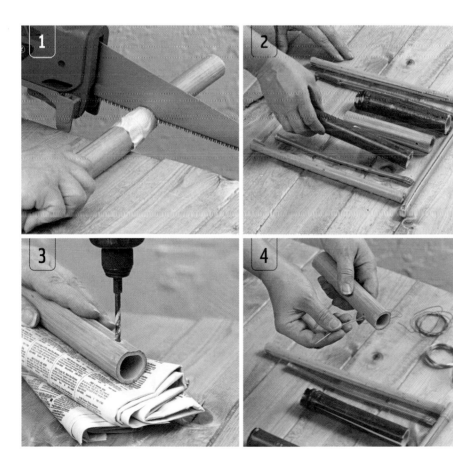

DESIGN PLANS

goal Muffle noise with the rhythmic sound of beaded bamboo chimes.

cost $1 to $9 per 6 feet of bamboo; $10+ for set of beads.

time 1 day

difficulty scale Cutting and drilling bamboo can be tricky.
◐●○○○

skill scale Have fun stringing bamboo and beads.
●●○○○

DECORATING

curtains for the porch
screens that look like elegant window treatments create a private zone

Sophisticated styling turns ordinary fiberglass screen fabric, available at hardware stores and home centers, into curtains that do double duty: They decorate while screening the porch. Bands of outdoor fabric border the edges, letting you select a color palette that suits your home's architecture and your personal taste. Pull them closed to shade views into the porch from the outside and to filter sunlight. Add to the charm of the veranda with coordinating fabrics and colors on outdoor furniture and throw rugs for a semi-private retreat.

CROSS CURTAINS (ABOVE) INTO GRACEFUL SWAGS BY LETTING GROMMETS SHARE A HOOK.

A SIMPLE HARDWARE ANCHOR (RIGHT) HOLDS THE CURTAIN CORD TAUT AND SAFELY OUT OF THE WAY.

hang the curtains

tools & materials

SPECIAL TOOLS: Clothes iron, sewing machine, grommet set, pulleys

- Outdoor fabric
- Fiberglass screening (widest available)
- 1-inch grommets
- 1-inch hooks
- Nylon cord

Bring down the curtain. Screen views from outside while allowing breezes to flow through and let you enjoy an adorned porch.

1 | miter borders For a 3-inch-deep border, cut four 7-inch-wide outdoor fabric strips: two 7 inches longer than the final curtain length, and two 7 inches longer than the final curtain width. Fold each strip in half lengthwise; press, creating a center crease.

Open strips and place them right side down on the work surface. To miter each end of one strip, fold corners in toward the center crease to form a triangle. Press. Trim the fabric ½ inch from the angle folds, making a point. Repeat the process until all four strips have points on each end.

With right sides of the fabric together, align one long strip with one short strip at the triangular ends; pin. Stitch using a ½-inch seam allowance, sewing on the fold. Repeat these steps until all of the strips are connected in a border

frame that's open along the inner edge to accept the screen fabric.

2 | encase screen Turn the border edge right side out; press at fold lines. Turn in raw fabric edges ½ inch, press. Cut the fiberglass-screen fabric to finished length. Sandwich the raw edges of the screen fabric inside the mitered border. Topstitch through all layers.

3 | hang panels Insert grommets in the top corners of the curtain panels. Insert one grommet about one-third of the length down from the top on one edge of the panel for the tieback cord. Screw the hooks into the porch overhang, one on each end and one in the center. Hang the curtains from the grommets for the tieback cord to meet at the center. The grommets at the top of the panels will share the hook in the center of the porch overhang, creating a swag effect.

4 | install pulleys Hang the pulleys from the corner hooks. Thread the nylon cord through the pulleys and the tieback grommets. Install hardware anchor pins on column bases or inside a porch rail to loop the tieback cord around to keep it from dangling.

SCREEN-FABRIC CURTAINS FRAME A PORCH (ABOVE) YET ALLOW THE HOMEOWNER TO CONTROL VIEWS.

PULLEYS ATTACHED TO THE RAFTERS (LEFT) ALLOW THE TIEBACK CORDS TO BE ADJUSTED EASILY.

DESIGN PLANS

goals Attractively enhance porch privacy, keeping insects at bay while allowing airflow.

cost about $1.50 per foot for fiberglass-screen fabric; $5 to $10 per yard for outdoor-canvas fabric, plus hardware.

time 1 weekend.

difficulty scale
Installing porch hardware is easy. Grommets require hand strength.
● ● ○ ○ ○

skill scale Straight stitching makes adding borders relatively easy; folding miters takes time.
● ● ○ ○ ○

ACCESS

Directing traffic. Here's how people can get from here to there at your home in a way that's inviting, practical, and safe.

ACCESS

Beautiful landscapes offer a sense of flow, including

easy entry to and movement around your home. The approach to your front door from the sidewalk and the street or other parking areas should be welcoming and harmonious with the design concept for the yard.

Designers consider access in two interactive ways: visual and actual. Visual access sets the scene and extends an invitation. Actual access provides a way to accept the invitation and step into the area.

There's more to creating access than simply putting in a path. Good access directs traffic—pedestrian and vehicular—to and through your yard. It shows people where you want them to go, and keeps them away from where you'd rather they didn't go. It uses directionals that might be obvious or subtle, such as the placement of a gate or the curve of a planting bed, to show the way. Good access takes convenience into account, as well as the type of usage, from foot traffic to movement of baby strollers, wheelchairs, or garden equipment such as wheelbarrows.

Think, too, about safety. Whether you have children or elderly relatives visiting, everyone should feel as though he or she can move through the yard without fear of falling or running into, or over, objects. Good surfaces and attractive and effective lighting are crucial.

HGTV designers have great ideas for helping your visitors make a grand entrance however they access your home or yard.

ARROW-SHAPE PEAKS ON SIMPLE LIGHT POSTS POINT THE WAY TO A DESTINATION ALONG A CURVING PATH, WELCOMING VISITORS WITH EASY AND INTERESTING ACCESS.

perfect pathways
walkways entice with points of interest

Getting there from here means following some kind of track. Many designers make a distinction between a walkway and a pathway.

A walk is the usual route from the public sidewalk, street, or parking area to the front door. It is more formal than a path. Comfort, safety, and a clear choice of direction are hallmarks of a well-designed walk.

The choice of material makes walks safe and visually interesting. They are often made of solid materials that provide safe footing when wet. Popular choices include concrete and brick or stone set in mortar. Concrete stains make dressing up a ho-hum walk with a punch of color easy, and texture makes it safer in wet weather than a slick surface. A single consistent

IF PEOPLE CUT ACROSS THE LAWN TO GET TO THE FRONT DOOR, CREATE A PATH FOR THEM (ABOVE).

level provides the most safety. If topography requires a slant, experts say a 5 percent slope is the safe maximum. Steeper slopes require handrails.

Low-voltage lighting guides walkers safely along the way. Safety strips that improve traction (some are reflective in the dark) adhere to the walk's surface.

Entry walks are generally 3 feet wide, which provides enough width for one person. Visitors should have enough room to walk and move their arms without feeling as though they are balancing on a tightrope. Walkways $4^{1}/_{2}$ feet wide going toward the front door are preferable, if space allows, letting two people walk side by side.

Landscapers suggest gently curving walks because nature prefers rounded edges. If, however, space for a walkway measures less than 20 feet long, or if you already have a straight sidewalk, HGTV designers have ways of turning it into a charming walk with shapely planting beds along the way.

Your beds can have curves that will turn heads. Fill them with colorful, fragrant plants that are on the same level as the walk or a little higher. Mix short and broad plants with tall and wispy ones. Anything more than 3 feet tall might make visitors feel as though they're walking through a tunnel, and create security concerns.

Garden paths are informal and often less permanent than walkways. They guide people while giving them close access to plants and landscape features. They often meander with twists that offer hints of mystery and whimsy. They may go nowhere near the house; instead they often are built simply for fun, or to make it easier to work a planting bed.

Materials should complement the landscaping. They include mulching materials, stone, or close-cropped grass. Rounded pea gravel makes a foot-friendly path with a crunch that adds sensory appeal, while homemade stepping-stones offer opportunity for

FOLLOW THE RED BRICK ROAD (TOP) THROUGH A VIVID ARCH THAT SHOWS THE WAY.

STEPPING-STONES (ABOVE) SHOW VISITORS WHERE YOU PREFER THEM TO WALK.

artistic flair. Some paths are practical, branching off walkways that provide access to the back door or a garden shed, and are made with materials such as compacted crushed stone. They are wide enough for transporting gardening supplies. Others are aesthetic, even artistic, with sweeping lines or dramatic curves that lead to surprise focal points in the garden.

A CURVING CARPET OF VELVETY GRASS (ABOVE)
WINDS SOFTLY UNDER AN ARBOR THAT ADDS
INTEREST AS IT SUBTLY SETS YOUR DIRECTION.

SHORT POSTS MARK A NARROW PATH (LEFT)
THAT INVITES VISITORS TO TAKE A RELAXING
STROLL THROUGH THE GARDEN.

moving through the yard

Let's get around to the backyard. You can get there if you take a path that's designed with that destination in mind.

Often you'll get there through the house. You'll probably step out onto a porch, a patio, or a deck constructed of concrete, wood, stone, or brick. Then you get clues from your surroundings on how to proceed. A lack of direction makes you feel as if you must stay put, while a path indicates that you can walk into the garden or wander over and take a seat on a settee under a shade tree.

Then there are times when going through the house is an awkward solution, such as when moving garden equipment or directing guests to a pool party. There may be a better route through an underused area.

Transitions. Side yards often take on the role of transition areas

BARKING UP THE RIGHT PATH. RED CEDAR MULCH GIVES A SPRING TO THE STEP WHILE IT COLORFULLY COORDINATES WITH BRICK EDGING.

connecting front yards and backyards. In deciding on walkways or paths, remember that people and equipment need access. When choosing materials, laying out flower beds, or placing gates to pass through on the way around back, imagine pushing a laden garden cart. A permanent walkway of bricks in a basket-weave pattern might fit the bill as a solid foundation with an informal style. Paths made of crushed stone or well-trodden bark mulch also provide firm footing and easy access.

In wide side yards, well-placed, vine-covered arbors take walkways from utilitarian tracks to entertaining elements. Maybe there's a blank house wall where a trellis under the eaves could hold small garden tools hanging on S-hooks, making them quickly accessible as you pass by, or a hose rack could go next to a water spigot. Strategic placement of garden art, peaking out from under a fern frond or looming large just around a bend, creates intrigue as it makes walks through the side yard an adventure.

Some side yards between buildings are narrow and dark. Consider using light-color paving to help brighten the space. Low-voltage path lights can show the way; some look like, and are installed like, border bricks and so won't snag objects being moved in tight quarters. Consult with neighbors on coordinating landscaping where property lines meet to avoid creating access problems for either party.

Backyards. Adding directionals and transitions to backyards changes the yard's character from flat expanse to desirable destination.

A bridge, either prefabricated or do-it-yourself, is charming over a pond, a creek emerging from a waterfall, or a dry creek bed. If wide enough, a bridge can hold a bench for relaxation and becomes a destination.

Give visitors a trail that goes to the garden. If you want something softer and more natural underfoot for paths, ground covers such as Irish moss are fairly sturdy and slow-growing.

Maybe you prefer flagstones or pavers but also want something growing in between. Using a base mix of sand and soil adds nutrients that allow you to fill gaps between stones with a hardy ground cover. Woolly thyme, blue star creeper, and baby's tears are good choices, depending on the amount of shade or sunlight. Woolly thyme likes sunshine and heat; blue star creeper wants dappled light; and baby's tears loves low light. Now your paths are truly part of the garden.

COBBLESTONES MEANDER ACROSS PAVING (FAR LEFT), VISUALLY TYING TOGETHER PLANTING BEDS.

AN APPEALING PIER (LEFT) IS ACTUALLY A BOARDWALK OVER A DRY STREAM OF GRAVEL.

SEND THE RIGHT MESSAGE with pathways. Straight lines are utilitarian, says landscape designer Dan Berger, while curves are more inviting and leisurely.

TAKE A ROUND TRIP AROUND THE YARD ON MOSAIC STEPPING STONES (ABOVE).

ENTER A FAIRY TALE (LEFT) THROUGH A PICKET GATE IN A PEAKED ARBOR DIVIDING THE YARD FROM THE STREET. A WINDING PATH OFFERS AN ENCHANTING INCENTIVE FOR WANDERING PAST A FRENCH-DOOR TRELLIS BEFORE REACHING THE FRONT DOOR. IF YOU'RE REPLACING A DRIVEWAY OR A SIDEWALK, CONSIDER SAVING THE CONCRETE PIECES FOR A CRAZY-QUILT PATH LIKE THIS ONE.

stepping out

Stepping-stones, either homemade or from a garden or home improvement center, have notable charm. Made of wood, tree stumps, tile, brick, stone, or concrete, they come as individual or interlocking pavers. Decorating them with paint or stain, and having fun with additions such as mosaic tiles, ceramic pieces, stained glass, marbles, and seashells turn practical stepping-stones into delightful accents.

Creating stepping-stones can be a fun family project. A variety of shapes and sizes of molds are available at garden and home improvement centers, as well as crafts stores and online sources. While the molds come with step-by-step instructions, you supply the labor and imagination.

Where to place stepping-stones can best be determined by you and other family members. Pets and people who often take shortcuts in reaching favorite areas forge trails across the lawn. If you find a timeworn track in your yard, take it as a clue that a much sturdier pathway belongs there.

Take into account your style and stride. If you are tall and long-legged, consider those family members or friends with shorter legs and then space the stones so they will be practical and comfortable for all. Designer Yoshi Kuraishi suggests walking across the area, then marking your footprints. These are the spots for stepping-stones.

After you know the spacing, and determine a style or pattern and the mold size, you'll know how many stepping-stones your path requires.

If the stepping-stones will be placed among pebbles, crushed rock, decomposed gravel, or bark or mulch, a border should be added to hold the material in place. Ready-made borders that can be found at garden stores are made of metal, rubber, vinyl, thin bender board (durable poly material that looks like wood), and scalloped concrete edging that comes in 2-foot sections.

You can make your own borders using large rocks; loose bricks set on their sides or ends; wood such as grape stakes, posts, or railroad ties; and tiles or flagstones set into the ground.

Creating the elements that you need to improve access, set direction, and mark transitions between landscaping areas is an enjoyable and worthwhile effort. In this chapter, you'll learn how to make your garden spaces accessible while reflecting your personality.

A GATED ARBOR, WITH TRELLIS "WINDOWS" AND WHIMSICAL "DOORBELL" (OPPOSITE), IMITATES A HOME ENTRYWAY AS IT CREATES A TRANSITION INTO A GARDEN ROOM.

A POSY ON THE GATE (BELOW) AND A GLIMPSE OF PATH EXTEND A WELCOMING INVITATION.

BRIDGING THE GAP CAN MEAN A FOOTBRIDGE ACROSS A DRY CREEK BED (ABOVE).

PAVERS, PEBBLES, AND POSTS (RIGHT) SET THE SCENE FOR A ROMANTIC CANDLELIT STROLL.

a crafty path leads the way
homemade stepping-stones make memories

Pathways encourage travel.
Without a defined route from one place to another, you're less likely to make the trip. So if an attractive and affordable way of drawing friends and family from, say, your front yard to a backyard deck or garden becomes an important goal—especially if a fence separates the two areas—consider a project like this one from HGTV.

In this design, a curving pathway of custom-made mosaic stepping-stones leads travelers through a gate from the front yard to the backyard deck.

Working with designer Dan Berger, the homeowners followed the construction sequence described on the following pages, but you can change the order to suit your own timetable. You may want to make stones in your workshop over the winter so they'll be ready to be placed outdoors come spring.

Low-growing flowers draw the eye downward toward the stones. 'Flower Carpet' roses are hardy to -20°F in Zones 5–9. Society garlic (*Tulbaghia violacea*) shows lilac flowers in Zones 7–10. Deep purple passion flower (*Passiflora edulis* 'Incense'), hardy to −10°F in Zones 6–9, provides tasty fruit as a bonus.

HOMEMADE STEPPING-STONES SET IN A MULCH PATH (RIGHT) EXPRESS THE PERSONALITIES OF THE FAMILY MEMBERS WHO MADE THEM.

SUNFLOWER STEPPING-STONES WERE CUT IN HALF TO CREATE SCALLOPED PATH EDGING (BELOW).

goals Define a walkway leading from the front yard to the backyard; give it a handcrafted look; make an arbor to frame the path with greenery; and end up with an affordable project.

cost $400 if you do it yourself vs. $2,400 for a professional (assuming stepping-stones are custom made).

time 2 weekends.

difficulty scale The overall project takes relatively little work, although you'll need lots of muscle power to bend rebar for the arbor.

● ● ○ ○ ○

skill scale All you need is a little creativity.

● ○ ○ ○ ○

DECORATING

BEFORE

A SOLID PLANK PRIVACY FENCE (ABOVE) MAKES A DAUNTING ENTRY INTO THE YARD. DIRT PATHS PROVIDE LITTLE DIRECTION AND EVEN LESS APPEAL.

a handcrafted path

stepping-stones

tools & materials

SPECIAL TOOLS: Masonry saw with diamond blade (optional—for border)

- Sand, 10 cubic feet for a 20-foot path, 3 feet wide, 2 inches deep
- Self-adhesive paper
- 4 reusable fiberglass molds
- Pieces of marble, stained glass, mirrors, small tiles, plastic beads
- Mold release oil (about $13 per can from masonry supply stores).
- Vinyl concrete patch mix (one 8-pound bag for four 18-inch molds)
- Quick-set aggregate concrete mix (one 10-pound bag for each 18-inch mold)
- Acrylic paint or concrete stain
- Masonry sealer

Step right up and have fun creating your own stepping-stones for leading visitors up the path. Figure on making nine stones for a 20-foot path.

1 | dig the path Measure a 3-foot-wide path, marking the outline directly on the grass or soil using landscaper's spray paint. Remove grass and dig out the path to a depth of 3 inches.

2 | sand the path Spread a 2-inch base of sand for embedding the stepping-stones.

3 | draw the pattern Start by placing a piece of self-adhesive paper right-side down inside the mold. Trace the outline of the portions of the mold that you want to fill with the mosaic onto the paper. Cut out the pattern.

Transfer this pattern onto a piece of cardboard and cut it out. Use this cardboard pattern to arrange your decorative pieces before transferring them into the mold.

AFTER

CUTTING OUT GRASS

A large portion of the path in this project led across several feet of lawn before ending at a deck. If you want to place stepping-stones within a lawn, lay out the stones about 6 inches apart for a comfortable striding distance. Score around each stone with a shovel or heavy knife and lift out the chunk of sod with a shovel. Dig out enough soil so the hole is about 3 inches deeper than the depth of the stone. Add 2 inches of sand and embed the stone so it's even with the lawn, adding sand underneath as necessary to make it level and stable.

4 | spray the mold Generously spray mold release oil. Place the self-adhesive paper pattern into the mold, sticky side up, and peel off the protective backing.

5 | place the pieces Transfer the pieces from the cardboard pattern into the mold, tacking the tops of the pieces, such as the glazed side of a tile, face down on the sticky paper.

6 | remove air bubbles Fill the bottom of the mold with a ½-inch layer of vinyl concrete patch mix. Tap the mold edges several times as you add the vinyl mix so that you distribute the mix evenly and remove air bubbles.

Fill the remainder of the mold with the quick-set concrete, again tapping the mold as you pour. After filling the molds, place them in a warm, dry spot (in the sun is ideal) for at least six hours. Avoid placing them in direct sun for more than eight

SAVING MONEY: MAKING YOUR OWN STEPPING-STONES

You can pay $60 or more for individual mosaic stepping-stones. If you plan to use 20 stones in your project, that's $1,200. Instead, consider what these homeowners did.
- **They bought reusable** fiberglass molds from a specialty garden store. Molds are also available online and in some crafts stores.
- **Molds come** in hundreds of designs and shapes, and range in size from 12-inch circles and squares to 22×24-inch rectangles.
- **Some designs** fill entire inside surfaces, leaving no room to add artistic objects. Look for molds that have open spaces.

- **This family** chose four designs: turtle, heart, butterfly, and sunflower. Molds were in the 16- to 18-inch size range. Total initial investment was $120. (You could stick with one mold in a favorite design, cutting costs further, though you'd be extending the completion date while you wait for each stone to cure before making the next one.)
- **They bought** two different concrete mixes for the base (one for weather-resistant flexibility; the other for a solid foundation) and collected materials for the mosaic—pieces of stained glass, mirrors, small tiles, marbles, and plastic beads.

a handcrafted path

stepping-stones
(continued)

hours, or you may have problems releasing the stones from molds and cleaning concrete from inside the reusable forms.

7 | remove self-adhesive paper
Release each stone by turning the mold upside down just above an area of grass or other cushioning surface. Tap gently if necessary. Pull off the self-adhesive paper.

8 | wash off mortar
Scrub off the excess vinyl concrete patch mix with water and a scrub brush, revealing the mosaic pattern. You can add details or highlights using acrylic paint or concrete stain.

9 | apply sealer
Brush on a coat of masonry sealer for a glossy shine and weather protection. Let the stones dry for two hours.

10 | set stones
Set the stones firmly in the sand. Make sure each stone is level and stable. Where the stepping-stones are surrounded by grass, make sure all the stones are level with the surface of the lawn.

11 | measure for tread
Set the stones about 6 inches apart to allow for a comfortable stride. Wait at least 72 hours before you walk on the stepping stones to give the concrete time to cure completely.

12 | create a border
In areas where you've dug out the pathway, fill around the stepping-stones with bark mulch, crushed stone, or pea gravel.

Paths made of mulching materials need borders to hold the mulch in place. One way is to make several extra stepping-stones, using the same pattern for each. Cut these stones in half using the masonry saw with the diamond blade. Decorate the half-stones with acrylic paint or concrete stain and let them dry.

Set the half-stone pieces along the path on the cut edges, overlapping them slightly to create a layered or scalloped border.

rebar trellis

tools & materials

SPECIAL TOOLS: Rebar benders, power drill

- 11 rebars, ½-inch diameter×20 feet long
- Aggregate concrete mix
- Wooden stakes
- Heavy fishing line

Arcs of appeal. Entwine simple arches with lush fragrant vines for lavish access accents.

1 | build a jig Build a semicircular jig for uniformly shaping the arches' rounded form by driving a stake into the ground as the center point of each arc.

2 | stake pattern Using the center point as a reference, drive a semicircle of stakes, each 22 inches from the center point, creating a 44-inch-wide arch, the width that spans the gate in this setting. Vary these dimensions as necessary for your site.

3 | bend rebar Center one 20-foot-long piece of ½-inch rebar against the stakes and, with one person holding each end, begin bending it gently by hand.

4 | use benders As the curve becomes tighter, use rebar benders to do the coaxing. You can find them at a concrete-supply store.

placing arches Before you set the arches in the ground, mark the spots where the legs will go. In this project, arches are clustered in groups of three for asymmetrical balance and creating a thick trellis for growing vines. Once you've determined placement, dig a hole 18 inches deep for each leg.

Shove the legs into the ground another 6 inches, resulting in a

below-ground depth of 2 feet. This prevents seasonal heaving yet still allows a comfortable head clearance.

Tie pieces of heavy fishing line between each arch and stakes in the ground and tighten the lines until the arch is plumb and stable. Then mix concrete and pour it into the holes; let it set overnight before removing the lines.

To frame a gate with the arbor, attach one arch to the gate posts. Use two or three strap hangers to hold each leg of the arch against the post. Predrill the mounting holes for the strap hangers and use deck screws to attach the hangers.

Allow the metal rebar to rust to a natural russet, or paint it to coordinate with flowers or stepping-stones.

AFTER

foot-friendly plants
let hardy ground covers serve as nature's mortar

Some ground covers thrive underfoot. These six plants, each good between flagstones, offer choices for sun or shade, wet or dry soil, and hot or cold climate.

■ **Barren strawberry** (*Waldsteinia fragarioides*) Yellow flowers stand out against a carpet of evergreen leaves in spring. In fall, the 4- to 6-inch-tall plants turn bronze. They thrive in full sun to moderate shade and well-drained soil. Hardy in Zones 4–7.

■ **Blue star creeper** (*Laurentia fluviatilis*) Tiny bright green leaves create a mosslike background for light blue, star-shape flowers in spring and summer. In hot climates, it prefers shade and regular watering. It grows 2 to 5 inches tall and is hardy in Zones 8–10 (except desert).

■ **Wild thyme** (*Thymus serpyllum*) In late spring and early summer, small purple flowers cover 4-inch-tall mats of dark green leaves. When thyme is walked on, a pleasant minty fragrance fills the air. Ideal for a hot, dry site, it grows best in full sun and well-drained soil. More cold-tolerant than woolly thyme, it grows well in Zones 4–9.

■ **Dwarf mondograss** (*Ophiopogon* spp.) It looks like grass but is an evergreen perennial ground cover. A spreading plant with slender shiny leaves and lilac flowers on spikes in summer, with blue pea-size fruit in the fall, it grows 6 inches tall. Hardy in Zones 7–10.

■ **Golden moneywort** (*Lysimachia nummularia* 'Aurea') Bright golden yellow leaves light up dark paths in full to partial shade. Slower growing than invasive green-leaf forms, golden moneywort creeps over bare soil, forming a mat 2 to 3 inches tall. A good choice for poorly drained sites, plants are hardy in Zones 4–9.

■ **Irish moss** (*Selaginella involens*) Irish moss forms a lush, mossy, vibrant light-green mat only an inch or two tall. Not a good choice for heavy clay soil, this evergreen ground cover grows best in a moist but well-drained site in partial shade. Hardy in Zones 6–10.

A MOSSLIKE GROUND COVER MAKES A SOFT PATHWAY THROUGH AN ARCH (OPPOSITE) TOWARD A HOT TUB.

A SUN-LOVING HERB, CREEPING RED THYME (ABOVE) IS IDEAL AMONG PATH STONES.

TUFTS OF DWARF MONDOGRASS (RIGHT) SPREAD INTO LUSH BORDERS AND MASS PLANTINGS.

A BLANKET OF STARS FORMS AS BLUE STAR CREEPER (FAR RIGHT) FLOWS AROUND PATHWAY PAVERS.

dwarf mondograss

blue star creeper

a transition garden
a bridge over a pond connects a deck with greenery

Landscape architect Louise Leff designed this water feature to soften the hard edge of the deck, blending it with the garden beyond.

Even the smallest water feature brings dramatic ambience to a landscape. An arcing footbridge gives those who cross a little lift.

Make sure the pond's overall size stays in proportion to the rest of your garden. If it's too large, it intrudes on living and play spaces. Downscaling creates a soothing pool that fits right in as it creates a transition point.

Ask local building officials if you need a building permit or if there are size and material restrictions. (Some communities require fences if ponds exceed a certain depth.) As a general guideline, in warm-weather states you can get by with a 12-inch depth; but if you live where the temperatures in winter drop to 10 degrees below zero, the necessary pool depth increases to

CONTROLLING ALGAE

Bridge over crystal waters. Slime and algae bloom turn ponds murky green. Help your pond stay clear, inviting guests to the edges for a closer look.

- **Feed fish** no more food than they can eat in a few minutes, and fertilize plants no more than once a month, using tablets formulated especially for water plants. Excess nitrogen encourages algae growth.
- **Allow plants** to cover one-half to two-thirds of the water surface, reducing the amount of sunlight available for fostering algae.
- **Use a nontoxic** blue dye that filters the sunlight algae need for growth.
- **Add a commercial** water clarifier that contains bacteria that consume ammonia, nitrates, and waste.
- **Float a barley ball** or add barley straw extract to the water for microorganisms that inhibit algae bloom.

WATER-WASHED STONES SOFTEN POND EDGES (RIGHT).

FEATHERY GRASSES, RUSHES, AND FLOWERS LURE VISITORS ACROSS THE BRIDGE (OPPOSITE).

SINUOUS LINES ON PLANTING BEDS (ABOVE) STRIVE FOR ATTENTION BUT GO FLAT AGAINST STRAIGHT-EDGED CONCRETE SLABS.

a transition garden
making the pond

24 inches; and if the lows sink to 30 below, you'll need a depth of at least 36 inches. Check with your local extension service for advice.

Attention-getter. A pond and bridge—wherever you put them—become a natural focal point. You want to place them where they will add the most life to your backyard garden and where you would like to draw attention.

Often the best site is the transition point where your patio or deck opens onto your yard or garden.

Water gardens turn a plain patch of lawn into calming, serene pools. A footbridge beckons visitors on a venture across the pond into the peace and beauty that awaits them on either side. Just be sure that the site you choose is on high ground or in an area that gradually slopes away from the house. Low spots collect runoff and may be difficult to drain.

Dig correctly. You can take on this project yourself even if you may not consider yourself a seasoned do-it-yourselfer. Building a water garden is not a particularly difficult task, even for a beginner. All you need are a few simple tools. As you begin building your pond, allow plenty of time for each step. Excavation is often the most taxing part, but you can pull this off. The key to whether it's fun or frustrating lies in how much you can do by yourself without overdoing it. Just take your time, follow the instructions, arm some friends with shovels and a wheelbarrow or two, and start digging.

Use proper digging technique, with a straight back and good posture, and knees bent to distribute weight to your legs. Scoop small amounts at a time. Lift with your legs and not your back. When carrying a shovelful of soil to the dump site, walk with your knees slightly bent to avoid back strain.

Check out more ideas from HGTV.com.
For water, water everywhere, see
■ www.hgtv.com/landscapemakeoversbook

making the pond

tools & materials

SPECIAL TOOLS: Scissors, shovel, string level, spirit level, masonry trowel
- Landscaper's paint
- Underlayment
- Sand
- 10×12-foot pond liner for a 5-foot diameter pond that's 12 inches deep
- Large, flat round-edged stones
- Mason's mix
- Sponge

Dig in. Determine the pond's location and size—the example pictured has a 5-foot diameter—and mark the pond's perimeter with landscaper's paint. Dig the pool 3 inches deeper than its final depth, allowing room for underlayment and sand. The depth required depends on whether you will be stocking your pond with fish and on how cold your region is in winter.

DESIGN PLANS

goals Add a feature to this large backyard that enlivens the space; create a transition from the house, deck, and patio to the rest of the yard with a bridge.

cost $750 if you do it yourself vs. $3,000 for a pro.

time 2 weekends.

difficulty scale You'll be carrying heavy stones and doing lots of digging.
●●●○○

skill scale The most tedious parts are cutting the arcs and forming pleats in the liner.
●●●○○

BUILDING

Dig a ledge around the pond 2 inches deep and a foot wide for the rock border that anchors the liner and edges the pond.

Smooth the ledge, bottom, and sides of the pond with the back of the shovel and remove protruding roots and sharp objects that could puncture the liner.

1 | level edges Stretch a line with a suspended string level from one side of the pond to the other side to check the level of the edges. If the edges are not even, the water will appear tilted in the pond.

Cut strips of carpet or commercial underlayment to fit the pond. Install this padding, extending it up the sides from the bottom to the outside edge of the ledge, with each strip overlapping its neighbor. Or spread a smooth 2-inch-deep layer of soft sand over the entire bottom of the pond, as well as a 1-inch-thick layer on the pond ledge.

2 | pleat liner Now comes the tricky part—getting a square liner to fit into a round hole. The 10×12-foot liner used for this project is fitted to the shape of the pond with pleats and folds so that it lies neatly along all the corners and ridges. This part

AFTER

of the job takes time and patience. (To make the liner as flexible as possible, open it up and lay it in sunlight for half an hour to warm.)

Begin installation by spreading the liner across the pond. Then fill it with water until it naturally sinks and stabilizes, temporarily holding the liner edge with stones or bricks so it doesn't slip into the water.

Along the edge of the pond, fold the liner in pleats so that it lies flat. Although it's OK to cut away some excess to make the liner easier to handle, it's better to wait until the pleating is complete to ensure there's enough liner to cover the edges.

3 | fill the pond Add more water to the pond while checking the folds in the liner and adjusting as necessary where gaps or leaking occur. Once you're satisfied with the liner, it's time for permanently setting the border stones.

4 | place stones Louise Leff chose large, flat pieces of California water-washed stone for this project because

the stones' rounded edges enhance the natural look of the pond. Any native stone with smooth edges will work. This edging also keeps the outline of the pond looking natural, as if the pond has always been there.

Dry-fit the stones, arranging them like puzzle pieces until a good fit is achieved. Leave a slight overhang along the inside edge of the pond to conceal the liner.

After all the stones have been laid, set the bridge (see page 74) in place, making sure it fits in the designated area. Lay a piece of flagstone on the lawn where the end of the bridge will be set. A stone base prevents

the wood from coming in direct contact with the soil, which would eventually rot the wood. Adjust the soil under the flagstone until it lies flat. Check it with a spirit level.

With the stones in position, mortar each one in place with mason's mix, which ensures a strong bond.

5 | clean the stone Remove excess mortar from the sides of the stones with a trowel; then clean the surface of each stone with a damp sponge before the mortar has a chance to set.

Trim excess liner extending beyond the stone edging. Then drain the pond, clean out debris, and refill it.

building a bridge

tools & materials

SPECIAL TOOLS: 6½-inch circular saw or jigsaw, compound miter saw, power drill with ⅜-inch bit

- 2 – 2×12s, 8 feet long
- 1 – 2×6, 8 feet long
- 5 – 2×6s, 8 feet long
- Masonry line and pencil
- Bender board or ¼-inch hardboard strip, 8 feet long
- 16d nails, deck screws, and 3-inch carriage bolts
- 2 – 1×2-foot flagstones or 4 concrete pavers

Plan the span Plan to locate the bridge across the pond's narrowest width. Bridges longer than 8 feet require special engineering and extra-sturdy materials. Use pressure-treated, redwood, cedar, wood-plastic composite, or other lumber rated for outdoor use.

draw top arc For two arcs that are each 8 feet long and 7½ inches high, start with two 2×12s, each 8 feet long. Measure 5½ inches from each end of one 2×12. Mark these points along one edge. Also mark the center point of the 2×12. (The curve of the top arc begins at the left mark, curves upward to the center point, then downward to the right mark.)

Lay the 2×12 flat on the ground. To scribe the arc of the bridge, use a compass made from a long piece of masonry line and a pencil. Attach one end of the line to a pivot point on the ground; tie the other end to a pencil. Start with a pivot point 6½ feet from the bottom edge of the 2×12. Adjust this distance until you can connect the three points in one graceful curve. Draw the line for the top arc.

Now mark the opposite edge of the 2×12 to create the bottom curve of the arc. Measure 9 inches in from each end to mark the ends of the bottom arc. (This leaves a flat surface at each end between the top and bottom of the arch.)

Then from points every 8 inches along the top arc, measure down 7½ inches perpendicular to the top arc and make a mark, creating a connect-the-dots curve.

1 | press bender Drive pairs of nails at the marks for the bottom curve. Slip a piece of bender board (or a strip of ¼-inch hardboard) between each nail pair.

2 | draw cut line Using the bender board as a guide, draw a pencil line connecting the marked points to form the bottom arc. Cut along this

line with a 6½-inch circular saw. (If you use a jigsaw, the job will take about an hour.)

After you've cut the first arched piece, sand the edges smooth and use it as a template for the second 2×12. Cut the second arched piece.

Next, cut a 2×6 into 18-inch lengths. Use two of these lengths as crosspieces to connect the bridge arcs at one end and at their halfway points with deck screws. The crosspiece at the other end will be installed later.

3 | attach deck planks Cut 2×6s into 24-inch lengths for decking. Screw the decking onto the top of the arcs. Each decking board will overlap the arched frame by about 1½ inches on each side. Check spacing between deck boards with a

16d nail. This spacing accommodates swelling and lets water drain.

4 | leave room to work Install all but the last two decking boards at the end without a crosspiece.

5 | prepare to install Temporarily place the bridge unit in its final location. Mark the locations of both ends of the bridge on the ground and also on the joist where the bridge attaches to a deck, if applicable.

If the bridge will not be attached to a deck, attach the final crosspiece and the last two pieces of decking. Also set flagstones at both ends of the bridge, not just one as was directed when building the pond (page73). Check that the deck edges rest firmly on the stones at both ends.

Both ends of the bridge need to be at the same elevation. If one end of the bridge attaches to a deck, the opposite end should be at the same elevation as the deck end. Dig out sod or soil on the end of the bridge where it meets the ground for the large flagstone or concrete paver. Stuff soil under the stone or paver until it is level and stable.

6 | install support If the bridge attaches to a deck, nail an 18-inch 2×6 to the deck joist at the location marked in Step 4. Position the 2×6 so that its top is 1½ inches below the deck's surface. Using a ⅜-inch bit, drill holes about 3 inches from the ends through the 2×6 into the deck joist for the carriage bolts.

7 | attach bridge Set the bridge in place. Check that the deck end fits snugly around the 2×6 and that the other end rests firmly on the stone. Nail the bridge to the 2×6.

8 | bolt support Anchor the 2×6 to the deck joist by inserting 3-inch carriage bolts in the holes you drilled in step 6. At the ends of the bridge flanking the 2×6, screw through the arcs into the 2×6 using deck screws. Attach the last two pieces of bridge decking.

HAMMERING TIPS

■ **For power,** grip the handle close to the end. Tap nail until set; then drive in with an arching motion.

■ **When you have no braces** to hold boards, try this: Set one board on a steady surface and drive the nails part way in. Hold the board to the other board and finish hammering through both boards.

After you've finished the bridge and pond in this project, choosing plants that highlight the features is like putting icing on the cake. Here, flower-filled containers on the deck visually tie the house and garden together, inviting visitors to cross the bridge and explore the lush plantings in and around the pond and in the gardens beyond.

Landscape architect Louise Leff creates a peaceful scene around this pool with green plants such as rush and sedge, natural companions near water. She also likes plants with interesting textures, such as foxglove, chosen more for its large beautiful leaves than for its flowers. She adds

spot color by repeating perennials from other parts of the garden, providing landscape unity.

If you build your pool in a sunny spot, you might prefer to landscape the water's edge with easy-care ornamental grasses such as prairie dropseed and fountain grass. In a shady site, hostas and ferns provide a natural-looking edging in calm, cooling shades of green.

Planting the pond. Water lilies, with their eloquent flowers and lush leaves, serve as the focal point in many water gardens, with bog plants such as dwarf umbrella palm (*Cyperus alternifolius*) in supporting roles. Here, cold-tolerant water horsetail (*Equisetum fluviatile*) stands at attention nearby as soft rush (*Juncus effusus*), which keeps its color all year, gently sweeps the bridge.

Place water plants in pots that allow good air circulation, such as lattice-type crates lined with burlap. Elevate them on bricks at the proper level.

Setting oxygenator plants, such as anacharis (*Egeria densa*) on the bottom of the pool provides oxygen for fish and keeps the water clear. Use one pot for every 2 to 3 square feet of water surface. In northern climates, add free-floating plants such as water hyacinth (*Eichhornia crassipes*). **Note:** The sale of some oxygenator plants is regulated in warm climates where escaped plants can clog waterways.

rush

horsetail

SOME LIKE IT WET

Bridging the bog is one solution to traversing a soggy spot in your yard. Plants also direct visitors around the wet area. Although most plants require good drainage for survival, here are a few that prefer wet feet.

Trees
- **Bald cypress** (*Taxodium distichum*), Zones 4–11
- **Swamp white oak** (*Quercus bicolor*), Zones 4–8

Shrubs
- **Buttonbush** (*Cephalanthus occidentalis*), Zones 5–11
- **Summersweet** (*Clethra alnifolia*), Zones 4–9
- **Winterberry** (*Ilex verticillata*), Zones 3–9

Perennials
- **Cardinal flower** (*Lobelia cardinalis*), Zones 3–9
- **Drumstick primrose** (*Primula denticulata*), Zones 4–7
- **Marsh marigold** (*Caltha palustris*), Zones 4–9
- **Meadowsweet / Queen-of-the-meadow** (*Filipendula ulmaria*), Zones 3–7
- **Pickerel rush** (*Pontederia cordata*), Zones 3–11
- **Swamp milkweed** (*Asclepias incarnata*), Zones 3–7
- **Turtlehead** (*Chelone lyonii*), Zones 3–7
- **Yellow flag iris** (*Iris pseudacorus*), Zones 3–9

COLORFUL POTTED PERENNIALS DRAW ATTENTION ACROSS THE BRIDGE (ABOVE LEFT) TO THE DECK.

WISPY BLADES CONTRAST WITH THE TEXTURE OF THE FLOWER HEADS ON THIS RUSH (FAR LEFT), MAKING IT A POINT OF INTEREST.

GREEN STALKS WITH BLACK AND PINK BANDS MAKE HORSETAIL A STRIKING FEATURE (LEFT).

MOSQUITO-BEATING TIPS

A water feature need not be a breeding ground for mosquitoes. Choose one of these easy ways to keep mosquitoes at bay:

- **Add a bubbler.** Moving water discourages mosquitoes from breeding.
- **Add mosquito fish** or goldfish to the water. For every 5 gallons of water, you'll need one small fish.

- **Float Mosquito Dunks** on the water's surface. An environmentally safe product, it contains bacteria (*Bacillus thuringiensis israelensis*, or Bti for short) that kill mosquitoes without harming pets or wildlife. One small doughnut-shape dunk is enough to treat 100 gallons of water for 30 days.

4
BRAND-NEW VIEW

Cover-up. Disguise visual shortcomings and enhance existing views by screening the unsightly and creating focal points.

a brand-new
VIEW

It could be that you have the garden equivalent of the basic black dress or blue suit: the lawn, the shade tree, the standard shrubbery, and the sturdy patio.

All you need are the perfect accessories, the gems that turn heads and provide focal points wherever the eye and foot may roam.

As you make landscaping plans, take advantage of existing views and consider how changes will alter the view. As you discover visual assets and shortcomings, take note. Perhaps you can cluster necessary but unsightly utilitarian items—garbage cans, compost bins, pool equipment, or heating and cooling units—into one area that can be attractively screened from view.

Consider the view from the yard toward the house too. That black hole under the deck can be made less stark with lattice panels as the background for a container garden. And just as you don't want to be spotted from windows above when using your deck or patio, you also don't want to look up and see gutters or vents. A vine-covered pergola disguises and shades the view from below as well.

Big empty walls are blank canvases for eye-popping attention-getters. Add a trellis, a mirror, some hanging plants, or an espaliered tree and see the change that comes over them. You can hide the unsightly and enhance the view with a good cover-up.

VIBRANTLY COLORED MOSAICS AND TALL SPIKY
PLANTS AGAINST A WALL MAKE A SMALL PATIO
FEEL MUCH LARGER AND MORE WELCOMING BY
DRAWING THE EYE UPWARD AND ARTFULLY
DISGUISING THE DRAB, UTILITARIAN CONCRETE.

A BRAND-NEW VIEW

get to the point
draw attention where you want it
with clever focal points

Divert attention and create a brand-new view by blocking, hiding, or camouflaging whatever is unsightly.

Screening unattractive views, such as dog runs, air-conditioning units, the neighbors' old cars, or a rusting chain-link fence, or dressing up an otherwise dull and drab yard, garden area, walkway, porch or patio, is easy with a little planning.

Planting, pruning, potting, and painting enhance views from wherever you and your visitors sit, stand, or stroll. By injecting a modicum of imagination and a megadose of excitement into your yard projects, you can have a landscape that's all dressed up as someplace to go.

Create a focal point. Focal points, such as a terraced planter in the corner of a courtyard or a wall fountain on a fence at the end of a garden pathway, offer the eye a place to rest. They also can divert views from the unsightly—so if there is something you don't want visitors to see, give them something else to look at instead. The secret to successful focal points is restraint. If the eye jumps from one point to another, focus blurs among distracting elements lost in space.

Focal points by their nature are objects or plants that stand out. For example, colorful objects set against neutral backgrounds garner attention. Specimen plants—any plant that has a unique shape or habit—create a sense of excitement. Allow a specimen tree to take center stage as the star attraction of its own space. Bring light to the shade under a more ordinary tree by planting colorful annuals in beds around its base.

Objects as focal points. Ornaments are part of the basic structure of the garden because they stay the same from season to season. They add dimension and color to a drab winter landscape, and make a statement among plants the rest of the year. They can serve a practical purpose, such as a birdbath or a feeder that attracts wildlife, or a sundial that keeps track of time. They can visually expand a garden, such as a mirror on a fence behind a fountain, which gives an illusion of depth and mystique. They can play artistic design roles by creating balance, such as a tall pillar or sculpture that offsets a tree, or a stone sphere that brings shape to a spread of flat ground cover.

A signature piece, such as a sculpture or something unique that makes your yard different from others on your block, reveals personality and brings a touch of appealing playfulness that gets noticed.

Check out more ideas from HGTV.com
For tips on creating focal points, see
■ www.hgtv.com/landscapemakeoversbook

SIMPLE COLOR (RIGHT) FROM HANGING RED GERANIUMS ABOVE BLUE IRIS CREATES A FOCAL POINT.

SCARLET POTTERY (BELOW) GIVES LUSTER AMID DRIFTS OF RED AND GOLD NASTURTIUMS.

A RED WALL MASKS GRAY CONCRETE (BELOW RIGHT) AND BECOMES A BACKDROP FOR A VIVID MOSAIC AND SCULPTURAL PLANTINGS.

LOOK AGAIN. IT'S A TENNIS RACKET (ABOVE) POSING AS A TRELLIS AMID A STAND OF LUPINES AND COLORFUL MIXED ANNUALS.

A BRIGHT BLUE BENCH (ABOVE) TUCKED AMID
THE GREENERY IMMEDIATELY CATCHES THE EYE
AND HELPS DRAW ATTENTION TO MORE SUBTLE
ELEMENTS, SUCH AS A BIRDHOUSE IN A TREE.
A SPLASH OF MAGENTA AND ORANGE FLOWERS
SURPRISINGLY WORK TO COOL THE INTENSITY
OF THE BLUE.

blank slates and cover-ups

New life. Give big blank walls, fences, or floors a fresh face with a little sprucing up. Trellised vines or espaliered trees give exterior walls and ordinary fences a new persona. Add some painted shutters, hanging baskets of flowers, a window box with trailing vines, an enchanting three-dimensional hand-painted trompe l'oeil scene, art objects, or a shelf for a collection of watering cans or old bottles. These attention-grabbers allow the walls to contribute to the overall ambience of the garden.

Jazz up a porch floor or patio pad by painting, staining, or resurfacing. Technology provides consumers with abundant product choices. Various techniques can help you create checkerboard designs; faux flagstones, slate, and brick; or swirls and curls.

Go for the gold, the silver, and the bronze. No need to cover up a dull patio or porch with furniture and potted plants when you can turn that ugly duckling into a preening swan with the flick of a paintbrush. Paint a whimsical patio or porch rug directly on the floor.

Concrete stains, which come in a variety of hues, transform dull gray concrete patios into outdoor floors that ooze old-world charm. If you want a real brick, slate, or flagstone patio but have gray concrete, there's no need to tear out the existing structure. The level patio can be the base for the new masonry surface.

Screening. Views of garbage cans, a utility pole, a vehicle in a carport, a pet pen, or an air-conditioning unit can ruin the look you hope to achieve. Think screens—you can build them, buy them, or grow them.

Garbage cans are a fact of life. We use them often and need easy access. Cans have to be rolled out to the end of the driveway on trash pickup days, and the cans should sit on a hard surface. You may store them just inside a gate, which hides them from outside the yard but leaves them on view for those in the backyard. Or you may have no choice but to leave them

in the front yard all the time. A homemade lattice screen topped with flower boxes that hold trailing vines and blooming plants becomes the master of disguise.

Latticework also helps camouflage air-conditioning and heating units. Ample air space and a way to get to the units for servicing should be taken into consideration when deciding how to screen the machinery. Lattice screens can also be used to hide a pool filter and pump, a compost pile, a woodpile, a play area, or the underside of a deck.

A lattice screen is ineffective for hiding a light pole. A tall tree, strategically placed, can do the job. If the light pole is yours, paint it a forest green that better blends with the garden. Train a vine on it that will climb, wind, and cover.

CONCRETE STAINS CAN GIVE NEW LIFE TO STEPPING-STONES (ABOVE).

PAINT A RUG ON THE FLOOR TO DRESS UP DRAB CONCRETE OR DECKING (RIGHT).

WALK ON WATER, OR AT LEAST SEEM TO DO SO, ON PAVERS IN A STREAMBED OF BLUE STONE (ABOVE). CRAFTSMAN-STYLE LIGHT FIXTURES INSPIRE THE PATH'S MOTIF.

HARLEQUIN PATTERNS AND BOLD COLORS (OPPOSITE), MAKE A SMALL SPACE UNDENIABLY SPECTACULAR.

"COLOR POSSESSES ME. I don't have to pursue it. It will possess me always, I know it. That is the meaning of this happy hour: Color and I are one. I am a painter."
—DIARY, ARTIST PAUL KLEE

cover-ups

(continued)

If you have a clothesline, screening it might be a little more difficult as it needs to have plenty of sun and a fair amount of air. Because they allow air circulation, lattice screen panels works in this area too.

Achieve partial screening along a carport by using bamboo posts and cross poles for trellising a vine. Buri (dried palm leaf) screens or reed mats also make nice baffles and are relatively inexpensive natural materials. Dog runs can be shielded from outdoor

DISGUISE CHAIN LINK FENCING BY COVERING IT WITH A TRADITIONAL WILLOW FENCE (BELOW) THAT GIVES FLOWERS A NATURAL BACKGROUND.

living areas by shrubs, short fences, or screens covered with plant material. A workhorse in the garden, the trellis provides an attractive screen and focal point. While wood is probably the most popular choice of materials, metal tubing, copper tubing, and even PVC pipe can be fashioned into trellises that are definite attention-getters.

Gazebos, gates, garden sheds, stone walls, and grape-stake screens can also be used to hide eyesores, create focal points, or provide backgrounds for focal points all at the same time. Unlike some plant material that may be used for screens, structures stay the same all year. They don't lose leaves or seasonally change color.

While contemplating cover-ups, remember that what can be seen from within a house can be as important as views from outside, especially during the winter months when more time is spent indoors.

When the curtain goes up or the blinds open at your house, make sure you have a pleasurable view. What is it your eye focuses on when you are standing at the kitchen sink looking out the window? A mature fig tree with a gnarled trunk would be intriguing. Replacing that splintery wooden fence might improve the view. When seated at the dining table, delight at the sight of a rose garden. While curling up in a chair near the bedroom window, look

out at a lush lawn or a woodland plant bed instead of the wooden fence that separates your side of a barren, crumbling patio.

It could be that something as simple as a water fountain of Mexican pots sitting amid pastel colored plants would make a calming sight. A well-placed specimen shrub or a hanging basket of flowers will make you want to leave the draperies open in your dining room all day long. Know what you want to see and the emotion you want to create.

If setting the scene in your garden requires structural work—and the use of hammers, saws, lumber, masonry skills, electrical work, or plumbing—determine what you can and are willing to do yourself.

Visit home improvement and garden centers to see what ready-made structures, such as water features,

screens, wood and plastic fence panels, reed mats, gazebos, stonework, and water features, are available. At the very least, you might be able to borrow some design ideas.

See things as they are, then think of them as they can be. Even if you opt against hanging a mirror in your garden, how others view your outdoor spaces is a reflection on you.

Check out more ideas from HGTV.com
Get fresh garden design and crafts tips at:
■ www.hgtv.com/landscapemakeoversbook

CONICAL TREES (ABOVE) BREAK UP THE VERTICAL SPACE OF A TALL, BLAND TWO-STORY HOUSE AND SOFTEN ITS EDGES. THE NARROW, UPRIGHT SHAPES LEAVE WINDOWS WITH CLEAR VIEWS AND PLENTY OF LIGHT.

A PAINTBOX OF IDEAS FOR GARDENERS

Color wheel. Gardening with color requires understanding concepts long followed by artists and designers. Create notable planting plans by using the color wheel.
■ **Analogous colors** are those colors adjacent to each other on the color wheel. They produce harmonious combinations.
■ **Contrast** comes from using colors opposite each other.
■ **Restful colors** are in the blue, violet, purple, and pink range.
■ **Vibrant colors** include reds, golds, and oranges.
■ **A tint** is a color that is mixed with white so it becomes softer.
■ **A shade** is a color that is mixed with black so it becomes subtle and more saturated.

AN ALLURINGLY ARTISTIC PATHWAY (LEFT) POINTS TOWARD A FOUNDATION THAT HAS BEEN DRESSED UP WITH BAMBOO SCREENING.

add a fountain to your view
decorative containers do more than hold plants—as fountains they spice up the view

When the view outside is less than appealing, you're missing an uplifting experience every time you glance out the window. Imagine, instead, filling that space on the other side of the glass with a gracefully flowing fountain surrounded by beautiful plantings. It's a prized extension of your inside living space—a window garden that brings the outdoors inside.

The owners of this project worked with Peter Parker to enlarge their bedroom window to gain light and a view. If you already have a large window to frame your garden, you have a head start on the process. But if your situation is like that of these homeowners, and you intend to replace a window, that should be the first step. Then you'll be able to stand or sit inside and admire your garden. In this example, the focal point of the new garden is a fountain made from a Mexican urn. The textures of the landscaping around it complement the fountain and complete the picture.

A CLAY JAR FROM OAXACA, MEXICO (LEFT), BECOMES A FOUNTAIN FOCAL POINT, EXTENDING THE VIEW FROM INDOORS ONTO A PATIO.

WHEN VIEWED FROM INDOORS, AN ARCHED WINDOW FRAMES THE FOUNTAIN (BELOW) MAKING IT SEEM A PART OF THE DECOR.

COBBLESTONES HIDING THE WATER RESERVOIR, PLUS SPIKY FERNS AND GRASSES, ADD TEXTURES THAT CONTRAST WITH PAVERS (RIGHT).

BEFORE

A PATCH OF LAWN, A FARAWAY TREE, AND SCRAGGLY TUFTS OF ORNAMENTAL GRASS OFFER LITTLE REASON TO LOOK OUTSIDE (ABOVE).

a fiesta fountain

tools & materials

SPECIAL TOOLS: Power drill with masonry bit, round rasp

- Mexican urn or other decorative container
- Sealant
- Pump box
- Submersible pump (rated at least 50 gph) with automatic fill/drain devices
- Flexible drain pipe, 2-inch diameter
- Glue
- ½-inch plastic electrical conduit and 90-degree elbow
- Flexible, high-strength poly tubing for water supply; hose-bib adapter
- Underlayment or old carpet
- 10×10 pond liner
- 1½-inch drain rock, 10½-cubic-foot bags
- ¾-inch PVC pipe, threaded bulkhead fitting, fitting nut, couplers, adapters, elbows
- Adhesive caulk
- Cobblestones

Water view Water spills over the lip of this fountain for a shimmering focal point. Have fun selecting a container for your fountain. The ceramic urn used in this project—2 feet in diameter and 3 feet tall—is from Mexico and cost $300. In areas without freezing weather, you can use this fountain all year. In cold climates, you will need to drain the fountain and bring the container indoors.

Prepare the fountain Because ceramic jars aren't meant for fountains, you may need to do some retrofitting. If the pot has no drainage hole, drill one in the center of its bottom. Smooth the edges with a round rasp.

Unless it is glazed, the pottery is probably porous. Cover the inside and outside of the container with two coats of stone sealant or similar product (ask at a home improvement center) to prevent leaking.

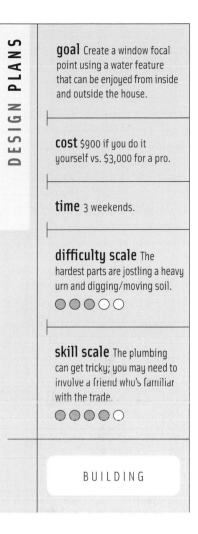

DESIGN PLANS

goal Create a window focal point using a water feature that can be enjoyed from inside and outside the house.

cost $900 if you do it yourself vs. $3,000 for a pro.

time 3 weekends.

difficulty scale The hardest parts are jostling a heavy urn and digging/moving soil.

●●●○○

skill scale The plumbing can get tricky; you may need to involve a friend who's familiar with the trade.

●●●●○

BUILDING

Excavating the site Outline the perimeter of the reservoir that surrounds the fountain, then excavate it. The reservoir should be about 5 feet across and 1 foot deep.

Next, dig a hole to house the pump box. The size of the hole for the pump box depends on the size of the box. This one is 2 feet square and 3 feet deep.

You'll also need to excavate a pair of trenches: one between the pump box and the house to carry the pump's wiring and incoming water feed and the other for the drain line that leads from the pump box to an exit site downhill from the box. Check local codes to determine how deep the trench for the water line has to be to

add a fountain to your view

fiesta fountain

(continued)

prevent freezing. The drain line and trench should come off the drain fitting on the back of the pump box.

1 | test pump box placement Set the pump box in its hole and check that it is level. Backfill with soil as necessary to level the box. Then remove the box from the hole.

2 | install drain Lay 2-inch flexible pipe in the trench behind the pump box to serve as the overflow drain. Glue it to the fitting on the back of the box.

3 | Thread an extension cord for the pump through the elbow and the

conduit. Cut a piece of ½-inch flexible plastic conduit long enough to reach from the pump box to an electrical outlet. Add a 90-degree elbow at the pump end.

4 | install the pump Use a submersible pump fitted with an automatic fill device, which works much like the float inside a toilet tank. Include an automatic drain mechanism that directs water away from the pump box through a 2-inch drain pipe when the water level in the box gets too high. Attach the automatic fill valve to the pump. Screw an adapter to the threaded end of a dedicated hose bib. Attach

AFTER

one end of a length of flexible tubing to the hose-bib adapter. Glue the other end to the fill-valve fitting on the back of the pump box.

5 | line the reservoir Level the top edge of the reservoir hole. Remove exposed roots and other sharp objects inside the hole that might puncture the liner. Lay old carpet or commercial underlayment, or spread 2 inches of moist sand, in the hole as a protective layer for the liner.

Position the pond liner in the hole. Gather extra material around the edge into pleats to create a good fit. (Butyl rubber is the heaviest and most expensive liner, but less-costly PVC and EPDM liners are effective; even low-density polyethylene works if it is kept out of direct sunlight.)

6 | add face plate Water needs to flow between the rock reservoir and the pump box. Cut a hole in the liner where it covers the opening on the pump box. Cover the cut edge of the liner with the box's face plate. Screw

the plate tightly to the box. Rinse the 1½-inch drain rock, then spread it evenly in the lined reservoir.

Fill the reservoir with 1½-inch diameter gray river rock, smoothing it to level it.

7 | make spout Glue a plastic bulkhead fitting to the end of a length of ¾-inch PVC pipe that will be the fountain's spout. Apply caulk to the bottom of the fitting's flange. Then slip the PVC pipe through the mouth of the urn.

8–9 | secure fittings Tip the urn on its side and have a helper hold the pipe in place with the threads of the bulkhead exposed through the hole in the bottom. Spread caulk on the nut. Screw the nut onto the bulkhead, drawing the bulkhead tight against the bottom of the container.

Glue an elbow, a coupler, and a threaded adapter to the end of the bulkhead. Clamp one end of the flexible tubing to the adapter, then attach the opposite end of the tubing to the pump.

Have a helper keep the tubing from crimping while you bury the base of the fountain in the rocks. Adjust the rocks under the fountain to ensure that the fountain is plumb, then turn on the spigot. Check the water flow and adjust it at the pump.

Top the rocks and cover the exposed liner on the edge of the reservoir with cobblestones. Put the lid on the pump box and cover it with cobblestones. Backfill the trenches for the drain line and electrical conduit.

VERSATILE CONTAINERS can be any of a variety of materials, including metal, ceramic, terracotta, plastic, and wood. Finding different ways of using them perks up vistas.

Choosing plants to play supporting roles makes the most of a beautiful focal point. Select plants that will complement your feature rather than compete with it. Foliage plants that emphasize texture, not color, make the best players. For example, to keep attention focused on the beautiful water feature in this garden, landscape designer Peter Parker chose ferns and other native woodland plants that create a natural-looking understory beneath the mature redwoods. Small white flowers add subtle highlights.

Leaf shape plays a big part in determining plant texture, sometimes described as the "visual feel" of a plant. Most ferns, ones with lacy leaves, have fine texture, while the bold leaves of hostas give that plant a coarse texture. By pairing plants with contrasting textures, you can add visual interest to your garden without detracting from the focal point.

Foliage foils. When searching for plants with interesting textures, don't limit yourself to the usual selection of bedding plants and perennials. Be sure also to browse through the houseplant aisles, where you will find a variety of leaf shapes and colorful foliage. Though not winter-hardy in most of the United States, tropical

plants play a great supporting role when grown outdoors as annuals.

Herbs have interesting textures that vary from the needlelike leaves of rosemary to the feathery foliage of dill.

Perennials for supporting roles. Many perennials are prized not for showy flowers but for their varied leaf forms and textures.

For shade
■ **Lungwort** (*Pulmonaria saccharata* 'Sissinghurst White'*)* Small white spring flowers and broad leaves speckled with silver shine in dark corners. Foot-tall plants like moist soil but tolerate dry shade once established. Hardy in Zones 3–7.
■ **Pacific bleeding heart** (*Dicentra formosa* 'Luxuriant'*)* Unlike old-

ORNAMENTAL GRASSES AND FERNS (ABOVE) PROVIDE SHAPE AND TEXTURE IN THE FOUNTAIN GARDEN.

OVERFLOWING WATER GLISTENS ON THE SIDES OF THE CERAMIC FOUNTAIN (RIGHT), CREATING A BRIGHT SPOT ON THE PATIO.

lady's mantle (medium texture)

Chinese rhubarb (coarse texture)

'Powis Castle' wormwood (fine texture)

fashioned bleeding heart, which disappears in summer's heat, the lacy blue-green foliage of fringed bleeding heart persists all season. Small cherry red flowers bloom on 15-inch plants. Zones 7–10.

■ **Hosta 'Krossa Regal'** Wide blue-green leaves stand 2 to 3 feet tall in an upright vase shape. Best growth is in rich, moist, well-drained soil. Hardy in Zones 3–9.

■ **Japanese painted fern** (*Athyrium nipponicum* 'Pictum') The fine, feathery texture of this fern is made even more special with subtle markings of lavender, silver, and red. Best in moist, humusy, well-drained soil, this fern grows about 18 inches tall. Hardy in Zones 4–9.

■ **Lady's mantle** (*Alchemilla mollis*) Gray-green scalloped leaves catch drops of dew and sparkle like jewels. Greenish yellow flowers add subtle color in summer. The plants grow 12 to 18 inches tall, adapting to almost any kind of soil. Hardy in Zones 3–9.

■ **Red barrenwort** (*Epimedium* × *rubrum*) Handsome heart-shape leaves emerge in spring with red tinges, turning dark green in summer, then bronze in autumn. Dainty red flowers

resembling tiny columbine blossoms top 10-inch-tall plants in spring. Best in fertile, well-drained soil, red barrenwort tolerates dry shade, such as beneath a tree. Hardy in Zones 4–8.

For sun

■ **Adam's needle** (*Yucca filamentosa*) Swordlike leaves grow in a clump 3 feet tall or more, thriving in sandy, dry soil. The bold gray-green leaves contrast beautifully with fine-textured companions. Hardy in Zones 4–11.

■ **Beach wormwood** (*Artemisia stelleriana*) Deeply divided leaves of silvery white give this artemisia a fine texture. Easy to grow in well-drained soil, it grows about a foot tall. Hardy in Zones 4–8.

■ **Blue oat grass** (*Helictotrichon sempervirens*) Arching leaves and a spiky habit make this 2-foot-tall grass a perfect partner for broader-leaved perennials. In autumn, the blue-green foliage turns golden. Easy to grow in well-drained soil. Hardy in Zones 4–9.

■ **Chinese rhubarb** (*Rheum palmatum*) Massive, fan-shape leaves form a 6-foot-tall green backdrop in moist soil. 'Atrosanguineum' has leaves that emerge red, then fade to green on top, rusty red underneath. Hardy in Zones 4–7.

■ **Lamb's-ears** (*Stachys byzantina*) Soft silvery leaves beg to be touched.

CONTRAST FOLIAGE WITH DIFFERING SHAPES AND GROWING HABITS FOR A STRIKING DISPLAY. LADY'S MANTLE ADDS SCALLOPED SHAPE. CHINESE RHUBARB ADDS HEIGHT. WORMWOOD ADDS THE LOOK OF SILVER FILIGREE.

Preferring well-drained soil, lamb's-ears spreads slowly to make a 10-inch-tall ground cover. Hardy in Zones 4–9.

■ **Willow blue star** (*Amsonia tabernaemontana*) Clusters of pale blue star-shape flowers in spring are pleasant, but it's the 3-foot-tall, willowlike leaves that make this plant a star in moist soil. In autumn, the green leaves turn golden yellow. Hardy in Zones 4–9.

Check out more ideas from HGTV.com
For tips on using foliage plants in a garden, see:
■ www.hgtv.com/lanscapemakeoversbook.com

a classy trellis
fool the eye with perspective and add depth to a narrow space

One of the toughest challenges for homeowners is to make a narrow walled-in space feel roomy. Often, the problem involves the skimpy what-do-you-do-with-this area sandwiched between your house and a nearby garage or fence.

The long, skinny entryway in this example begins with an attractive gate and has good proportions, but an imposing house wall enclosing one side of the courtyard seems as if it's closing in. The wall needed some kind of feature to break up its expanse while visually enlarging the space.

Enter landscape architect Louise Leff and this trompe l'oeil trellis.

French for "fool the eye," trompe l'oeil is a technique that uses realistic detail to trick the viewer. In this example, the trick uses the concept that things appear smaller as distance increases. To mimic that effect, the trellis uses progressively smaller parts joined by tapered components that are placed closer together as they seem to disappear in the distance. A special object, such as a wall fountain, at the vanishing point catches the eye.

FORGETTABLY FLAT. A TRIO OF NARROW TOPIARIES (ABOVE) ONLY CALLS ATTENTION TO THE VAST BLANKNESS OF A LONG COURTYARD WALL.

making the trellis

tools & materials

SPECIAL TOOLS: Narrow-crown pneumatic stapler, table saw, chop saw, compound miter saw, jigsaw, framing square

- Fountain and recirculating pump
- 32 redwood laths, 1½ inches×6 feet
- Exterior paint primer
- Narrow-crown staples, ½-inch
- Exterior latex paint
- Galvanized screws

Central feature Pay particular attention to scale and proportion when planning a trompe l'oeil trellis. One that's too large could overwhelm the wall; a too-small trellis would throw off the scale and the trellis would look insignificant. And it would lose its effectiveness as a space expander. This trellis is 6½ feet tall and 8 feet wide. The wall is 8 feet tall and about 30 feet long.

Select an interesting item to use as a focal point in the center of the trellis—a statue, fountain, sculpture, wall-mounted planter, or other artwork. It's important that the object be in scale with the trellis. One that is one-third the height of the trellis is about right.

1 | measure for center
Measure and mark two spots on the wall—one indicating the center or vanishing point toward which the eye will be directed, and the other showing where the legs of the trellis will go. These should be equidistant from the vanishing point.

2 | prepare slats and panels
Sand and prime the redwood lath strips. After the primer dries, cut 10 strips to 5½-foot lengths to use for the verticals. Then cut 24 – 2-foot lengths for crosspieces.

Find a flat area on the ground, such as a driveway or patio, and dry-lay the two rectangular side-

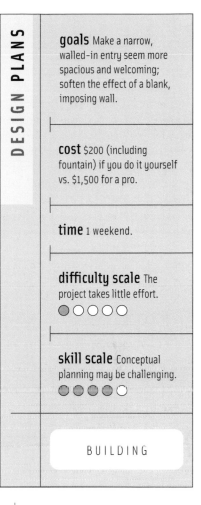

a classy trellis

making the trellis
(continued)

panel frames. Each consists of two 5½-foot verticals and two 2-foot crosspieces. Place the good sides facing the ground and the crosspieces on top of the verticals.

3 | check for square Using a framing square, check for accurate angles, and adjust as necessary.

4 | complete side panels Staple through the crosspieces into the verticals at the corners. Evenly space 10 crosspieces, good side down, on top of the verticals and staple them to the verticals. For each panel, center a vertical strip underneath the crosspieces; staple in place through the crosspieces. Using two more vertical strips for each panel, center one on each side of the middle vertical. Staple through crosspieces.

5 | begin layout Mark a spot on your work surface to represent the vanishing point. This will be your center for laying out the side panels, illusion panels, and the arch. Set the side panels on either side of the mark, about 4 feet apart.

6 | create illusion panels Each panel consists of three 5½-foot-long verticals and 12 short crosspieces. Start by ripping two vertical strips to 1¼ inches wide, using a table saw. Rip two more verticals to 1 inch wide, and two final verticals to ¾-inch wide strips.

Lay the verticals on the ground, leaving 2 inches between the first, widest, vertical and the inside of each side panel; 1½ inches between the first and second or 1-inch-wide vertical; and 1 inch between the

second and third, ¾-inch, vertical. Because objects look smaller and appear to head toward a vanishing point the farther away they are, this combination of narrowing space and shrinking verticals creates the illusion.

Now determine the position and size of each crosspiece for the illusion panels. Use a straightedge to draw pencil lines from the corresponding crosspieces on the side panels across the illusion verticals toward the vanishing point.

To determine the length of each crosspiece, measure the distance from the side panel to the outside edge of the narrowest illusion vertical.

7 | add illusion crosspieces Cut each crosspiece to length. Using a jigsaw, taper the crosspieces lengthwise from the 1½-inch width

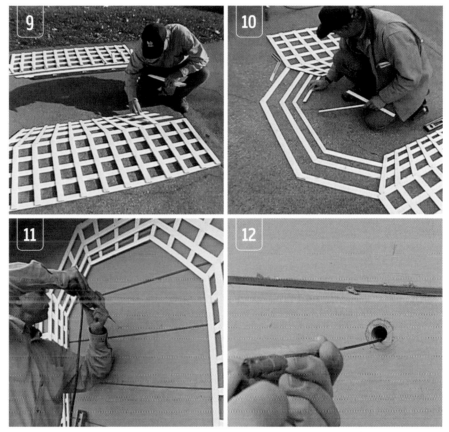

at the end that meets the side panel to ¾ inch at the other end. Number the backs of the crosspieces and their position on the verticals. Cut the ends of the crosspieces at an angle flush with the edges of the verticals.

8 | trim excess Set the first crosspiece in place. Mark its position on the verticals, then cut the excess.

9 | align crosspieces Lay out the crosspieces in their numbered spaces, angling them from where they meet the side panel crosspieces across the illusion-panel verticals toward the vanishing point. Staple into place.

10 | create the arch The top layer of the arch is wider and longer than the lower layers, which become narrower and shorter as they get closer to the vanishing point. The verticals and crosspieces taper and angle toward the vanishing point. Each piece will be cut to its specific size as you create the layout.

Start by creating the top of the arch. Angle a 1½-inch wide lath strip upward from each inside edge of the side panels. Staple a horizontal lath

across the top. Slip the ends of the two angled pieces beneath the side panels and staple them in place. For this example, the structure should now be 6½ feet tall.

Each piece for the next two layers of the arch will be ripped ¼ inch narrower than the one above it. Each crosspiece will be placed ½ inch closer to the previous layer. Each will be a narrower length. When they're cut to size, taper each piece as in Step 8. Align them as you did for the top layer by angling them from the illusion-panel verticals toward the vanishing point. Staple them in place.

Cut and taper nine lath strips to use as arch verticals. Angle them toward the vanishing point and staple them in place. Cover the finished trellis with two coats of

exterior latex paint and let it dry. Attach the finished trellis to the wall with galvanized screws.

11 | add fountain supports Drive a screw into the wall at the spot you marked for the hardware in Step 1. Attach mounting brackets, if any.

12 | wire the fountain Hide and protect the pump's electrical cord by running it indoors through the wall. To keep the hole as small as possible, cut off the plug. Drill a hole in the wall to insert the cord. Have a helper hold the fountain in place while you snake the cord through the hole. Install the fountain on its mounting hardware. Attach a new plug on the cord and plug into an outlet. Fill the fountain with water and turn it on.

Color and texture are important considerations in creating the optical illusion of depth and space. For example, landscape architect Louise Leff chose fine-textured plants with dainty foliage, which appears farther away, making the area seem bigger. Pastel and cool colors such as blue and purple enhance the feeling of greater space because they appear to recede into the distance.

On the trellis, 'Cécile Brunner' climbing roses with pale pink blossoms help dress up the wall. They also make the small planting area appear taller by drawing the eye up. 'Cécile Brunner' roses are hardy in Zones 6–10. In colder areas, you could get a similar look by substituting perennial sweet pea (*Lathyrus latifolius* 'Pink Pearl'), hardy in Zones 3–9.

For the bed at the base of the trellis, Leff chose pastel cottage-garden favorites including delphinium, bacopa (*Sutera*), and lavender (*Lavandula pinnata*), hardy in Zones 9–10. In colder climates, substitute 'Hidcote' lavender (*Lavandula angustifolia*) hardy in Zones 5–9. Where lavenders aren't winter-hardy, 'Lady', grown as an annual, is a good alternative. An All-America Selections award winner, this variety blooms the first season from seed.

Check out more ideas from HGTV.com
For tips on using color in the garden, see:
■ www.hgtv.com/landscapemakeoversbook

'CECILE BRUNNER' ROSES CLIMB THE TROMPE L'OEIL TRELLIS (BELOW), ADDING DIMENSION AND DRAWING ATTENTION UP THE GRID. TALL FLOWER STALKS POINT TO THE FOUNTAIN SET AT THE VANISHING POINT.

PERENNIALS TO FOOL THE EYE

Dress up the blank wall in your narrow entryway and welcome your guests by planting some of these easy-care perennials. Small enough to fit in the tiniest of garden beds, all have dainty foliage and pastel blooms that help give the illusion of greater space.

- **Alpine aster** (*Aster alpinus* 'Wargrave Park') Purple-tinged pale pink daisylike flowers bloom in early summer on plants 6 or 8 inches tall. Hardy in Zones 4–7.
- **Basket-of-gold** (*Aurinia saxatilis* 'Gold Ball') Dwarf globe-shaped 8-inch-tall plants boast canary yellow flowers in spring and gray-green foliage. Zones 3–7.
- **Candytuft** (*Iberis sempervirens* 'Little Gem') Clear white clusters of tiny flowers cover the 5- to 8-inch tall evergreen foliage in spring. Hardy in Zones 4–8.
- **Cheddar pinks** (*Dianthus gratianopolitanus* 'Bath's Pink') Soft pink daisylike flowers bloom in early to midsummer on mats of blue-green grasslike foliage that grows to 6 inches tall. Hardy in Zones 3–8.
- **Pincushion flower** (*Scabiosa columbaria* 'Butterfly Blue') Soft blue long-stemmed flowers stand about a foot high, dancing from spring through fall above low mounds of gray-green leaves. Hardy in Zones 4–9.
- **Pink coreopsis** (*Coreopsis rosea* 'Sweet Dreams') Blooming throughout the growing season, the pink and white daisies contrast nicely with handsome needlelike foliage. This perennial grows about a foot tall. Hardy in Zones 3–9.

cheddar pinks

basket of gold

'Sweet Dreams' coreopsis

lavender

TRUE BLUES

Blue, the most sought-after of all flower colors, enhances the feeling of space. Here are a few "cool" blues to try in your small-space garden:

- Azure monkshood (*Aconitum carmichaelii*), Zones 3–7
- Balloon flower (*Playcodon grandiflorus*), Zones 3–7
- Blue false indigo (*Baptisia australis*), Zones 3–8
- Blue flax (*Linum perenne*), Zones 4–8
- Bottle gentian (*Gentiana andrewsii*), Zones 3–7
- Great blue lobelia (*Lobelia siphilitica*), Zones 4–8
- Plumbago (*Ceratostigma plumbaginoides*), Zones 5–8
- Siberian squill (*Scilla siberica*), Zones 2–7

colorful wall treatments
simple, inexpensive techniques enliven the view

A concrete wall made this patio seem like a prison to the homeowner, who longed for a serene area with the feeling of a Zen garden. Designer Marguerite Stamos transformed it with a coat of subtle pale green stucco trimmed in yellow.

Stuccoing is within the skill set of many do-it-yourselfers, but it is a job for which you may prefer to hire a professional. An easier way to a similar appearance is to use decorative painting techniques such as sponging.

Decorative painting. These techniques involve painting a base coat on a wall, then applying glaze over it. Glazes may be oil- or water-based. Glazes tinted with regular or acrylic paint (also called universal colorant) give depth to surfaces. Glaze tinted with acrylics has a translucent finish; with regular paint, it is cloudy. Techniques differ in how the glaze is applied.

AN UNADORNED RETAINING WALL CREATED AN UNAPPEALING VIEW AND AN UNWELCOMING SPACE (ABOVE).

faux stucco

tools & materials

SPECIAL TOOLS: Sea sponge, pointed brush
- Trisodium phosphate (TSP)
- Light-color exterior paint
- Glaze
- Artist's acrylic paints in yellow ochre, mossy green, and raw sienna
- Gel retarder

Create the effect of stucco with a technique that involves color washing and sponging. Brush off the wall, then wash it with TSP. Rinse and let dry. Apply light-color exterior paint as the base coat.

1 | tint glaze Mix 1 part yellow ochre acrylic paint to 4 parts glaze. Glaze fresh out of the can looks milky, but it will dry translucent. Add the gel retarder according to label directions. Stir until color is uniform.

2 | color wash Using a circular motion, rub tinted glaze onto the wall with a sponge. Vary the pattern and thickness of the glaze for the textured effect. Start at the top of the wall and work in 3×3-foot sections.

3 | sponge on moss Tint another batch of glaze with mossy green paint. Think of areas where moss would likely be. Dab the green onto the wall at those spots with the sponge, lightly bouncing the sponge against the surface.

4 | add character With the pointed brush and raw sienna paint, draw cracks. Add age spots: Dip a toothbrush in the raw sienna, then run your finger down the bristle to splatter paint on the wall.

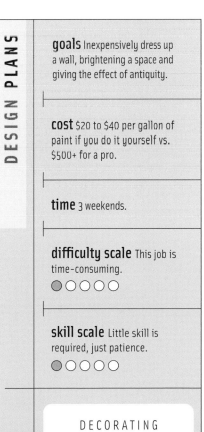

A NEW WALL FINISH AND COLORFUL TILES BRING LIFE TO THE PATIO (ABOVE).

ASIAN-INSPIRED DETAILS SUCH AS A KIMONO MOSAIC AND CONCRETE PLANTERS FILLED WITH BAMBOO, HORSETAIL, AND PAPYRUS (FAR LEFT) COMPLETE THE PICTURE AND SOFTEN THE EDGES.

GLAZED CERAMIC POTS (LEFT) AND A SIMPLE FOUNTAIN COMPLEMENT THE COLORS USED IN THE MOSAICS.

DESIGN PLANS

goals Inexpensively dress up a wall, brightening a space and giving the effect of antiquity.

cost $20 to $40 per gallon of paint if you do it yourself vs. $500+ for a pro.

time 3 weekends.

difficulty scale This job is time-consuming.
●○○○○

skill scale Little skill is required, just patience.
●○○○○

DECORATING

a stylish way to hide the "uglies"
keep utility items out of sight, but still in reach, behind an attractive crisscross screen

Garbage cans and recycling bins are rarely known for their beauty. And although you may be fortunate enough to have a storage shed or garage where you can stash them, there's something about the aroma of days-old garbage in a hot, enclosed space that compels you to keep everything out in the open.

Then there are eyesores you can't move—things like air-conditioning units, well-pump structures, and on-ground electrical boxes. But you can hide them from sight behind this simple but attractive lattice screen from designer Scott Soden.

Check out more ideas from HGTV.com
For ways of covering up eye sores, see:
- www.hgtv.com/landscapemakeoversbook

FLOWER BOXES DRESS UP A LATTICE SCREEN THAT HIDES TRASH CANS (RIGHT), MAKING A UNIT THAT IS STYLISH ENOUGH FOR THE FRONT YARD.

ALTHOUGH NEATLY ARRANGED ON THEIR OWN PAD (ABOVE), GARBAGE CANS AND RECYCLING BINS LACK WELCOMING AMBIENCE AT THE HOME'S ENTRY.

LATTICEWORK PANELS come in many sizes and in a number of natural woods, including redwood, as well as in durable plastic, making them useful in countless practical ways.

lattice cover-up

tools & materials

SPECIAL TOOLS: Gravel rake, hand tamper

- 1 – 2×4, 10 feet long
- 1 – 2×4, 8 feet long
- 3 – 4×4 posts, 8 feet long
- 2 – 1×8s, 6 feet long
- 2 – 2×4s, 10 feet long
- 5 – 1½-inch-wide laths, 8 feet long
- 1 – 1×6, 8 feet long
- 2 – 4×8-foot lattice sheets
- Screws
- Wooden stakes
- Landscape fabric
- Decomposed rock, such as granite
- Gravel
- Concrete mix
- 3 cedar flower boxes
- Spray primer and exterior latex paint

Undercover is where they belong—those practical, but often unsightly, objects like air-conditioner units, utility boxes, compost bins, and trash cans. This lattice screen is such a terrific coverup, you can even locate it in the front yard without embarrassment.

1 | prepare the site Position the items to be hidden at the rear of the space (in this example, against an existing fence). Measure the distance from the fence to the front of the largest container. Double that figure and add about a foot to determine the depth of the overall area.

DESIGN PLANS

goals Devise an attractive unit to screen garbage cans and recycling containers from view, make access to containers easy, and create a design that's compatible with the surroundings.

cost $300 if you do it yourself vs. $1,200 for a pro.

time 2 weekends.

difficulty scale Hauling decomposed rock and digging holes require labor.

●●○○○

skill scale Average do-it-yourselfer experience will do fine.

●●●○○

BUILDING

A LATTICE COVER-UP THAT COULD BE TAKEN FOR A GARDEN FENCE HAS PROPORTIONS THAT STAIRSTEP DOWN FROM THE HOUSE ROOF (LEFT). ITS FACADE PROVIDES AIRY CONTRAST TO THE SOLID GARAGE DOOR.

hiding the "uglies"

lattice cover-up
(continued)

Pound small stakes in the ground at the four corners to mark the perimeter. (In this example, it's 6×9 feet). Dig trenches that are 2 inches wide and 3½ inches deep where the lattice screen will be placed. Because this example is an L-shape, trenches are along the front and one side of the staked area.

2–3 | form the frame
Position pressure-treated 2×4s alongside the stakes, forming a simple frame. If the 2×4s won't stay in place, screw them to the stakes. If a tree or other object blocks the path of the frame, use benderboard to work around it.

4 | prepare base
With the 2×4s as borders, remove 2 inches of soil from the boxed-in area and level it. Lay weed barrier fabric over the excavated area. Use landscapers pins to hold the fabric in place.

Pour in 2 inches of decomposed rock. Rake it level with the tops of the 2×4s. Wet the surface to set the particles, and use a hand tamper to pack it down. This will give you a surface that's smooth, sturdy, and mud-free, yet much less expensive than concrete.

5 | mark postholes
This three-sided unit needs only two walls—one 3 feet long, the other 6 feet long—which form an L.

Mark locations for the 4×4 posts. The two outer ones are 3 feet from the wall and 6 feet apart. The third is against the fence opposite the opening of the unit. Dig holes 2 feet deep and 6 inches in diameter. Shovel 2 inches of gravel into the holes and stand the posts in them.

AFTER

6 | add temporary braces
Check the posts for plumb, then temporarily stake and brace them. Prepare concrete mix and pour concrete into the holes, stirring it as you go to eliminate air pockets. Let the concrete set overnight, then remove the braces.

7 | add kickboard
After measuring the distance between the front two posts, cut a 1×8 to that length, slip it between the posts at the bottom, and toe-screw it into the posts. Do the same for the kickboard between the post next to the fence and the outer post in front of it.

Cut bottom rails from 2×4s the same lengths as the kickboards, lay each one flat on top of the corresponding kickboard, and toe-screw both to the posts.

Saw off the tops of the three posts 4½ feet above the ground. Cut two more 2×4s for the top rails.

8 | attach top rails To make the junction where the two rails meet more attractive, miter the ends at 45-degree angles. Screw these two rails down on top of the posts.

9 | attach lattice frame Nail or screw 1½-inch-wide pieces of redwood lath to the inside faces of the posts, the bottom of the top rail, and the top of the bottom rail, flush with the front edges of all four members. This edging will hold the lattice in place on the front side. Use the circular saw to cut one lattice sheet for the front of the unit and another for the side, each to fit inside the rectangles formed by the rails and posts. (This project calls for premade redwood lattice sheets. The designer suggests using an architectural grade because it's thicker, stronger, and less likely to split or chip.)

10 | install the lattice Rip one 1½-inch redwood lath strip to 1 inch wide. Cut this into lengths that fit snugly inside the lattice frame. Insert the lattice sheet from the inside, pushing it against the laths installed in Step 9.

11 | make it decorative Attach the lattice by running the 1×1-inch lath strips around the edges and nailing them to the posts and rails.

12 | add flower boxes Use premade cedar flower boxes available at a garden supply or home improvement centers. Or make your own boxes. Spray the boxes with two coats of primer.

After the paint is dry, screw them to the top rails. Spray a primer coat on the entire lattice unit and allow it to dry. Finish with two coats of exterior latex paint.

a patio makeover
paint, mirrors, and pocket planters give fading concrete personality

Can a concrete wasteland morph into a secluded hideaway? That's what landscape designer Mike Guttman accomplished with this makeover for a neglected walled patio.

Previous owners left concrete rubble from unfinished projects. The new homeowners found the patio to be a useless eyesore—too hot and in desperate need of personality.

Now queen palms planted in pockets along the wall break up the stark bareness of the concrete. Colorful annuals tumble over a terraced rock planter built into one corner. Fresh paint on the patio shows off a new stenciled design that brightens the entire space. A mirror mosaic

A QUEEN PALM AMID A POCKET OF MARIGOLDS (RIGHT) ADDS COLOR AND TEXTURE.

RED PAINT (FAR RIGHT) AND A STENCILED DESIGN MAKE THE PATIO PAD VIBRANT AND INTERESTING.

A MIRROR MOSAIC (BELOW RIGHT) REFLECTS LIGHT, BOUNCING SPARKLES ACROSS THE AREA.

BETWEEN THE RUBBLE AND FADED PAINT (ABOVE), THIS PATIO HAD NO APPEAL.

reflects the beauty of the surrounding plants and serves as a dazzling focal point for the massive white wall of the house. As a finishing touch, ivy geraniums cascade from planters hung from stair railings and colorful annuals spill from containers.

Each project is easy and inexpensive to do as well as to personalize. The shape of the mosaic is drawn freehand. Its simple pattern prevents the design from overpowering the space. The color of the patio paint complements that of the home.

Check out more ideas from HGTV.com

For tips on patio makeovers, see

- www.hgtv.com/landscapemakeoversbook

A PAINTED BENCH (RIGHT) AND PLANTS DRAW THE EYE AWAY FROM A FAUCET, HOSE, AND ELECTRICAL OUTLET ON THE WALL.

CONCRETE STAIN is an easy option for updating a patio. It comes in a wide variety of colors and, as an added benefit, it protects surfaces from salt, UV rays, water, and foot traffic without peeling, fading, or flaking.

PERFECT PATIO TREES

Queen palm trees (*Syagrus romanzoffiana*) dress up this sunny California garden, but many other trees would do just as well. Look for ones that grow less than 30 feet tall, have few serious pests, and no surface roots to buckle concrete or messy fruit or twigs to sweep up. The following candidates will grow in cold as well as warm regions:

- **American hornbeam** (*Carpinus caroliniana*) Leaves open red in spring, become dark green in summer, and turn orange or yellow in fall. Graceful form and slate gray bark ensure winter interest. Trees grow 20 to 30 feet tall. Zones 3–9.
- **Japanese tree lilac** (*Syringa reticulata*) Creamy white blossoms appear in June after those of shrub lilacs fade. A handsome tree 20 to 30 feet tall, it develops a graceful, arching shape with age. Zones 3–7.

- **Paperbark maple** (*Acer griseum*) Cinnamon-colored exfoliating bark makes this 20- to 30-foot tree a winner in all seasons. In autumn, its leaves turn a pretty russet red. Zones 5–8.
- **Seven-son flower** (*Heptacodium miconioides*) Clusters of white flowers in late summer and early fall give way to showy rose-purple sepals lasting into November. This tree has lovely exfoliating bark. It grows 15 to 25 feet tall. Zones 5–8.

Japanese tree lilac

terraced rock planter

tools & materials

SPECIAL TOOLS: Jackhammer, circular saw equipped with a diamond blade, or a heavy-duty wet saw with a diamond blade

- Large stones
- Well-amended topsoil (the amount depends on how large you intend to make your planter)

Add life to a patio corner with an easy-to-build terraced planter. The concrete wall serves as the back of the planter. The design will work well with any masonry backstop. Avoid building the bed against a wooden wall; moist soil will rot the wood. Cut a planting space into the concrete with a jackhammer or saw. The front edge can be any shape you like.

1 | start rows Place large stones along the front edge of the planter. Fill the area behind them with topsoil, up to the tops of the stones.

2 | build up Place a second row of stones 12 inches behind the first.

3 | add soil Partially bury the rocks, filling in behind them and between rows 1 and 2.

4 | back corner Set a final row of rocks 12 inches behind row 2, again filling with soil to the new level. Gently firm the soil with your fingers. Plant the bed and water well.

BEFORE

AFTER

DESIGN PLANS

goal Find a place to grow plants on the patio without taking up more room.

cost $200, including plants.

time 8 hours.

difficulty scale Cutting concrete requires steadiness and strength. Stones are heavy.
● ● ● ○ ○

skill scale Cutting the shape is the project's most difficult part.
● ● ● ○ ○

GARDENING

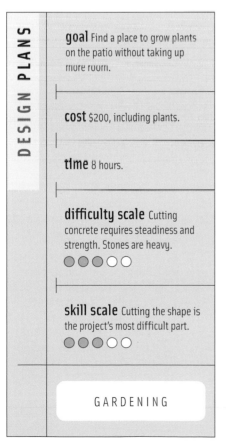

painted patio

tools & materials

SPECIAL TOOLS: Jigsaw, paint roller with extension handle, deck brush or power washer

- Trisodium phosphate (TSP)
- Paint
- Plywood

Before painting, clean the patio with a brush and TSP, or use a power washer; then let it dry completely.

1 | apply base coat Use an exterior paint that is recommended for use on concrete. Prime the floor if painting it for the first time. Apply two coats if you're changing its color. Let the paint dry for several days before adding the design.

2 | Make stencil Draw the design on a piece of plywood. A simple pattern is easier to transfer and the final effect will be less busy. Cut out the pattern with a jigsaw.

3 | paint Lay the stencil on the patio floor and brush on the design in a contrasting color. Move the stencil to another spot and repeat until design is scattered across the patio floor.

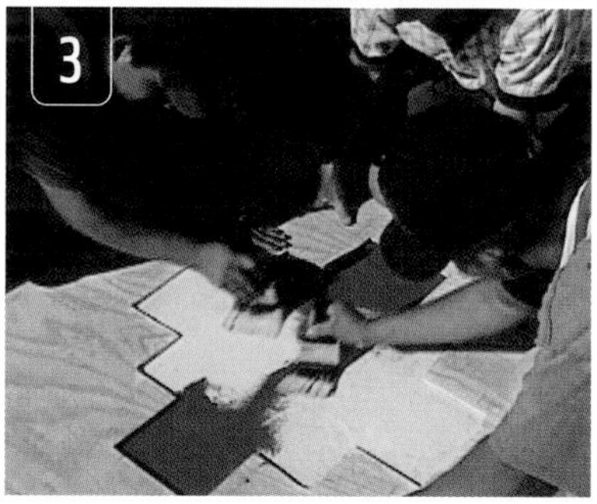

DESIGN PLANS

goal Brighten a boring patio with color that complements the house and a stenciled design that adds impact.

cost $30 to $40 for each gallon of concrete primer and paint.

time 1 weekend.

difficulty scale A long-handled roller avoids knee bends.
●○○○○

skill scale If you can paint or stencil a wall, you can do this project.
●○○○○

DECORATING

mirror mosaic

tools & materials

SPECIAL TOOLS: Point-notched trowel (the mastic container will specify point size), grout float, hand and eye protection

- Trisodium phosphate (TSP)
- Pieces of mirror, glass, tile, marbles, dishes, and other colorful items
- Mastic
- Grout
- Latex additive for the grout
- Sponge

Dress up a wall with this easy-to-make focal point.

1 | mark the outline Clean the wall by brushing it, then washing with TSP. Draw the shape of the mosaic on the wall.

2 | break the mirror Wrap the mirror in a sheet and hammer it into

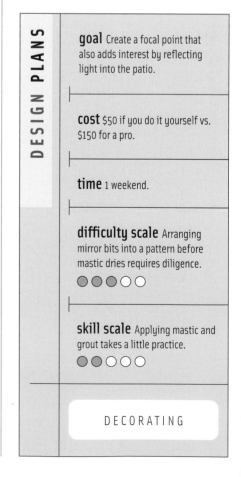

DESIGN PLANS

goal Create a focal point that also adds interest by reflecting light into the patio.

cost $50 if you do it yourself vs. $150 for a pro.

time 1 weekend.

difficulty scale Arranging mirror bits into a pattern before mastic dries requires diligence.
●●●○○

skill scale Applying mastic and grout takes a little practice.
●●○○○

DECORATING

pieces. Wear protective goggles and gloves as you work. Aim for a variety of sizes from large to small. For accents, break colored glass, such as wine and soda bottles, and dishes.

3 | trowel Smear mastic on the wall with the notched trowel. Use long strokes for an even surface.

4 | set pieces Arrange the glass on the mastic, setting the pieces in a random pattern. Start with the largest pieces of mirror and fill in with smaller ones and other items. Set each piece with a slight twist to ensure it adheres fully to the mastic. Avoid sliding the tile into place; doing so squeezes mastic into the joints.

5 | grout Let the mastic set for 24 hours (or longer in humid weather).

Try to move a glass piece. If it doesn't move, you're ready to grout.

Clean mastic off the glass with a damp sponge. Mix grout with latex additive to the consistency of toothpaste. (In this example, white grout matches the white wall, but grout can be tinted to suit other masonry colors.) Let grout mixture sit for 10 minutes, then stir again.

With a grout float, spread grout over the glass, pressing it into the joints. Hold the float flat and work diagonally on the wall. Remove excess grout by holding the float at an angle to the wall as you swipe the area.

6 | clean up Wipe the glass clean with a damp sponge, frequently rinsing and wringing out the sponge. Allow the surface to dry, then buff away the haze.

BEFORE

AFTER

create a colorful mosaic entry
resurrect a worn entryway with a
rustic multicolor stone pattern

Old concrete patios and entryways—now stained and pitted—may have been attractive when they were new but fail the charm test now. You could break them up, haul away the pieces, and start over. Or, as this homeowner did, consider taking advantage of a salvageable base and simply giving it a new face.

The example shown here is just one of several ways you can transform a worn entry into a fresh and colorful greeting for family and friends. If this one doesn't attract you, the next two projects will show you other ideas for resurfacing concrete to give a worn but solid pad a new lease on life.

Designer Scott Soden created this new surface from large sections of flagstone in several colors and small multicolored stones and pebbles. The completed project blends beautifully with the rustic American Arts and Crafts style house adjoining it and introduces lots of color and texture to the landscape.

Follow up with complementary plantings, and you have a winner.

Check out more ideas from HGTV.com
For mosaic techniques and uses, see
- www.hgtv.com/hgtv/landscapemakeoversbook

COBBLESTONES STACKED AND GLUED ON TOP OF EACH OTHER (ABOVE) CREATE A FUN HOSE GUIDE.

COLORFUL STONES EMBEDDED IN MORTAR (FAR LEFT) CREATE A NATURAL MOSAIC FOR A WALKWAY.

WAVY PATTERNS OF BLUE STONES COOL A FLAGSTONE PATH THAT RUNS ALONG TROPICAL PLANTS IN HOT COLORS (LEFT AND OPPOSITE). THE DESIGNER CHOSE ARIZONA FLAGSTONE IN TWO COLORS—ROSE AND PEACH. TOO MANY LARGE SPLOTCHES OF COLOR WOULD OVERWHELM THE DESIGN.

PLAIN CONCRETE IN POOR CONDITION (ABOVE) RADIATES HEAT AND PROVIDES NO CONTRAST FOR THE PLANTS.

create a colorful mosaic entry

mosaic entry

tools & materials

SPECIAL TOOLS: Circular saw with diamond blade, hand grinder with diamond blade, mason's hammer, cold chisel, eye and ear protection, concrete mixer, rubber mallet, damp sponge

- Large and midsize flagstones, 1 to 2 inches thick
- Cobbles and colored rocks
- Mortar mix
- Brown powder tint (optional)
- Phosphoric acid
- Masonry sealant

Prepare the surface Thoroughly hose off the concrete, then let it dry.

AFTER

Draw the mosaic design directly on the concrete surface with chalk. Aim for a natural, fluid look with curves and leaf shapes. If you need to make an area appear more spacious, include several large shapes in your design.

1 | place and mark flagstones

Work on one small area at a time during the layout and cutting stage. Set each large piece of stone in place on the chalked design (get someone to help with the heavy ones). Then mark on the stone where to cut it to fit the space.

2 | cut flagstone

Cut each piece as you go, so you can dry-fit the entire surface before you mortar. Wear protective glasses and earplugs as you work. Score along the marked line with a circular saw.

3 | chisel flagstone

Using the cold chisel, cut through all layers.

4 | break flagstone

Finish the job by slipping wedges under the portion of the slab you'll be using and gently separating the scored chunk with the mason's hammer.

DESIGN PLANS

goals Convert a concrete entryway into a colorful mosaic with sweeping lines and graceful curves; work with natural materials that complement the Arts and Crafts architecture of the house.

cost $1,200 if you do it yourself vs. $4,000 for a pro.

time 3 weekends.

difficulty scale The flagstones are heavy and sometimes difficult to position.
●●●○○

skill scale Cutting masonry requires patience and dexterity with a circular saw and hand grinder.
●●●○○

BUILDING

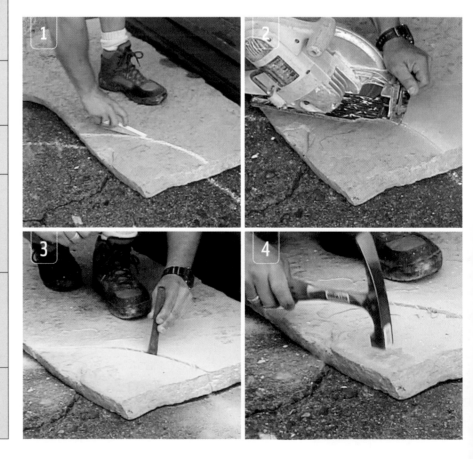

WHICH TOOL TO USE?

For the longer, rougher cuts, plan to use a 7-inch or 7¼-inch circular saw fitted with a wet or dry diamond blade; substitute a hand grinder, also equipped with a diamond blade, for those neater, more precise cuts.
To save wear and tear on the expensive diamond blades, keep a mason's hammer and cold chisel handy to do part of the work.

5 | chip edges Create an old-world hand-chiseled look by chipping the edges with the back of a mason's hammer. Continue placing large stones, adjusting the layout as you go to accommodate special pieces.

6 | cut small pieces Using a hand grinder, create the smaller, leaf-shaped pieces, making several passes along the chalk line. Use the hammer to knock off excess stone.

7 | fill spaces After you've cut and set the flagstones—big and small—begin filling in the spaces with cobbles and colored rocks, placing groups of colors together to create a flowing pattern.

8 | mortar Plan to use at least a 1-inch-thick layer of mortar under the thickest flagstones. Thinner stones will need a deeper bed of mortar under them to raise them to the same level. For a big job like this one, you may want to rent a mixer (about $30 a day). To give the mortar a warmer tone, add a brown powder tint to the mix.
  Working with one flagstone at a time, spread out the mortar, then set the stone in it. Tap it with a rubber

mallet to seat it well and to drive out air bubbles. As you set additional stones, continually check with a straightedge to make sure you're maintaining a consistent height throughout. Once the large flagstones and the small leaf-shaped pieces are mortared in place, fill in the remaining gaps with mortar and position the smaller colored rocks. When you're satisfied with the designs you've created, sink each rock into the mortar. As each section is completed, use a big damp sponge to wipe away excess mortar. Then leave the surface alone for three days while the mortar sets.

9 | clean up Sponge the mosaic with diluted phosphoric acid, then wire brush it to remove remaining mortar. Wear goggles and chemical-

resistant gloves as you work. Take your time and do a thorough job.
  After the surface is dry, spread three thin coats of masonry sealant onto the entire surface to help protect it from weather and add a beautiful gloss that brings out the rich colors in the stonework.

reshape and resurface a patio
soften an old concrete slab with woodsy hues

Sometimes concrete patios can be too big. They may have been the right size for previous homeowners, but, as in this example, a 12×28-foot chunk of concrete can overwhelm a small backyard. Its dull gray look is reason enough for taking the effort to convert it into a beautiful asset.

Louise Leff, the designer of this dramatic transformation, suggested reducing the overall size to a more workable 12×16 feet and cutting off the corners to create a gently curved shape. Then, to complete the project, she recommended covering the concrete with the natural beauty of flagstone. Other options are slate or half bricks.

You might want to duplicate this patio even if you don't have the existing slab. If so, you'll need to pour a base first, boosting the total cost. But if the concrete is already there—and as long as the slab is fairly level and free

from major cracks and buckles—you have the beginnings of a classy, affordable project.

Once the patio itself is completed, you can hide the raw edges with closely spaced plantings. If you wish, create a matching walkway of stepping-stones leading away from the patio by placing individual flagstones about 6 inches apart through planting beds or lawn.

A CIRCULAR FOUNTAIN (RIGHT), ECHOING THE ROUNDED SHAPES, SOUNDS LIKE RAINFALL IN THE FOREST.

ROUND EDGES AND CURVING WALKWAYS MAKE GENTLE FRAMES FOR PLANTING BEDS (BELOW). SOFT NATURAL HUES IN THE FLAGSTONES CREATE A SENSE OF WALKING ON A LEAF-COVERED WOODLAND TRAIL.

COLORED BLOCKS IN MOSS GREENS AND RUSSET TANS (ABOVE) ENLIVEN WHAT ONCE WAS DINGY LEADEN GRAY CONCRETE.

A VAST EXPANSE OF CONCRETE OVERWHELMS THE LANDSCAPE AND UNDERWHELMS GUESTS (ABOVE).

remade patio

tools & materials

SPECIAL TOOLS: Jackhammer; circular saw or large heavy-duty wet saw, both with diamond blades; hand grinder with diamond blades; mortar trowel; joint trowel; rubber mallet; mason's hammer, masonry bag, sponge

- Flagstones
- Premixed masonry mortar
- Premixed masonry grout
- Masonry bag
- Powdered coloring

1 | shape old concrete Use chalk to outline the new shape for the patio. This homeowner simply rounded off the old square pad. Rent a jackhammer, unless you have the strength and patience to use a big chisel and hand sledge. Break through the concrete along the new outline. Save the debris for a crazy-quilt walkway or stepping-stone path, or haul them away. Hose down the remaining concrete and scrub it thoroughly with a stiff broom.

2 | select flagstones Sort the flagstones by size.

3 | dry-fit large stones Dry-fit the larger pieces first. Keep the gaps as small as possible for an informal look. Continue until the entire area is filled with large and mid-size stones. You'll undoubtedly need to cut some of the slabs to get a good fit.

4 | cut to fit Use chalk to mark a gentle curve around the edge of the new flagstone top. You'll want to extend the new surface just a bit past the existing concrete underneath. Then use the larger saw to score along this cut line. Finish by knocking off excess pieces with a mason's hammer. For the larger cuts, score the stones with either a standard circular saw equipped with a diamond blade or a heavy-duty wet saw, also with a diamond blade, which you may need to rent. Knock off excess pieces with a hammer. You can fill gaps with smaller stones.

5 | grind edges To make the tighter, more precise cuts, use a hand grinder fitted with a diamond blade. Mark the backs of specially cut pieces so you'll know where they fit in the puzzle.

DESIGN PLANS

goals Revitalize an old, drab concrete slab by giving it a more graceful shape and adding a natural surface; introduce a more informal appearance to the overall design.

cost $1,500 if you do it yourself vs. $3,200 for a pro.

time 3 weekends.

difficulty scale Whether you use a jackhammer or break up the concrete by hand, the work is grueling; big chunks of flagstone require a strong back and a helper or two.
○○○○○ ○

skill scale Operating the jackhammer, wet saw, and hand grinder require technique.
○○○○○ ○

BUILDING

6 | place mortar Using a mixture of cement and sand or premixed masonry mortar, spread the mortar 2 inches deep.

7 | embed the flagstones Wet the stones beforehand so they don't absorb water from the mortar. Set each stone in the mortar by tapping it with a rubber mallet. Continue until all of the big and midsize pieces are mortared in place. Be sure to clean off excess mortar as you go, rather than waiting until the job is finished. Use a long spirit level or 2×4 to check that each stone is on the same plane as its neighbors.

8 | add smaller pieces Fill gaps with the smaller precut pieces. If necessary, chip the stone with the pointed end of a mason's hammer to get a better fit. Let the mortar dry at least 24 hours.

9 | apply grout Mix prepackaged grout with coloring pigment that complements the flagstone. Use a masonry bag to push the grout into the cracks.

10 | shape grout Using a special trowel to work the grout, make it

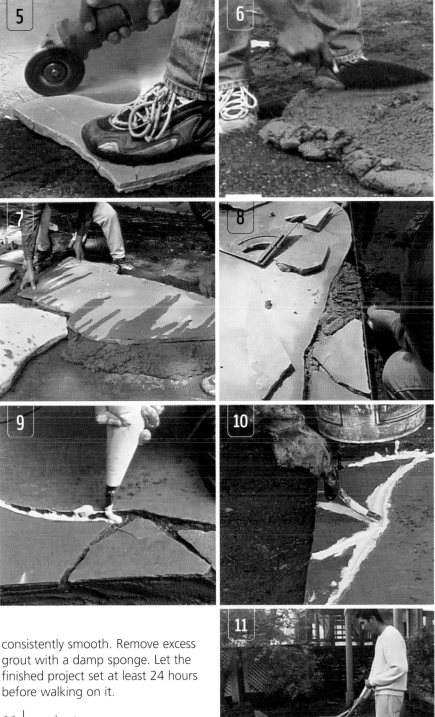

consistently smooth. Remove excess grout with a damp sponge. Let the finished project set at least 24 hours before walking on it.

11 | wash stones After the mortar has cured, hose down the flagstones to wash away debris and bring up the color and luster of the stones.

concrete cover-up
give an old patio a new life with a new look

There's no denying the beauty of flagstone, but some homeowners would rather find another way to salvage old concrete than to go through the expense and physical labor a flagstone project requires. Here's a solution to consider from Yoshi Kuraishi, especially if you live where extreme temperature changes are rare.

The process involves applying two coats of a special concrete mix to the old surface with a trowel. When you spread the second coat, you have the opportunity to produce a texture that resembles a variety of rock products. In this particular example, the family wanted to come up with a look that complemented their Japanese garden. So their contractor created a slate finish, then gave it a mottled look by spreading two different paint colors across the surface in an uneven pattern to mirror the boulders in their garden.

The results are dramatic. If you choose to try your hand at duplicating the procedure, be sure to practice. You can produce a host of interesting textures just by experimenting with your trowel stroke and with other materials in addition to the trowel to embellish the surface. You might even create a unique design of your own.

TRANQUIL CURVES OF PEBBLES AND BARK MULCH RIPPLE AWAY FROM A FAUX-SLATE PATIO, RELAXING HARSH LINES (ABOVE). MOUNDS OF SHRUBBERY FEATHER OUT THE EDGES, AND STEPPING-STONES LEAD TO A STONE FOUNTAIN AT THE BACK.

RESURFACING WITH A FAUX-SLATE FINISH SUITS THIS PATIO'S LOCALE (LEFT).

FLAT, PLAIN CONCRETE (ABOVE) HAD LITTLE IN COMMON WITH THIS HOME'S JAPANESE GARDEN.

FAUX FINISHES are all about the imaginative use of color and texture. Think beyond slate to any look you like: tile, flagstone, brick, or pavers in a starburst pattern—almost anything is possible.

faux slate

tools & materials

SPECIAL TOOLS: Power washer, mixing paddle, steel finishing trowel
- Masonry coating or concrete resurfacer
- Concrete colorant
- Clear lacquer base

Clean slate This technique gives concrete a rocklike finish.

1 | prepare the surface Use a power washer to rid the old concrete of dirt and debris, which could keep the new surface from bonding properly. Allow the concrete to dry two hours before proceeding.

2 | mix base coat Attach a mixing paddle, which you can rent, to a drill and stir up a batch of concrete coating. This coating is a blend of sand, concrete, and acrylic resin, and is available from masonry suppliers. Add water to make it the consistency of pancake batter.

3 | pour base coat Use this batch for the first coat, pouring it out in little puddles. Spread a smooth base coat with a trowel to a depth of about ⅛ inch or a little thicker. Even though you'll be mixing several batches and troweling them out, this part of the project goes pretty quickly. Allow about an hour before you apply the second coat. Keep any leftover base mix to use in Step 6.

4 | second coat Mix the mortar to a thicker consistency—like pudding—and spread it to a thickness of ¼ inch with a trowel.

5 | create texture Pat and scrape the coating with the trowel to texturize the surface. Or use any other technique to create an appealing texture. Allow the second layer to dry.

6 | color and seal the surface Water down the base mixture you used earlier, thinning it to the consistency of gravy. Tint each batch with the colorant. Tan and gray were used for this project. Daub the colors onto the concrete with a sponge, as if you were sponge painting. This process is called "veining." The goal is to produce a mottled look, reminiscent of slate.

After the veining has completely dried, seal the surface by sponging on a clear lacquer base.

If the concrete surface ever cracks, you'll be able to repair it easily by forcing some of the base mix into the cracks and blending it in with a trowel, matching the rugged surface that surrounds it. Touch up with paint if necessary to match the rest of the surface.

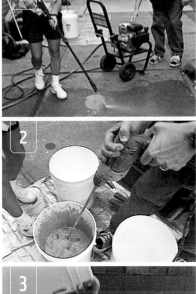

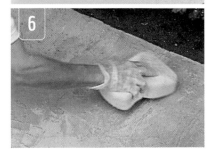

DESIGN PLANS

goals Convert an old concrete slab into a fresh new element that complements the adjoining Japanese garden; create a surface that imitates natural slate.

difficulty scale The physical part is mainly lugging around bags of mortar mix.

●●○○○

cost $1 to $2 per square foot if you do it vs. $3 to $7 per square foot for a pro.

skill scale If you practice, this project is more fun than taxing.

●●○○○

time 1 to 2 weekends, depending on square footage.

DECORATING

5

LANDSCAPE SMART

Landscape challenges. Solving landscape problems requires you to understand the site and the range of options available to you. Most often, the solution is to grow plants that thrive in such problem areas.

landscape
SMART

In a perfect world, having a yard and garden you could love would be easy. There would be just the right amount of water and sunlight, and little worry of wildfires.

Temperatures would always be pleasant and breezes would always be gentle. Critters would venture into your garden to admire the plants and not eat them.

But reality has challenges. When there are setbacks, you regroup and rethink. Challenges motivate you to strengthen your resolve, dig in your heels, roll up your sleeves, and try again.

Solving landscape challenges is about understanding the site and the range of options. Often plants are the solution. Selecting the right plants for the site—one that's shady, or hot and dry, or wet—makes a world of difference. Sometimes the challenge requires a design solution, such as installing a path that stairsteps down a slope.

Many times, the solution uses a combination of plantings and structures. For example, planting a slope is about holding soil in place and avoiding erosion. Plants alone could do the job, but terraces and retaining walls hold the slope and provide more useable planting and living space. Small spaces can be made to appear more expansive by using landscape design tricks that fool the eye. Safety in areas prone to wildfire requires creating landscape zones in which both structural and plant materials are chosen for their fire-resistant qualities.

RISE TO THE CHALLENGE AND CREATE A BEAUTIFUL LANDSCAPE ON A DIFFICULT SITE. THIS YARD IN A HOT, DRY CLIMATE BRIMS WITH FEATHERY ORNAMENTAL GRASSES, ROSES, LAMB'S-EAR, CATMINT, AND NEW ZEALAND FLAX, GIVING NEW MEANING TO BRINGING THE DESERT INTO BLOOM.

wow a ho-hum space
use tricks of the designer trade in a small yard

Many factors come into play when turning a small ho-hum yard into a *wow*!

Fooling the eye is nothing new. In your home, you use soft colors to make areas look larger and roomier. You might paint the porch ceiling sky blue. You use correctly proportioned furnishings and position them in the right places. You might use other tricks that include varying accessory heights and placing mirrors.

The same techniques apply outdoors. White and pastels make a garden appear spacious and restful. Using the sky as the ceiling for a patio or reading niche gives an airy lightness. Give a planting area depth by placing medium-textured foliage in the front and fine-textured plants in the back.

Strategically placing a pathway and gate creates the illusion of a secret garden. Mirrors on fences or walls,

GO FLAT FOR FABULOUS SPACE-SAVING SHAPE: ESPALIER A TREE AGAINST A WALL (BELOW). FRUIT TREES ARE MOST COMMONLY USED FOR ESPALIER (FRENCH FOR TRELLIS), BUT ALMOST ANY PLANT CAN BE TRAINED IN A CLASSIC FORM. HERE, PYRACANTHA IS TRAINED INTO A CORDON, OR HORIZONTAL SHAPE.

tucked among greenery, or placed behind a fountain, arbor, garden art, or specimen tree enlarge space.

Artists have long used the technique called trompe l'oeil, French for fool the eye. Charming scenes, such as garden gates and benches or ivy vines clinging to stone create the illusion of depth when painted on fences and walls. A row of arbors, beginning with the tallest and graduating to the shortest, creates long perspective in a small yard even though the structures are close together. Anything graduating in size, such as plant pots, pillars, or statues, accomplishes the same purpose.

Designers agree that perspective requires focal points. Plantings that grow up arbors, trellises, obelisks, and walls add dimension. Vertical plants that take up little space in width are excellent candidates for small yards. Keep the design simple in a small space, because with one scan of the eye, every detail can be detected.

The way outdoor furnishings are grouped can give an open or cramped look. Wrought-iron furniture appears airy and provides focal points during the winter. Raised planters provide seating, eliminating furniture that

ELIMINATE THE LAWN (ABOVE). A BOARDWALK IN A PLANT-FILLED COURTYARD GIVES A SMALL SPACE BIG CHARM.

crowds the space. Elevated beds, planted berms, or pots in various sizes and colors give height and scale to an otherwise flat area. Slow-growing small and dwarf trees and shrubbery prevent the yard from looking overgrown.

Treat a diminutive yard as a courtyard. Stone and brick laid on the diagonal from one corner to another make a small area appear larger. Container gardens work well in very small yards because they look clean and attractive, are low-maintenance, help control plant growth, and are portable. Pots and planters in similar tones unify the space. Fewer but larger pots work better than a lot of little pots. Every pot should earn its space.

Creating individual spaces for particular activities such as reading, eating, and entertaining helps the yard look larger. The smaller the yard, the more important it is to define spaces.

Check out more ideas from HGTV.com
For tips on small-space landscaping, see:
- www.hgtv.com/landscapemakeoversbook

A MIRROR INSIDE AN ARCHED TRELLIS (ABOVE) CREATES THE ILLUSION OF GREATER SPACE.

A BOWLING BALL THAT LOOKS LIKE POLISHED MARBLE ATOP A SCULPTURAL BASE (FAR LEFT) BECOMES A STRIKING FOCAL POINT.

PATIO FURNITURE WITH AN OPEN GRID PATTERN AND NEARLY INVISIBLE GLASS TABLETOP (LEFT) GIVES AN AIRY FEEL AS IT SERVES AS DINING AREA AND FOCAL POINT.

challenging sites

A sloping yard poses landscape difficulties, but also offers tremendous opportunities. If designed well, slopes add visual interest, screen views, buffer noise, direct the eye, and create ample living and planting areas. Some flat landscapes could benefit from having a slope created. A well-designed slope makes a small yard appear to move endlessly toward the horizon.

If, however, slopes are carelessly planted or left untouched, they can limit outdoor living space and create serious problems, including soil erosion and drainage difficulties.

Retaining walls, terraces, decks, and stairs increase living and planting space, control water runoff, hold soil, and make it safer and easier to traverse and maintain the property. Stairsteps built of natural materials such as pebbles or mulch rather than solid surfaces absorb water and are soft underfoot.

Building on a slope. Take advantage of the view, but remember that a structure on top of a slope becomes the dominant element. Winding paths and mixed plantings soften the view from below. Think about side views of the slope. Taller plants at the base draw the eye upward. Consult with local building officials on height and drainage regulations and permit requirements before beginning building projects.

When landscaping on slopes, finding plants that help hold the soil is important. Those with dense, fibrous roots, such as English ivy, winter creeper, and daylilies, are good choices. Landscape fabric controls erosion while the plants are filling in. It lets water in but keeps sunlight out, controlling weeds. Slit the fabric to place plants. Plant material, rather than lawn grasses, should be used on steep slopes because mowing an embankment can be difficult and dangerous.

If your plans require changing soil levels, or grades, around a mature tree, build a wall or well around the tree to avoid damaging its roots.

Solutions for shade. The pattern of sun and shade in your landscape changes throughout the day, with the seasons, as plantings mature, and as structures are built.

SHADOW AND SLOPE COMBINE FOR A LANDSCAPING CHALLENGE, BRILLIANTLY MET HERE WITH A SPECTRUM OF COLORS THAT BRIGHTEN TREE-SHADED SLOPES AS THEY HOLD SOIL IN PLACE (ABOVE AND RIGHT).

If your problem is too much shade, consult with a tree specialist about trimming trees to let in more light. Choose plants that tolerate shade. Ferns are a natural choice. Shade gardens also can embrace vivid color. Understory trees such as dogwood, redbud, and Japanese maple, provide seasonal color. Annuals, perennials, and bulbs—such as nicotiana, astilbe, and caladium—bring bright flowers or foliage to shady areas.

In choosing stone or mulching material for planting beds or paths,

pick a light color. If nothing grows in an area under a tree, wrap a deck around the trunk; be sure to leave enough room for water to get through to the tree and for the tree to expand.

Solutions for hot, dry, windy sites. Walls or hillsides that face south or west trap sunlight and heat and create a desertlike microclimate. Plant trees for cooling shade; build overhead structures for shade while trees grow.

Wind pulls moisture from plants and carries away soil. A windbreak is a structure or plant material, wider than it is tall, that slows or redirects the wind. Evergreens and ready-made or homemade screens shield yards. A solid screen is less effective than one that lets some air through because it compresses air, which can cause turbulence on the leeward side.

Lawn grass needs too much water for arid areas, but many ornamental grasses hold soil and take less water. Succulents are good, but plant choices also include drought-tolerant plants such as salvia, stonecrop, and yarrow.

Xeriscaping describes planting strategies that conserve water. Success comes from good soil preparation. Well-amended soil holds more water. Thick layers of mulch help retain soil

moisture, control weeds, and nourish plants. Drip irrigation takes water directly to roots, using less water than sprinkling. Water features such as fountains near plantings help to humidify them. Using cool colors on walls and fences as well as in plant materials helps create cool views.

Seaside solutions. Wind, salt, and sandy soil are hard on plants. Planting in containers lets you control soil conditions. Some hardy plants that can survive in-ground planting at the seaside include barberry, cedar, cosmos, hostas, juniper, lamb's-ears, lavender, and sedum.

RETAINING WALLS (ABOVE) TAME A SLOPE, EXPAND OUTDOOR LIVING SPACE, AND CREATE AREAS FOR PLANTING.

ORNAMENTAL GRASSES THAT HELP RETAIN SOIL THRIVE IN A HOT, DRY, WINDY CLIMATE (LEFT).

Wildfire solutions. Beauty and safety can be combined if you live in an area prone to wildfires. The right kind of landscaping can help defend your house from fire. Seek advice from local fire prevention agencies, master gardener organizations, nursery workers, and professional landscapers. Safe landscaping requires keeping weeds and flammable plantings, such as pine, cedar, juniper, eucalyptus,

shrubs and flowers that deer don't like to eat—plants with pungent or prickly foliage, such as rosemary, or plants with thorns, fuzzy textures, and gray leaves. These include maiden grass, sage, viburnum, foxglove, rugosa roses, and false indigo. Any list of deer-resistant plants must be tempered with the knowledge that deer may eat that plant if they're hungry. Deer also rub their antlers on tree

REDUCE FIRE RISK by keeping the area next to the house free of plants. Plant juicy succulents next to the plant-free zone. Native vegetation adapted to local climates is placed farthest from buildings.

cypress, bougainvillea, and ornamental grasses, away from the house and other structures. Near the house, plant lawns and more fire-resistant low-growing vegetation. Plants that store water in their tissues are good choices in fire-prone areas. These include succulents and ground covers such as ice plant (*Delosperma* or *Lampranthus*).

When incorporating landscape structures and features such as decks, fencing, and mulches, avoid using flammable wood. Think stone, concrete, gravel, and metal.

Wildlife solutions. Deer are beautiful creatures when admired from afar. That is just the way you want them to view your garden: from afar. Keeping them at bay, which is away from flowers and plants, can be challenging. Ask those in your area who have had some success about their specific solutions. One source of information are local fish and wildlife professionals.

Experts say that the longer the deer have been munching in an area, the more difficult it is to get rid of them. Some suggestions include planting

bark, which can damage the bark and expose the tree to insects and disease.

Ways to keep out deer include physical barriers and repellents. Erect fences as high as 12 feet if permitted, but avoid sharp points that could impale a leaping deer. Netting around or over plants helps deter deer and birds from feeding. Wrap trees and shrubs with galvanized hardware cloth or wire mesh to help deter damage from deer, rabbits, and raccoons.

Wildlife repellents include the family dog, electronic devices that emit sounds that scare off animals, and motion detectors that shoot sprays of water. Milorganite, composted sewage sludge, nourishes plants and helps ward off deer. Spraying predator scents, such as coyote urine, around plants is said to act as a deer deterrent. Check pet stores, zoos, and garden centers for availability; they must be reapplied frequently to be effective. Bar soap or bags containing blood meal or human hair hung from tree limbs are sometimes effective. A scarecrow—moved around the garden as deer become used to it—also helps.

Whatever method you try, you must be vigilant to succeed.

A STONE FOUNDATION AND PATIO PAVING CREATES A FIRE-RESISTANT RING AROUND A HOUSE (ABOVE). CONTAINER PLANTS CAN BE MOVED QUICKLY IF WILDFIRE RISK INCREASES.

Check out more ideas from HGTV.com
For tips on protecting your landscape, see:
- www.hgtv.com/landscapemakeoversbook

DEER-RESISTANT PLANTS

Hungry deer forced into residential areas by increasing housing development often find garden plants delicious. Some may even nibble those plants that top deer-proof lists. Here are some worth a try:

- Bee balm (*Monarda*), Zones 3–7
- Butterfly bush (*Buddleia*), Zones 5–9
- Catmint (*Nepeta*), Zones 4–7
- Maiden grass (*Miscanthus*), Zones 4–9
- False blue indigo (*Baptisia*), Zones 3–8
- Fescue grass (*Festuca*), Zone 4
- Fountain grass (*Pennisetum*), Zone 5–9
- Foxglove (*Digitalis*), Zones 3–8
- Lavender (*Lavandula*), Zones 5–9
- Lavender cotton, Zones 6–8
- Ornamental onion (*Allium*), Zones 3–9
- Rugosa roses, Zones 2–7
- Russian sage (*Perovskia*), Zones 5–9
- Salvia, Zones 3–10
- Summersweet (*Clethra*), Zones 3–9
- Viburnum, Zones 4–8
- Wormwood, Zones 3–9

bee balm

OUTDOOR LIVING BY THE SEASIDE (LEFT) IS ENHANCED BY A GARDEN FILLED WITH SALT-TOLERANT PLANTS, SUCH AS THE LILY-OF-THE-NILE (FOREGROUND).

fern grotto
the landscape for a shady space is filled with woodland plantings

Bald spots beneath the trees on your shady lot can take on the look of the lush green growth of the forest floor. That's where landscape designer Dan Berger found inspiration for a fern grotto that mimics nature's handiwork.

Imagine yourself walking in the woods, Berger advises. In this hillside yard, two curving walkways—a timber path and a narrower flagstone path—preserve the natural feel of the yard, encouraging casual strolls around the waterfall and plantings. A welcoming patio serves as a popular destination. Ferns add the perfect touch, giving the hillside a leafy woodland feel.

Check out more ideas from HGTV.com
For tips on under-tree landscaping, see:
- www.hgtv.com/landscapemakeoversbook

A TERRACED STONE AND TIMBER PATH (RIGHT) LEADS TO A PEACEFUL SHADY SPOT WITH A WATERFALL AND WOODSY PLANTINGS.

DESPITE A FEW BRIGHT PLANT POTS, THE SHADY DECK REMAINS FORLORN (ABOVE).

SHADY SECRETS

- **You can create** the illusion of light by including lots of white and gold accents. White bloomers such as bugbane and hostas with gold foliage, for example, work wonders in shade.
- **When shade is so dense** that nothing will grow, increase the light that reaches the ground by elevating trees or by thinning some of the overhead branches.
- **Add mirrors** or gazing balls, or give found objects a coat of bright paint.

hillside path

tools & materials
SPECIAL TOOLS: Power saw, drill with ½-inch bit

- Railroad ties
- Rebar, ½-inch diameter
- Landscape fabric
- Drain stone, ¾ inch

A stone and timber path makes access easy by terracing a slope.

1 | clear and grade Excavate steps with a 6-inch rise. The tread, or flat part, should be 3 to 5 feet deep, depending on the grade of the hill.

2 | cut ties For a rustic path wide enough to accommodate two walkers, use railroad ties cut to a 4-foot length as the risers. For a path wide enough for one person, cut the ties to 2-foot lengths.

3 | place ties Set a tie into a carved-out step.

4 | drill hole Drill a ½-inch hole through each end of the tie.

5 | anchor tie Hammer 2-foot lengths of rebar through each hole and into the ground, anchoring ties.

6 | level tread Check risers for level. Adjust as necessary.

7 | lay landscape fabric Place a double layer of landscape fabric between the dirt steps and wooden risers to serve as a weed barrier.

8 | fill with gravel Cover the landscape fabric with a 2-inch layer of drain rock.

finishing touches Use flagstones, if desired, on the landings. Grade the landings so that they're level. Cover with landscape fabric. Set the flagstones. Use larger pieces for easy stepping-stones and fill in with smaller stones.

DESIGN PLANS

goals Add style to a shady yard and improve access through it.

cost $1,000 if you do it yourself vs. $3,900 for a pro.

time 3 weekends.

difficulty scale There is heavy lifting.
●●○○○

skill scale Keeping steps level is most important.
●●●○○

BUILDING

fern grotto
staghorn fern and patio

A staghorn fern hanging from a tree mimics the look of ferns that grow on tree trunks in the wild. Staghorns are epiphytic, or air plants. Rather than getting nutrients through soil, they absorb them from the air, as orchids also do.

These shade-loving plants like to be moderately moist, but overwatering can encourage a fungus that can kill the plant. Watering once a week in periods without rain is enough.

Ideal temperatures for this fern are between 60 and 80°F. Freezing harms staghorn ferns, so be sure to overwinter them indoors.

AFTER

A BENCH ON THE PATIO NEAR A WATERFALL (ABOVE) IS THE PERFECT PLACE TO RELAX WHILE ENJOYING THE SHADY FERN GROTTO.

mounting a staghorn fern

tools & materials
- 6×18-inch piece of decay-resistant wood, plus a few small scraps
- 12×12-inch corkboard, 1 inch thick
- 1 small bag sphagnum moss
- 1 staghorn fern
- 4 feet plastic-coated telephone wire
- 8 coated, 1½-inch deck screws

Imitate nature by growing a fern in a tree. Soak sphagnum moss in a water before making the frame.

1 | cut frame Cut a 4-inch square from the center of the corkboard. Set the cork on the 6×18 wood piece. Drill pilot holes at each corner into the wood.

2 | place roots in hole Squeeze excess water from a large handful of sphagnum and place it in the hole of the corkboard. Slice the fern's root ball and gently spread the roots apart. Set the fern on the moss and place extra moss around the roots.

3 | attach screws Fasten the corkboard frame to the redwood with deck screws, leaving ½ inch of each screw protruding from the front. Screw through the pilot holes.

4 | finish the project Loop wire in an X between the screws to hold the fern in place. (As the plant grows, it will cover the wire.) Attach a couple of pieces of scrap wood below the fern to help support its weight.

Mount the frame in a tree in a spot that is out of direct sunshine and sheltered from wind. Once a year, place fresh moss between the board and the plant.

DESIGN PLANS

goal Enhance a shady spot by mounting a fern to a tree to grow as some species do in the wild.

cost Mature ferns can be expensive, running about $45.

time 1 weekend.

difficulty scale Frame construction is simple.

● ○ ○ ○ ○

skill scale If you can drive a screw, you can do this project.

● ○ ○ ○ ○

DECORATING

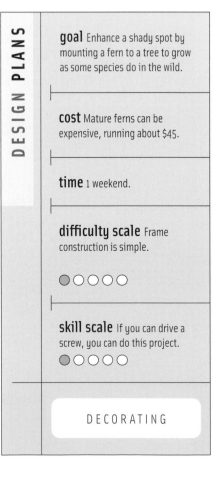

a stone patio

tools & materials

- Landscape fabric
- Gravel, ³/₈ inch
- Flagstones and fieldstones

A simple patio at the base of the terraced hillside path has the feel of a forest glen.

1 | level area Dig out and level an area for the patio, such as this 8×8-foot example. Carve out the hillside for a simple retaining wall of stacked fieldstones.

2 | stack fieldstone Dry stack the fieldstones, fitting them together securely. In this example, the designer chose Sonoma stone. Pockets between the rocks make ideal spots for planting small ferns, lichens, or mosses to create a natural mortar.

3 | lay landscape fabric Cover the entire base of the patio with landscape fabric. A double layer works best as a weed barrier.

HOSTAS, QUEENS OF SHADE

As plant breeders develop hostas in endless variations of showy foliage, the old-fashioned plantain lily has reached new heights as America's favorite perennial for shade. You can choose varieties with blue, green, or gold leaves that are smooth or puckered, plain or variegated. Heights range from 3 inches to 4 feet tall. Lilylike blossoms of lavender, purple, or white add to the show.

Some popular choices include 'Piedmont Gold', 'Francis Williams', 'Krossa Regal', and 'Sum & Substance'.

4 | place flagstones Set the flagstone directly on the fabric in a random pattern with the best-looking sides facing up, leaving 1-inch gaps between stones. Use a level to make sure the stones create a flat surface. Chisel the flagstones as necessary so they lie evenly. Position larger pieces in areas of heavy foot traffic for greater stability.

5 | fill gaps After setting all the flagstones, fill in around them with the gravel.

DESIGN PLANS

goals Create a patio area that joins the two pathways uphill from a waterfall with a view of the fern grotto.

cost The stone patio makes up about a third of the total project cost, which includes the stairs ($1,000 vs. $3,900).

time 2 weekends.

difficulty scale Shifting rocks makes for heavy work.
●●●●○

skill scale Setting the random flagstone pattern takes patience.
●●○○○

BUILDING

Tips for ferns.

Ferns grow best in rich, organic soil, so plant them in a 50-50 mix of peat moss and native soil. Ferns like full to partial shade. Mulch to conserve soil moisture in dry weather. By mixing ferns in different shades of green and with contrasting forms and textures, you can create your own fern fantasy. Here is a sampling of ferns to get you started.

■ **Christmas fern** (*Polystichum acrostichoides*) These leathery evergreen fronds grow 2 feet tall, combining well with other woodland perennials and providing cuttings for holiday decorations. Hardy in Zones 3–9.

■ **Cinnamon fern** (*Osmunda cinnamomea*) Both elegant and robust, this moisture-loving fern has erect center fronds that look like cinnamon sticks in spring. Hardy in Zones 2–10.

■ **Hay-scented fern** (*Dennstaedtia punctilobula*) Adaptable and easy to grow, this fern with graceful, tapering fronds forms attractive clumps 2 to 3 feet tall. In fall, the fronds turn a soft shade of yellow. Hardy in Zones 3–8.

■ **Japanese painted fern** (*Athyrium nipponicum* 'Pictum') Thanks to the wine-red stems and silver markings, it looks like someone took a paintbrush to the fronds of this 12- to 18-inch-tall fern. Hardy in Zones 4–9.

■ **Male wood fern** (*Dryopteris filix-mas*) Sturdy and masculine compared to the delicate painted fern, this plant grows to 4 feet tall. It is an adaptable fern that tolerates drying and poor soil. Hardy in Zones 4–8.

■ **Marginal wood fern** (*Dryopteris marginalis*) With familiar deep-green fronds that serve as a staple in florists' bouquets, this gently arching evergreen fern grows about 24 inches tall. Hardy in Zones 4–8.

■ **Maidenhair fern** (*Adiantum pedatum*) This 18-inch-tall fern with shiny black stems and light green fronds that are delicate and lacy is considered one of the most elegant. Hardy in Zones 3–8.

■ **Ostrich fern** (*Matteuccia struthiopteris*) A vase-shaped fern, it can grow 4 to 6 feet tall. It spreads rapidly and will

maidenhair fern

GRASSES AND GRASSLIKE PARTNERS

Most ornamental grasses require full sun, but a few prefer some shade. By including a few grasses in your shady space, you can add an interesting contrast of form and texture as well as the movement and sound of rustling leaves. Here are a few to consider:

■ **Hakone grass** (*Hakonechloa macra*) Zones 5–9
■ **Mondo grass** (*Ophiopogon japonicus*) Zones 6–9
■ **Purple moor grass** (*Molinia caerulea* 'Variegata') Zones 4–9
■ **Sedge** (*Carex* spp.) Zones 5–9

easily naturalize on a shady hillside. It does best where summers are neither too hot nor too dry. Hardy in Zones 3–7.

Check out more ideas from HGTV.com

For informative details about ferns, see

■ www.hgtv.com/landscapemakeoversbook

cinnamon fern

Evergold' sedge

FLOWERING PLANTS FOR A SHADY SPACE

A shady garden can have more shades than just green. Many flowering plants can light up your shade garden with bright blooms. Here's a sampling:

Perennials

- **Allegheny foam flower** (*Tiarella cordifolia*) Zones 3–9
- **Blue-eyed grass** (*Sisyrinchium angustifolium*) Zones 4–9
- **Bugbane** (*Cimicifuga racemosa*) Zones 3–7
- **Coral bells** (*Heuchera sanguinea*) Zones 3–9
- **Forget-me-not** (*Brunnera macrophylla*) Zones 3–7
- **Heart-leaf bergenia** (*Bergenia cordifolia*) Zones 4–8
- **Narrow-spiked ligularia** (*Ligularia stenocephala*) Zones 5–8
- **Navelwort** (*Omphalodes cappadocica*) Zones 6–8
- **Old-fashioned bleeding heart** (*Dicentra spectabilis*) Zones 4–6
- **Siberian bellflower** (*Campanula poscharskyana*) Zones 4–7
- **Spiderwort** (*Tradescantia virginiana*) Zones 4–9
- **Yellow corydalis** (*Corydalis lutea*) Zones 5–7

Annuals

- **Browallia** (*Browallia speciosa*)
- **Coleus** (*Solenostemon scotellarioides*)
- **Impatiens** (*Impatiens walleriana*)
- **Wax begonia** (*Begonia semperflorens–cultorum* hybrids)

Shrubs

- **Azalea** (*Rhododendron* spp.) Zones 4–8
- **Bigleaf hydrangea** (*Hydrangea macrophylla*) Zones 6–9
- **Black jetbead** (*Rhodotypos scandens*) Zones 4–8
- **Kerria** (*Kerria japonica*) Zones 5–9

impatiens

siberian bellflower

japanese kerria

plants for a dry, windy site
tough, lovely survivors can take the heat

In yards blasted relentlessly by hot, dry winds, plant survival can be difficult. Plants that thrive without coddling in such harsh conditions are an important landscape consideration. You can also use plants or structures to help block the wind. The plants used in this landscape stand up to hot temperatures and drying winds.

Flowering plum (*Prunus × blireana*) softens the setting and screens sunlight with fine leaf texture and purple foliage. This tree is hardy in Zones 5–8. In colder areas, you could substitute purple-leaf sand cherry (*Prunus × cistena* 'Big Cis'), hardy in Zones 3–6.

Plants with flowers or foliage in restful colors of purple, gray-green, and lavender visually cool the landscape. This garden features rose of Sharon (*Hibiscus syriacus*), hardy in Zones 5–9, and lavender (*Lavandula angustifolia*), hardy in Zones 5–8. In colder areas, you could substitute 'Frau

Dagmar Hastrup' rugosa rose (*Rosa rugosa*), hardy in Zones 3–7, and 'Lady' lavender, a variety that grows successfully as an annual in all regions because it blooms the first year from seed.

Most ornamental grasses stand up well to heat and drying winds. Purple fountain grass (*Pennisetum setaceum*), repeated throughout this outdoor garden room, thrives in Zones 8–10. In colder regions, you can provide the same fountainlike form (but not the purple foliage) with either perennial fountain grass (*Pennisetum alopecuroides*), hardy in Zones 5–9, or prairie dropseed (*Sporobolus heterolepis*), hardy in Zones 3–8. Or grow purple fountain grass as an annual.

HEAT AND WIND DON'T BOTHER THE PLANTS IN THIS SOUTHWESTERN LANDSCAPE (RIGHT). THE MOSTLY GRAVEL PATH LETS WATER SOAK INTO THE GROUND WHEN IT RAINS.

A LIVING WINDBREAK

Searing winds require lasting solutions. Start by spacing shrubs closely enough together that, when mature, their branches will touch. Best bet: Plant a mix of several kinds of shrubs, so pests or disease would be less likely to wipe out the whole stand.

Make sure the shrubs you choose can tolerate hot, dry winds. Here are some good candidates:
- **Common lilac** (*Syringa vulgaris*), Zones 3–7
- **Privet** (*Ligustrum amurense*), Zones 4–7
- **Siberian peashrub** (*Caragana arborescens*), Zones 2–7
- **Spreading cotoneaster** (*Cotoneaster divaricatus*), Zones 4–7

siberian pea shrub

russian sage

MORE PLANTS FOR A DRY, WINDY SITE

Shrubs
- **American elder** (*Sambucus canadensis*), Zones 3–9
- **Bush cinquefoil** (*Potentilla fruticosa*), Zones 2–6
- **Fragrant sumac** (*Rhus aromatica*), Zones 3–9
- **Japanese barberry** (*Berberis thunbergii*), Zones 4–8

Perennials
- **Russian sage** (*Perovskia atriplicifolia*), Zones 4–9
- **Showy sedum** (*Sedum spectabile*), Zones 3–9
- **'Silver Mound' artemisia** (*Artemisia schmidtiana*), Zones 3–8
- **Yarrow** (*Achillea millefolium*), Zones 3–10

Annuals
- **Fan flower** (*Scaevola aemula*)
- **Moss rose** (*Portulaca grandiflora*)
- **Mexican zinnia** (*Zinnia haageana*)
- **Vinca** (*Catharanthus roseus*)

rock cress

fountain grass

MAKE THE MOST OF SOIL MOISTURE

When water is short, preserving soil moisture is critical.
- **Before you plant,** spread a 2- to 4-inch layer of organic matter such as compost on the soil and dig it in. Organic matter acts as a sponge, soaking up excess water, then giving it back to the plants when they need it.
- **After planting,** spread a blanket of shredded bark or other mulch on the soil around the plants to keep soil moisture from evaporating.

expand a small space
a faux gate gives a backyard the illusion of depth and secret spaces as it dresses up a fence

A gate suggests that there's a destination on the other side. That is the theory behind this fanciful project. The homeowners wanted to find a way to make their limited backyard appear more spacious, so they enlisted the help of creative designer Nancy Driscoll, who devised this clever faux gate, complete with an "entrance arbor" that draws the eye.

The yard already was bordered by a wooden privacy fence that served as a logical location for the gate. The designer worked with the existing fence, tweaking it until it would accommodate the new faux portal. You probably will have to make some minor revisions on your own fence, as well. If you have to build a fence, you will be able to customize the

A FAUX GATE AND OVERSIZE STEPPING-STONES (RIGHT) CREATE AN ILLUSION OF GREATER SPACE IN A SMALL BACKYARD.

A NARROW, PLAIN BACKYARD (ABOVE) GAVE THE HOMEOWNERS LITTLE REASON TO SPEND TIME IN IT.

PLAY TRICKS WITH SMALL
SPACES BY USING OVERSIZED
ELEMENTS SUCH AS THESE
GIANT STEPPING-STONES,
WHICH FOOL THE EYE INTO
SEEING EXTRA SPACE (ABOVE).

DESIGN TIPS

To make the most of your small space,
follow these tips.

- **Avoid a cluttered appearance** by keeping
your landscape plan simple. Repeat some of
the same plants or materials throughout the
landscape to provide unity.
- **Use dense planting** to make the garden
appear larger.
- **Make the most** of vertical space.
Grow vines on trellises, arbors, and walls.
- **Create a sense** of tranquility with a tiny
pool or other water feature.
- **Include plants** with contrasting textures
and year-round beauty.
- **Keep scale in mind.** For example, a small
ornamental tree may be more appropriate
than a large shade tree.
- **Use a focal point,** such as a statue or a
fountain or a plant with strong vertical lines,
to pull the garden elements together.

design to effortlessly accept the gate and its accents.

The project pictured incorporates used wood for the gate. Check with architectural salvage yards and watch for ads in the paper for such finds. Or use redwood or cedar, which age into an attractive silvery patina.

Enhance the illusion of unlimited spaciousness begun by this faux garden portal by adding an oversize flagstone pathway that leads toward the gate. Surround the pathway with a curving stone wall and planting beds filled with small trees, shrubs, and flowers and foliage that show bright spots of color.

Check out more ideas from HGTV.com
For making the most of small spaces, see:
- www.hgtv.com/landscapemakeoversbook

RUSTIC DETAIL FROM SALVAGED HOBNAILS CREATES AN OLD-WORLD EFFECT FOR THE ARCHED GATE (BELOW LEFT).

FLOWERING VINES CLIMBING THE PORTAL ARBOR (BELOW) USE VERTICAL SPACE AND SUGGEST THERE MIGHT BE A SECRET GARDEN BEYOND THE FALSE GATE.

A SINGLE PROMINENT FEATURE does more to visually expand a small space than scattering a number of pieces, which can cause a sense of claustrophobic clutter.

arbor, lattice, and faux gate

tools & materials

SPECIAL TOOLS: Circular saw or beam saw, reciprocal saw, table saw, compound miter saw, jigsaw, nail gun, drill with 24-inch electrician's bit
- 2 – 6×6s, 10 feet long
- 1 – 6×6, 8 feet long
- 1 – 6×6, 10 feet long
- 1 – 4×4, 8 feet long
- 2 – 4×4s, 12 feet long
- 2 – 2×2s, 12 feet long
- 11 – 2×2s, 8 feet long
- 2 – 2×4s, 8 feet long
- 3 – 1×8s, 6 feet long
- 2 – 1×6s, 6 feet long
- 1 – 1×12, 6 feet long
- 1 – 1×10, 6 feet long
- 2 – 1×3s, 6 feet long
- 4 – threaded rods or rebar, 18 inches long, ⅜-inch-diameter

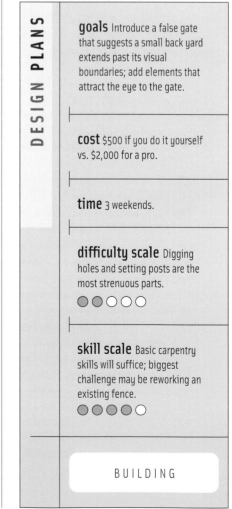

DESIGN PLANS

goals Introduce a false gate that suggests a small back yard extends past its visual boundaries; add elements that attract the eye to the gate.

cost $500 if you do it yourself vs. $2,000 for a pro.

time 3 weekends.

difficulty scale Digging holes and setting posts are the most strenuous parts.
●●○○○

skill scale Basic carpentry skills will suffice; biggest challenge may be reworking an existing fence.
●●●●○

BUILDING

- Pea gravel
- Concrete mix
- Antique or handmade gate handle and hinges
- Antique hobnails

Dress up a fence and visually expand a small yard with an arbor, a false gate, and a trellis topper for the fence. This homeowner used a combination of pressure-treated and salvaged lumber to build the unit along with redwood where looks were important. You will find it helpful to build the arbor gate near the posts supporting your fence.

Set arbor posts This arbor uses two 9-foot-long 6×6 posts (cut down from 10-footers), which provide a final arbor height of 8 feet after the posts are sunk and the arbor is topped with the caps and lintel. The length of posts you will need depends on the height of your fence and how deep the posts must be sunk in the ground in your climate. The goal is for the lintel to be even with the top of the lattice.

Dig two 24-inch-deep holes 4 feet apart and 2 feet from the fence. Pour 2 inches of pea gravel into each hole. Stand a 6×6 post in each hole, plumb it, and temporarily brace it. Fill each hole with concrete and let the concrete set up for 24 hours.

1 | add a step and build a lattice frame Cut a 6×6 in three pieces to form a step leading to the gate. One piece should fit between the two posts, flush with the ground and the other two between the posts and the fence to form a rectangle. Toenail the 6×6 to the posts. Fill the box with pea gravel.

build lattice frame You'll be constructing two sections of lattice—one on each side of the arbor gate. Start by building a frame to hold the

lattice. First, extend the height of the fence posts at the end of the fence (or at the point where you will end the lattice) and the ones near the arbor gate. To do this, toenail a 2-foot-long 6×6 to the top of the existing posts. Brace each one with a 4-foot-long 2×4, which will run from the top of the post down 2 feet past where the extension meets the post, screwing it to the back of the post.

If existing fence posts are not well-located in relation to the arbor gate, install new posts. These should be in line with the existing posts and extend 2 feet above the fence.

2 | cap the frame Measure the length of the fence on both sides of the gate. Cut a 4×4 to those lengths. Place the 4×4s on top of the two posts and toenail or toe-screw them to the posts.

3 | attach verticals Cut 2×2s to the dimensions of the lattice frame. You'll need enough to place one every 12 inches along the length of both lattice sections.

Stand each upright flush with the back edge of the the top of the fence and the 4×4 cap. Check that each is plumb with a small level. Use a nail gun to toenail them into the top of the fence and the bottom of the cap.

Snap a horizontal chalk line on the uprights halfway between the fence and the 4×4 cap.

4 | add crosspiece For both sections of lattice, cut a 2×2 to fit horizontally between the lattice frame posts. Center it on the chalkline. Screw or nail-gun it to the uprights.

arbor, lattice, and faux gate
(continued)

5 | decorate ends Make a decorative cap for each of the two arbor posts. With a reciprocal saw, notch the ends of two 14-inch lengths of 6×6. In the project pictured, each notch is 2 inches tall and about 4¼ inches long (see the "after" photo at right).

Top each post with a cap, notches facing down, and temporarily attach the caps by toenailing them with a nail gun or toe-screwing them to the posts.

Next, cut a 2×2-inch square notch at both ends of a 6-foot length of 6×6. This will be the lintel.

6 | set lintel Place the lintel on the caps and temporarily toenail it in place. Make sure notches point down and that the amount of overhang is the same on each side.

Using a 24-inch electrician's bit (also called a bellhanger bit), drill two ⅜-inch holes through each lintel and cap and about 8 inches into the top of each post.

7 | attach lintel Drive a threaded rod or length of rebar into each of the four holes flush with the surface of the lintel.

Next, lay out the gate planks. For the vertical gate planks, lay out 62-inch-long 1×6s and 1×8s, side by side, to produce a width of 32 inches, or whatever dimension suits your gate. You may need to use a table saw to rip one of the boards to arrive at the correct width. In the end, the planks will be held together by the kickboard, arch, and side trim.

AFTER

8 | create kickboard From a 12-inch-wide board or two 1×6s, cut a kickboard that is as long as the gate is wide. Then cut a 3-inch-wide-by-2-inch-deep notch at the top corners to accommodate a vertical trim piece.

9 | attach kickboard Set the kickboard on top of the gate planks. Line it up with the bottom and sides of the planks, then secure it to them with deck screws.

10 | cut arc guides It may be hard to find one piece of wood large enough for the 6-inch-wide arc at the top of the gate; you can make it from two pieces of 1×10. Cut one end of each 1×10 at a 45-degree angle. Position the pieces on the top of the planks with the angled ends placed together to form an inverted "V." Drill a screw partway into the plank 16 inches directly below the apex of the inverted "V."

11 | draw and cut arc Use a steel tape measure as a compass. Hold the tape on the screw, and draw an arc with a pencil over the top edge of the "V." Move the screw down about 6 inches and mark the bottom arc of the curve.

Cut along the marks with a jigsaw. Also cut out notches at the bottom corners to match those in the top corners of the kickboard.

12 | attach arch Screw the two arcs to the top of the planks. Cut off plank ends extending beyond the arch, using the arch as a guide.

Cut two 3-inch-wide boards to fit snugly between the notches in the arched top and kickboard and screw them to the gate.

PLACEMENT MAKES ALL THE DIFFERENCE

Select a location for your faux garden portal, or an accent feature such as dramatic garden art, that logically fits the purpose of the piece. Plunking a gate or a statue in the center of an area dominates the space, making it feel smaller. Tucking the same piece into a corner visually expands the space along a diagonal, creating an illusion of spaciousness.

Enhancing the sense of size also comes from using the concept that a straight line is the shortest distance between two points. A meandering path that draws the eye toward the focal point, therefore, must be longer.

13 | attach side trim Screw 1×3s between the arch and the kickboard for a finished look.

14 | attach gate Screw the gate to the fence with the arched top above the top of the fence. Complete the rustic look with a rustic gate handle and hinges, and hobnail trim.

A simple plan plus a large dose of creativity works magic in a small-space landscape. You can create an open, airy feel, for example, just by manipulating the textures and colors of plants. Also try experimenting with the shape and height of planters and beds to discover other ways to create a more spacious effect.

Tricks with texture. The shape, size, and feel of foliage, flowers, and other plant parts all contribute to a plant's texture. For example, the small frame and finely divided leaves of a Japanese maple give that tree a fine texture. A lilac, on the other hand, with its bold branches, large flower clusters and undivided leaves, has a coarse texture.

In this small backyard garden, landscape designer Nancy Driscoll created the illusion of more space by choosing plants with coarse texture for the foreground and plants with fine texture in the background.

Color considerations. Color offers another way to visually expand a small space. A monochromatic color scheme unifies an area and makes it appear larger. Cool blues, greens, and purples, which appear to recede, give the illusion of space. Warm oranges, reds, and yellows, on the other hand, clamor for attention and may overwhelm a small area.

If you want to include warm colors, fool the eye by planting the bright colors in the forefront and saving the soft colors for the background.

Form that fits. For an easy way to decide on the shape and height of planters and beds, collect cardboard boxes in a variety of shapes and sizes. Then experiment by moving boxes around to see where they give the best illusion of more space.

Take advantage of changes in elevation to make an area appear larger. A raised bed or steps down from a deck, for example, often creates the illusion of more space.

COMPOSE WITH SHAPE AND COLOR. PRUNING AN ORNAMENTAL TREE AND SHRUBS INTO THE SAME ROUND SHAPE CREATES UNITY (BELOW). THE COOL PURPLE CLEMATIS SEEMS TO RECEDE AND MAKES THE SPACE LOOK LARGER.

USING SEVERAL SHADES OF ONE COLOR (NEAR RIGHT) VISUALLY EXPANDS AND UNIFIES SPACE.

CONTRASTING TEXTURE WITH TUFTS OF FESCUE IN FRONT OF A CRINKLY-LEAF PERENNIAL GERANIUM (CENTER RIGHT) CREATES AN ILLUSION OF DEPTH.

TRAINING A VINE (FAR RIGHT) TO LIE FLAT ON A FENCE USES VERTICAL SPACE TO ADVANTAGE AND ENLARGES A SMALL AREA.

A MULTIHUED STONE WALL
(ABOVE), TOPPED WITH A
MADCAP MIX OF GRASSES,
ROSES, AND FOLIAGE
CONTINUES THE PLAY WITH
TEXTURE, MAKING A RAISED
PLANTING BED APPEAR LARGER.

6

CHILDREN'S GARDENS

Fun for all ages. Give the children in your life a space of their own that lets their imaginations flourish, and add some fun spots for grownups too.

children's
GARDENS

Before there were speed bumps, there were signs in residential areas that said, "Slow down: children at play." Before there were outdoor rooms, families gathered on

front porches and children played kickball on front lawns. Before there were video games, children engaged in imaginative play under the shade of a sprawling tree.

You can create a place that sparks the imagination and demonstrates the wonders of nature in your own backyard. It can be a special place where children can play games, romp with pets, have a teddy bear tea party, make mud pies, and learn how fascinating it can be to watch something grow in a garden that grows along with them.

What children want, say landscape designers, are structured areas for unstructured play. They want spaces in which to be kids, where they can run around, ride on a swing, pick the flowers, eat strawberries, fill their dump trucks with sand, and splash water.

If fresh air is going to compete with TV and video games, children need a reason to go outside. They need more than their parents' patio table and bottles of bubbles to blow. They need furniture that fits them and garden tools that are comfortable in their hands. They need a place that beckons to them, fills their senses, and lets them explore. But most of all, kids just want to have fun.

A CHILD-SIZE WHEELBARROW FILLED WITH
SMILING PANSIES MAKES IT FUN FOR YOUNG
ONES TO HELP OUT IN THE GARDEN, ESPECIALLY
IF THE GARDEN IS DESIGNED TO GROW ALONG
WITH THEM.

children's gardens
turn everyday yards into wondrous havens of enjoyment that spark young imaginations

Seeing play through the eyes of a child and getting creative yourself make a garden special. Large play structures may be a dream for your children, but in reality many yards lack the space. Visiting parks that have swing sets, jungle gyms, slides, and swinging bridges becomes a treat. Yet with careful planning, small yards can accommodate many fun elements.

String up a swing on a big tree or under an arbor. Set up a portable soccer goal. Start an old-fashioned game of leapfrog on the lawn. Think

A FLOWER-LINED WALKWAY DOUBLES AS A SPEEDWAY FOR A REMOTE-CONTROLLED CAR (ABOVE). MULTIPURPOSE AREAS ARE FUN, PRACTICAL, AND COST-EFFECTIVE.

like a child, but plan as a grownup, and the possibilities for fun and learning become endless.

Even small yards can accommodate a 6×8-foot play area. Corners make good play sites where fencing helps give children the feeling of enclosure and a secret "no adults allowed" space. Where fencing is impractical, a partial screen with plants in raised beds or structures such as split-wood railing can define the space as well.

Ask children for their ideas for play spaces. Landscape designers say children have good suggestions and should be encouraged in drawing pictures as best they can of what they want their spaces to look like. The children's input could result in a compromise or alternative that works well and with which everyone will be happy.

Soliciting children's ideas and then letting them plant their own gardens or create play areas makes the space their own. If they feel ownership, the space will be more meaningful and used more frequently.

As well-intentioned as parents and grandparents may be, they sometimes must suppress their own inner child in place of the children's longings and imagination. Kids' interests may differ from what their elders' were at the same age.

Designers say that thoughtful planning means more than making something elaborate or expensive. Recycle useful things from your yard or garage in the play area. Children learn from you the benefits of reusing rather than discarding.

With scrap lumber and old sheets you can build a frame where swaths of fabric provide cover for a tent or curtains for a theater. Turn large planters into simple sandboxes that become planters again once the children have grown. Let a gazebo go from being a castle or a fort back to an

attractive garden feature years later. A potting shed does double-duty as a kitchen for making mud pies.

Playhouses and forts, potting benches, wheelbarrows, rakes, shovels, and trowels specifically for children are on the market. Offering a child a pair of brightly colored garden gloves and a wide-brimmed straw hat that fits just right may help produce a love for the garden.

Children love to climb. A short retaining wall could make a good rock wall for a child. If the wall is wide enough, it may make a nice seating area or a place to walk. An assortment of smooth rocks makes a child's rock garden and defines space.

A STURDY COVER FOR A SANDBOX (OPPOSITE) KEEPS SAND CLEAN AND DRY WHEN THE KIDS AREN'T PLAYING IN IT. THE LID CAN BE A STAGE WHEN THE SANDBOX IS CLOSED.

COMFORTABLE CURVES AND IMAGINATIVE PATTERNS IN BRIGHT COLORS MAKE THIS SWING DOUBLE THE FUN (BELOW).

Consider play area surfaces during the planning stage. Understand, too, what activities will be played on the surfaces. A soft yet sturdy green lawn makes an ideal place for games such as croquet and kickball. Sand makes a soft landing pad at the end of a slide.

Fine-ground decomposed granite, foam-rubber-like carpet, bark mulch material, manufactured turf, and interlocking rubber pieces in 2×2-foot squares are available at home improvement and garden centers and provide cushioned safety. Hard surfaces are good for tricycles, scooters, pedal cars, and games of hopscotch or foursquare.

A PERGOLA BECOMES A SWINGSET WITH THE ADDITION OF HEIGHT-ADJUSTABLE, WEATHERPROOF PLASTIC SWINGS (ABOVE).

PLAN WALKWAY SURFACES TO MEET THE SPECIAL NEEDS OF THOSE WHO WILL BE USING THEM (LEFT) FOR A USER-FRIENDLY LANDSCAPE.

Water works. Water is a big draw for children. Depending on the ages of the children, including a water feature makes for a splash of fun.

A simple sprinkler attached to a hose provides comic and hot-weather relief to youngsters and their parents who might be inspired to join in the fun. Older kids enjoy water fights with mega water blasters mounted on posts.

Show kids the practical use of water in the garden. Demonstrate proper methods, from the correct use of watering cans to the best times of day to water plants. If you have a pond, let children discover how it fits into the ecosystem. Watching a waterbug skitter across the surface, or listening to frog song, is a nature lesson.

Preformed ponds are good water features for older children. The pool can sit above ground surrounded by plants and rocks. When the kids grow tired of it, simply remove it.

The more portable the play area, the easier changing the space will be when the children outgrow it. For example, the Whimsical Garden on page 150 can be torn down in an afternoon. Plan ahead for multipurpose areas or features.

Kids' plants. Gardening with kids teaches them a skill they can use throughout their lives. Perhaps when children grow up they will have gained appreciation for recycling, fresh air, water, planting, weeding, harvesting, sunshine, rain, and seeing things grow and, yes, seeing them die. Maybe one day they'll want to provide such experiences for their own children.

Show them that garden chores can be a fun time of playing in the dirt, and point out the benefit of the tasks when plants bloom or yield fruit.

Let them help select what will be planted. Plants with bold color, such as cannas, and patterns, such as coleus or variegated foliage, elicit curiosity. Plants with familiar shapes, such as a purple ball atop a jumbo allium, attract attention. Cinnamon-scented carnations have nose-appeal. Edible flowers make gardening a treat when a salad can be topped with nasturtium petals or a candied violet can top a cupcake. Golden bamboo can be pruned and the sticks used to write in the dirt, as magic wands, and to build pretend log cabins—or whatever lies in the child's imagination.

Special places. Create a safe environment where young children feel secure. Put play areas where they are visible from the house but not from the street. If Mom or Grandpa supervises play, provide comfortable seating for her or him.

Considering the interests of the children is important. Providing children with their own outdoor space gives them a sense of responsibility. If your children love reading, provide a sitting nook in the garden ideal for curling up with a book. Let them plant an area based on a favorite story or nursery rhyme. Let a budding gardener pick the cherry tomatoes for dinner or cut flowers for a bouquet.

Game time. Teens and adults, too, should have special places in the yard to have some fun. Consider games such as badminton and croquet, which are played on lawns; volleyball, which can be played on grass or sand;

IMAGINATIVE SETTINGS: A CORRUGATED PLASTIC "SNAKE" TOPS A CURVY WALL AROUND A PLAY AREA (BELOW LEFT) AND AN OLD HAIRPIECE IS A LION'S MANE.

SUNFLOWER STOOLS (BELOW RIGHT) AND STARS PAINTED ONTO THE PATH ADD TO THE FANTASY OF PLAYING IN AN ENCHANTED GARDEN. BRIGHT PRIMARY COLORS STIMULATE THE SENSES.

TURN A SMALL PATIO INTO A CHECKERBOARD (ABOVE) WITH COLORED PAVERS. PAINT OLD TIRE RIMS TO RECYCLE THEM INTO OVERSIZE CHECKERS.

COAX CHILDREN into gardening by planting their playhouse in a garden. Tell them playing in the dirt is OK.

shuffleboard, which is played on asphalt or concrete; horseshoes, which are pitched in dirt or sand pits; and bocce ball, which is played on clay surfaces. Putting greens also are popular in some backyards.

Whatever backyard sport you want to engage in, learn how much space it needs, how much equipment will cost, and whether the project is one you can do yourself or one with which you will need help. Make it as attractive as you can. Learn about plant placement and decide whether you are willing to sacrifice some blossoms to errant balls. You may determine that the fun is well worth the price. Shrubs and flowers are replaceable.

Like families, backyards are ever-changing landscapes as they fulfill the measure of their creation. When babies are born, yards change. Teenagers emerge and there is change again. When the nest empties, the landscape takes on another look. And, just when it appears as a seasoned, mature landscape, grandchildren arrive on the scene, ready for discovery and adventure in the garden.

The circle of life in the garden continues, and holds as much promise for the next generation as it did for the former. The child in everyone deserves a place to be cultivated and nurtured, a place where imaginations and spirits soar, a place that is unhurried and where the sign still reads, "Slow down: children at play."

Check out more ideas from HGTV.com
See tips on introducing children to the garden at
■ www.hgtv.com/landscapemakeoversbook

GARDEN ART LETS CHILDREN'S IMAGINATIONS SOAR. A FANTASTIC WINGED WATERING CAN IS READY FOR TAKEOFF FROM THE POINT OF A PLAYHOUSE ROOF (TOP).

A MYSTERIOUS BOOK LETS CHILDREN PRETEND THEY HAVE ACCESS TO THE HOGWARTS SCHOOL LIBRARY (ABOVE).

CHILDREN'S GARDENS

149

a whimsical garden
give your kids this fairy-tale garden

As you know, one of the best ways to introduce children to the joys and rewards of gardening is to offer them their own patch of ground to develop as they see fit. But you can make their experience even more rewarding if you help them give the garden a personality all its own by adding fun features that make the space special. An excellent example of this concept is the project pictured here in which the grandmother, with lots of input from her granddaughter,

worked with designer Dan Berger to develop a kids-only retreat full of light-hearted elements that appeal especially to the young gardener-to-be and her friends.

The key to success is involving children at the very beginning of the project. Their input is what will make the finished product a lasting source of enjoyment. In this example, the 12-year-old and the designer put their heads together and came up with the ultimate "outdoor playroom,"

featuring a central pond, funky planter boxes, a personal storage unit, a couple of close-to-the-ground barrel chairs, and a low, wavy fence that defines the entire area. Help yourself to any or all of these ideas.

A WHIRLIGIG FLOWER, A BLUE PARROT, AND A FUN FENCE INVITE YOUNG ONES INTO A GARDEN OF THEIR OWN (BELOW) WHERE PEA GRAVEL CRUNCHES DELIGHTFULLY UNDER SMALL FEET. A WATER GARDEN AND FOUNTAIN HIGHLIGHTS THE SPACE FOR OLDER KIDS.

BARRELS OF FUN COME FROM BARREL CHAIRS, A GNOME GARDEN WITH ITS TINY GNOME HOME, AND PLANTS IN A MURAL (ABOVE).

WHERE'S THE FUN IN AN EMPTY PLOT OF GROUND? (ABOVE)

water pond

tools & materials

SPECIAL TOOLS: No special tools required

- Preformed liner
- Stones, 8 to 12-inch diameter
- Pump kit with fountain head and fittings

Playful pond This preformed pond makes an easy addition. Let the kids help.

1 | install a central pond Choose a pond shell from a variety of shapes and sizes. Place it in the center of the new garden area, level it by slipping loose dirt under it where needed, and fill it halfway with water to keep it in place.

2 | dry-stack wall Disguise the shell with a wall of dry-stacked rocks. Working with head-size rocks, lay the bottom row around the base of the shell, leaving enough space between the rocks and the base that by the time you reach the top row, the wall will touch the top edge of the shell. Shovel fill dirt behind each layer as you go.

install pump Fill the pool with water, then set the pump on a brick in the water. Plug the pump into a GFCI outlet. Adjust its flow according to manufacturer instructions.

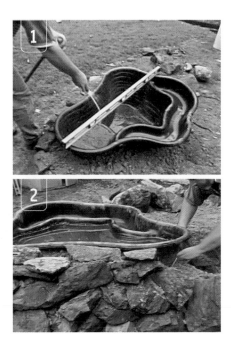

DESIGN PLANS

goals Create a magical backyard garden retreat for children; include elements that reflect the children's interests; use features that can be changed or removed as the children's interests and curiosities evolve.

cost For all elements, $450 if you do it yourself (assuming a low-cost storage unit and a stash of salvaged wood) vs. $2,000 for a pro.

time 3 weekends.

difficulty scale Hauling the rocks and moving the storage unit are the two most physically demanding tasks.
●●●○○

skill scale You can involve your children in many steps.
●●○○○

BUILDING

hypertufa planter

tools & materials

SPECIAL TOOLS: Steel finishing trowel, power drill with masonry bit

- 2 corrugated cardboard boxes
- Galvanized metal mesh
- Peat moss
- Perlite
- Portland cement
- Scrap wood for stakes

Box it up Select an outer box that's the same size as the planter to be or make your own box by cutting scrap cardboard to size and taping it together. The second box should be 2 inches shallower than the first and leave a 4-inch gap on all sides when set inside the outer box. Cut a strip of metal mesh to fit around the small box. Crease the mesh to follow the outside contour of the inner box. You'll use this piece in Step 3.

1 | form planter base Remove the inner box. Place the outer box where you want the planter. Check for level. Mix 3 parts peat moss, 3 parts perlite, and 2 parts Portland cement. Add water and mix to the consistency of cottage cheese. Add a 1-inch layer of this hypertufa mix to the bottom of the larger box and tamp it down with a trowel.

2 | form mesh base Cut a second piece of mesh to the size of the bottom of the large box. Lay the mesh on top of the hypertufa mix, then spread a 1-inch layer of the mix on top and tamp it.

3 | form sides Center the small box inside the large box. Insert the creased mesh between the boxes. The outer box may bow out from the pressure of the hypertufa. Hold its sides in place by pounding stakes into the ground at the center of each side, flush with the box.

4 | form planter walls Fill the gap between the boxes with the hypertufa. Smooth the top with a trowel.

5 | cure planter Cover the planter with a tarp for three days, allowing mix to cure. Then remove stakes and peel off cardboard forms.

6 | drill holes Drill five or six holes in the bottom of the planter for drainage.

potting bench and fence

tools & materials

SPECIAL TOOLS: Sledgehammer, jigsaw, belt sander

- 2 – 2×6s, 8 feet long
- 1 – 2×2, 8 feet long
- Wood screws
- Cedar log
- Salvaged wood for fence, or cedar boards
- Storage unit, such as an old set of lockers
- Paint

Build a potting bench. One end of the potting bench is attached to a cedar log leg, the other to the storage unit. If your whimsical garden will not include a storage unit, use a second leg and attach the bench to the fence. Salvaged 2×6s from another project will work fine for a shelf. Cut 2×6s to the length that fits your setting. The shelf in this example is 6 feet long.

Place 2×6s flat on the ground, side by side, to create an 11-inch-wide surface. Screw four 2×2 crosspieces to both 2×6s, one 6 inches in from each end and the other two equally spaced between them. Use four deck screws for each crosspiece, two per 2×6. When the shelf is finished, the crosspieces will be on the bottom. Have your young gardeners show you how high the shelf should go, and mark the side of the storage unit. Attach a 2×2, 11 inches long, as a support piece (sometimes called a cleat or ledger) horizontally to the side of the storage unit at the mark. This supports one end of the shelf. To support the other end, cut the log to fit between the ground and the crosspiece nearest that end.

1 | place shelf Lift the shelf into place and rest one end on top of the ledger attached to the storage unit.

2 | attach shelf Drive four screws down at an angle through the top of the shelf into the ledger. At the

opposite end, slip the log under the crosspiece and drive several screws up at an angle through the log into the crosspiece.

3 | make waves Salvaged cedar boards were used for this fence. Cedar boards weather beautifully and resist rot.

Mark a curvy path along the ground for the fence. Drive the boards, one by one, into the ground with a sledgehammer. It helps if someone steadies the boards while you swing the sledge. Don't worry if the boards don't line up precisely; that's part of the charm. Once all of the boards are in place, ask your children to draw the wavy cut line on them for you. Using a jigsaw, cut along the pattern. Smooth the cut edges with a belt sander.

4 | paint and decorate Turn your children loose with several colors of paint and a sponge. Let the decorating begin.

Low-maintenance shrubs planted in open areas give the play area a sense of privacy, while plants with bold, colorful leaves, such as striped 'Tropicana' cannas, provide a magical feel. Other ideas for children's gardens include these:

Container gardens. Fill hypertufa planters with potting soil. Plant favorite vegetables, herbs, and fruits, along with bright-colored annuals. Be sure to select compact varieties. Include foods for snacking, such as cherry tomatoes, everbearing strawberries, and sugar snap peas.

For success growing in troughs or containers, use rich soil. Best bet: Mix two-thirds potting soil with one-third compost. Fertilize vegetables every two weeks with an organic liquid fertilizer, such as fish emulsion, mixed according to package instructions. Mulch to conserve soil moisture.

When growing root crops such as carrots, expect better results than when they are planted directly in the ground. Root crops often grow bigger and straighter in containers because the soil is not compacted.

Plan to harvest several crops from each container during the growing season. For example, in early summer replace cool-season favorites such as lettuce and sugar snap peas with warm-season crops such as peppers.

Water plants for kids. A simple water garden makes a great place to grow kid-pleasing plants. Fill small plastic crates lined with a porous material such as burlap with ordinary garden soil. Then add plants. Sink the crates so water covers the top of the pots by an inch or two.

Here are a few easy-to-grow water plants with unusual shapes and textures. Even the names are fun.

- **Dwarf horsetail** (*Equisetum scirpoides*)
- **Dwarf papyrus** (*Cyperus profiler*)
- **Parrot's-feather** (*Myriophyllum aquaticum*)
- **Water snowflake** (*Nymphoides* spp.)
- **Water sensitivity plant** (*Neptunia oleracea*)

EXPLORATION AND DISCOVERY ARE TWO IMPORTANT ELEMENTS OF A CHILDREN'S GARDEN. A COMICAL TOY BUG (RIGHT), EXCITES CURIOSITY AND MIGHT EASE FEARS ABOUT THE REAL THING.

TEXTURE, SCENT, AND COLOR TEASE THE SENSES. WALL PAINTINGS (BELOW) DEVELOP ARTISTIC ABILITY AND CREATE LASTING MEMORIES

CREATING A GNOME GARDEN

Spark imagination by setting a scene. Fill a half whiskey barrel with potting soil. Add creeping plants such as alyssum, thyme, rock cress, and heron's-bill. Trim rosemary into a miniature evergreen forest. Tuck in a thimble planter, doll-size tools, and a few gnomes to "live" in a minuscule cottage garden. In this garden are brown-and-green coleus, sedge, and ferns.

MAKING THE MURAL

With buckets of latex paint in several colors, small rollers or brushes, and a few sponges, older children can easily personalize their special space. Here, a masonry wall that adjoins a garden is being painted. After the paint dried, the kids dipped leaf-shape sponges in latex paint and dabbed randomly to create a pattern of falling leaves.

A CHILDREN'S GARDEN

Creating a special place for children means including them in all phases of the project so they develop a sense of ownership. Most of all, a child's garden should be enjoyable with a special magic all its own. A few tips for success include:

■ **Size.** Take a furnishing lesson from Goldilocks and the bears' chairs. Acquire kid-size garden tools so children can use them comfortably. Build a playhouse that's small enough for a child but tall enough that an adult can comfortably take tea.

■ **Interests.** Today it might be mud pies and insects. Next year, who knows? Be flexible, remembering that interests often change.

■ **Color.** Create a happy mood with bright colors. Select plants in shades that attract butterflies and hummingbirds.

■ **Safety.** Round edges and soft ground covers protect from "ouchies." Low fences allow adults to monitor without intruding.

■ **Fun.** Keep it simple. A tire swing hanging from a tree on pivot hardware is fun. A toad house fosters ecological inquiry.

child-friendly plants
grow "eggs" among the veggies and dinosaur food among the foliage just for fun

Landscape designers David and Isis Schwartz know the importance of giving children their own little piece of the world. They also know that kids love cozy spots. When they decided to build a play area for their son, they chose a secluded corner. This playhouse, built with a 5-foot door and an 8-foot peak in the ceiling, is small enough that adults have to duck to come in when invited, but large enough to allow an adult to fit comfortably once inside. A concrete patio provides a play place outdoors, surrounded by a magical garden.

Choosing child-friendly plants. Create a child-pleasing feeling of enclosure by surrounding a play area with large shrubs such as lilacs. Or to grow hedge tall quick-growing annuals such as sunflowers or Mexican sunflower (*Tithonia rotundifolia*). Include some blueberries, strawberries, or other plants with edible berries in

their "jaws" when pinched, and pansy faces. Plants that remind kids of animals, such as turtlehead (*Chelone* spp.) and zebra grass (*Miscanthus sinensis* 'Zebrinus'), are always a hit. Other fun choices include balloon flower (*Platycodon grandiflorus*), a dependable perennial with starlike blossoms and buds that mimic balloons, and wishbone flower (*Torenia fournieri*), with stamens that form a wishbone shape.

Many vegetables make fun crops for kids. What kid wouldn't be fascinated by all the little white "eggs" hanging from 'Cloud Nine' eggplant, or the multicolored harvest of 'Easter Egg' radishes? Cotton, another great crop for kids, grows on large handsome plants closely related to hibiscus. It can be grown as an annual by planting seeds early indoors.

Older children find fascination in plants like four-o'clock (*Mirabilis jalapa*), with blossoms that open every afternoon, and moonflower (*Ipomoea alba*), with huge fragrant blossoms that open at nightfall. The seeds of both of these plants are poisonous, so leave them out of your landscape if you have young children.

IF YOU BUILD A PLAY AREA in the center of the yard, the magic is gone, say designers David and Isis Schwartz. Corners are cozier.

stevia

your landscape, so kids can forage for food.

Arouse children's interest with plants that have odd foliage. Kids love the dramatic leaves of elephant's ear (*Colocasia esculenta*) and "dinosaur-food" rhubarb (*Gunnera manicata*). Unusual-looking grasslike plants such as corkscrew rush (*Juncus effusus* 'Spiralis'), fiber-optic grass (*Scirpus cernuus*, also called *Isolepsis cernua*), and New Zealand hair sedge (*Carex comans* 'Frosted Curls') grab the kids' attention.

Even very young children are intrigued by snapdragons, which open

ELEPHANT'S EAR (BELOW) RESEMBLE THE EARS OF THEIR NAMESAKES, LETTING CHILDREN IMAGINE JUNGLE SCENES OR A TRIP TO THE CIRCUS.

AN HERB THAT'S SWEETER THAN SUGAR, STEVIA (ABOVE) IS A PLANT WITH LEAVES THAT CHILDREN CAN SAFELY CHEW.

SUNFLOWERS (RIGHT) GROW QUICKLY AND DELIGHT KIDS WITH THEIR HUGE BLOOMS AND EDIBLE SEEDS.

sunflowers

elephant's ears

Appeal to kids' senses. All plants appeal to the sense of sight, but what about the other senses? Children love plants that are fun to taste, touch, smell, and hear.

Tasty plants include chocolate mint and stevia, an herb that's used as a sugar substitute.

What kid can resist petting the soft, furry leaves of lamb's-ears or the spring catkins of pussy willow? Sensitive plant *(Mimosa pudica)*, with leaves that roll up when touched, also will please the children.

Along with fragrant flower favorites such as sweet William and garden phlox, be sure to include some plants with fragrant leaves, such as lemon verbena and pineapple sage. Another fun choice: A small collection of scented geraniums, which come in your choice of 200 different scents from citrus to spice to coconut.

The leaves of tall ornamental grasses, such as feather reed grass or switchgrass, rustle in the wind, delighting children with the sound. Consider adding wind chimes or a small fountain for more of nature's music.

CHILD-SIZE TOOLS MAKE DIGGING IN THE GARDEN FUN (RIGHT), AND MAY HELP CHILDREN DEVELOP AN APPRECIATION FOR GARDENING

MORE FUN FOR THE KIDS

■ **Hang a large blackboard** inside the kids' hideaway. Or use a piece of slate to provide a natural chalkboard for the kids to draw on. You could also embed some slate in the ground for drawing a hopscotch grid.

■ **Create a fun** and unique setting by adding objects such as barrel chairs, a decorative windmill, small water sculpture, ceramic animals, or brightly colored pails filled with flowers.

PLANTS THAT ENGAGE THE SENSES INCLUDE SCENTED GERANIUM (RIGHT). ITS SCENTS INCLUDE APPLE, MINT, AND CHOCOLATE.

SOFT LAMB'S-EARS (CENTER RIGHT) IS FUN TO FEEL; IT'S ALMOST HUGGABLE.

scented geranium

POISONOUS PLANTS

Teach children to eat only those plants they know are safe. If any part of a plant is poisonous, don't include it in a garden for young children. Little kids love to gather tiny "treasures" such as yew berries and castor beans, and might be tempted to taste. Here are some common poisonous plants you'll want to avoid:

- Angel's trumpet (*Brugmansia*)
- Caladium
- Cardinal flower (*Lobelia cardinalis*)
- Castor bean (*Ricinus communis*)
- Daffodil (*Narcissus*)
- Delphinium
- English ivy (*Hedera helix*)
- False indigo (*Baptisia*)
- Flowering tobacco (*Nicotiana*)
- Foxglove (*Digitalis*)
- Holly (*Ilex*)
- Hydrangea
- Jack-in-the-pulpit (*Arisaema triphyllum*)
- Lantana
- Lily-of-the-valley (*Convallaria majalis*)
- Monkshood (*Aconitum*)
- Persian buttercup (*Ranunculus*)
- Poppy (*Papaver*)
- Privet (*Ligustrum*)
- Spurge (*Euphorbia*)
- Squill (*Scilla*)
- Windflower (*Anemone blanda*)
- Yew (*Taxus*)

lily-of-the-valley

lamb's-ears

sensitive plant

SENSITIVE PLANT (LEFT) FOLDS UP AT THE SLIGHTEST TOUCH OF A FINGER.

a backyard putting green
teach your children the sport, and practice your own game at home

Whether or not you're a whiz with a putter, it's nice to stay in the swing of things with your own practice green just steps from the back door. And it's a great training spot for your children too. The good news is that you don't have to have an unlimited bankroll to create this little bit of paradise. The biggest requirement is space—especially if you want to practice those long putts that try your nerves at the golf course. The synthetic turf used in this project from designer Jeff

Castro comes only in 12-foot-wide rolls, which limits the width of your green to about 11 feet, allowing for the rock edging. So if you want to practice 20-foot putts, you'll need to lay out a space about 25 feet long. (The green pictured is about 30 feet long.) Once you've set aside a nice flat area about that size (or smaller if your needs are simpler), it's just a matter of designing an asymmetrical shape and surrounding it with randomly placed plantings to mimic the wonderful irregularity of nature.

If the best site for your putting green is not flat, you may have to level out an area and put in a retaining wall between the higher elevation and the site to keep dirt and other debris from washing onto the green. And you'll want to sink a perforated drain line alongside the wall to help the higher land drain quickly and keep standing water off the green. Once your site is flat and protected, you're ready to become your own course designer.

A SOFT 'ROUGH' (ABOVE) OF SILVERY BLUE FESCUE TUFTS MIMICS THE SHAPE OF THE ROCK EDGING.

SUN-YELLOW VARIEGATED FOLIAGE LIGHTS THE WAY TO THE CUP AS A ROCKY RETAINING WALL HOLDS BACK THE SLOPE (OPPOSITE).

USE YOUR PRIVATE PUTTING GREEN FOR TEACHING YOUR KIDS THE FUNDAMENTALS AND ETIQUETTE OF GOLF (ABOVE).

A RIVULET OF GREEN APPEARS TO RUN FROM UNDER A BRIDGE (RIGHT), CREATING A PLEASANT PLACE TO PRACTICE.

A BARREN SLOPE IN DEEP SHADE (ABOVE) ONCE HELD LITTLE PROSPECT FOR FUN AND GAMES

a backyard putting green

putting green

tools & materials

SPECIAL TOOLS: Sod cutter, plate compactor

- Landscaper's paint
- 12×30 feet synthetic turf
- Golf cups (one for each hole)
- Finely crushed gravel, 90 cubic feet
- Fine sand, 1,200 pounds
- Cement
- Decorative rocks

Hole in one. Have family fun on your own backyard practice green.

1 | outline shape Remove grass from the area. Smooth the soil and outline the perimeter of the green with landscaper's paint. Spread crushed gravel (called quarter-bide dust in some regions), 2 inches deep.

2 | screed surface Drag a long board across the entire site, leveling the fine gravel for an even surface.

3 | wet gravel Hose down the gravel to help settle it.

4 | compact base Run a plate compactor over the gravel until it's very firm.

5 | put down second layer Add a 1-inch layer of fine gravel, screed it, wet it, and compact it. Fill indentations.

6 | roll out turf Cut turf edges with a utility knife, matching the irregular shape as outlined.

7 | dig holes Decide where to locate holes. Mark the spots. Roll back the synthetic turf at each location and dig out enough soil to accommodate the cup.

8 | install cups You can buy authentic 4¼-inch inside-diameter cups, or make your own by cutting a 6-inch section of 4-inch PVC pipe and tamping it into place. Plumb each cup in its hole. Pour a dry mixture of two parts fine gravel and one part cement around each, taking care that the top of the cup is flush with the mix surrounding it.

9 | moisten concrete mixture Set mixture by slowly adding water with a slow dribble from a hose until the concrete absorbs the fluid and becomes completely wet.

DESIGN PLANS

goals Design and create a backyard putting green for the entire family; landscape it tastefully.

cost $2,000 if you do it yourself vs. $7,000 for a pro. Plate compactor rents for about $60 a day.

time 4 weekends.

difficulty scale Both the plate compactor and turf are heavy; you'll also be moving lots of sand and crushed gravel.

● ● ● ● ○

skill scale It's a matter of time and patience.

● ● ○ ○ ○

BUILDING

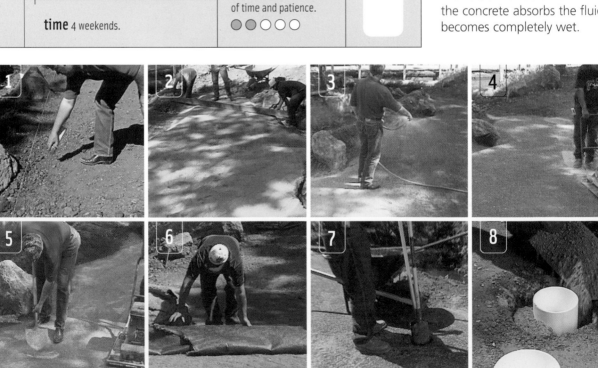

AFTER

10 | **replace turf** As you roll the turf back into position, mark it to indicate the center of each hole. After the turf is rolled out, cut an "X" in the center of each mark and extend the legs of the "X" to the inside edge of the cup. Cut out the circle so that the turf overlaps the top edge of the cup.

11 | **form putting surface** Pour fine sand on top of the turf and sweep it into the grass with a stiff push broom. The sand provides the firm surface that keeps your putts rolling along. The turf fibers hold the sand in place

Continue adding sand and sweeping it in until only about a ⅛-inch nap is left above the surface of the green. This project requires brushing in about 1,200 pounds of sand.

12 | **decorate edges** Cover the exposed edges of the synthetic turf with decorative rocks or pebbles. Blend the green into the landscape by planting a bed of hardy shrubs and perennials around the green. This homeowner used heavenly bamboo (*Nandina domestica*), Zones 6–9; blue fescue (*Festuca glauca*), Zones 4–8; and sun azalea (*Rhododendron indicum* 'Pink Lace'), Zones 5–9.

a groovy swing

get back in the swing and have fun with the kids on this curvy seat suspended from a tree branch

Remember third grade.

It's recess time. First stop, the swings!

OK, so you're not in third grade anymore, and you're not real big on squeezing between rusty chains. That shouldn't keep you from doing the swing thing. Be the grooviest grownup in the neighborhood by adding this funky two-person tree swing to your backyard.

This project is loads of fun and easy to make. You won't break your back—or the bank. This wavy swing transforms almost any sturdy tree branch into a favorite place to play for the kids—and for you too! The nylon rope and lag screws allow you to adjust the height of the swing as the children grow taller.

Before you get to sawing and drilling, make sure you have a place to hang your swing. Pick a sturdy branch on a hardwood tree. Be sure to pick a healthy limb that's at least 8 inches in diameter at the point the swing will be attached. Pick a tree with a branch that hangs over a soft landing area, or put down soft mulching material just in case of falls or leaping dismounts.

What if there are no sturdy tree branches for hanging the swing, or you'd rather not drill holes in a limb? That's easy! This swing can be installed from the rafters of an enclosed porch, a sturdy pergola, or a car port (just be sure to create a soft landing area if there's a concrete floor).

If installed indoors, allow enough room for swinging so feet don't kick the walls. Soft carpeting or rubber mats on the floor make soft landings.

HANGING AROUND

An old-fashioned tire swing gets a modern update by using an accordion shock boot with a pivot joint (available at tire dealers and automotive supply centers) that safely allows full 360° motion. It, too, can hang from a tree, or build a simple sturdy frame. Center the accordion boot on the limb or crosspiece and secure it with heavy lag bolts. Attach a strong carabineer clip to each bolt. Drill three equidistant holes in the tire. Secure a heavy lag bolt in each hole. Using three lengths of 5/16-inch galvanized chain, attach each chain to the carabineer above. You're ready to take a spin!

DAD AND DAUGHTER HAVE TIME FOR FUN ON A SIMPLE-TO-MAKE SWING DESIGNED FOR TWO (OPPOSITE).

LET THE CHILDREN PICK THE COLORS (RIGHT) AND IT BECOMES A TRUE FAMILY PROJECT.

HANG TIME

Prepare to install the swing.
Select a hardwood tree limb that's a minimum of 8 inches in diameter. Drill three ³/₁₆-inch holes distanced to match the pairs of holes in the seat. Install and secure the lag thread screw eyes in each hole, eye side down.

With a flat-sided ball on top of the seat, lace one end of the nylon rope through the ball into one end hole, up through the adjacent hole and through another flat-sided ball. Pull the rope taut under the seat and even up the ends above the seat. Thread a rounded ball over both ends of the rope. Repeat for the holes in the middle and on the opposite end of the seat.

Position swing seat beneath the limb and thread each of the three doubled pieces of rope through the lag screw above it. Adjust the ropes to level the swing seat. Tie secure knots at the lag screws.

THERE'S PLENTY OF ROOM FOR A FRIEND, BUT THE CENTER SUPPORT ROPE (RIGHT) KEEPS THE SWING BALANCED EVEN FOR A SOLO FLIGHT

IT DON'T MEAN A THING if it ain't got that swing, as the Duke Ellington classic says. An old-fashioned homemade tree swing with a jazzy new look continues to be fun for children and grownups.

make the swing

tools & materials

SPECIAL TOOLS: Jigsaw, wood burner, drill with $^3/_{16}$-, $^1/_2$-, $^5/_8$-, and 1-inch bits, math compass

- 2×12 fir plank, 8-feet long
- $^1/_2$ inch rot-resistant nylon rope
- 6 wooden balls, $1^1/_2$-inch diameter or larger with flat side
- 3 wooden balls, $1^1/_2$-inch diameter or larger
- 3 lag thread screw eyes, $^3/_8 × 4^1/_2$ inches
- Sanding block and sandpaper
- Wood stain, oil-based, in four colors
- Clear polyurethane exterior wood sealer

Swingin' colors. This example uses violet, gold, blue, and green stains, but choose colors you like and that won't fade in the sun. Ask your sales associate for help in selecting color pigments that will hold up.

1 | gather materials The wooden balls can be found at crafts shops. The flat-sided ones are used to make doll's heads. You'll need enough nylon rope to suspend the seat 18 inches above the ground with doubled-over lengths at the three points where it hangs from the tree branch.

2 | create curve Cut the plank to length (the one in this example is 4 feet). Draw an even pattern for a gentle curve on the wood. Using the jigsaw, cut the curves. Sand edges.

3 | drill holes Using the $^5/_8$-inch bit, drill two holes on each end of the swing seat plus two in the center for the rope, at least 1 inch from the edges. Drill 1-inch holes through the rounded balls, and $^1/_2$-inch holes through the flat-sided wooden balls.

4 | draw design Using the math compass, draw five large circles on the seat. Draw a line down the center of each circle. Using the wood burner, outline the circles and the center lines. This defines the color sections and stops stains from bleeding into each other.

5 | apply stain The stain is applied to the wooden balls and to the swing seat. In this example, the balls are all the same color, but you can mix them up. Stain each section of the swing seat a different color. Let the stain dry. Apply several coats of polyurethane sealer. See "Hang Time," opposite, for instructions on hanging the swing with lag thread screws and nylon rope.

DESIGN PLANS

goals Make a tree swing with a seat for two-persons and decorate it with unique patterns and colors.

cost About $40.

time 1 weekend.

difficulty scale Requires cutting simple curves, which might take practice.
●●●○○

skill scale Basic carpentry and painting.
●●○○○

BUILDING

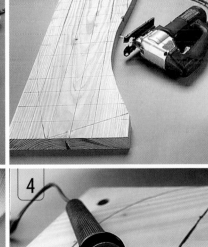

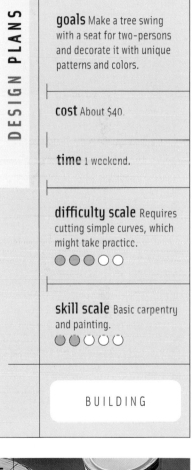

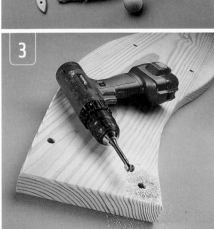

7 COMFORT & CONVENIENCE

Creature comforts. Outdoor living spaces can be designed to make you feel right at home.

PROJECTS

comfort &
CONVENIENCE

When it comes to your personal outdoor space,

creature comfort means more than a patio pillow for your dog. Outdoor

rooms need to be comfortable, cozy, and convenient to cater to your own creature comforts. If they are less than intimate and personal, it matters little how well-maintained, how well-designed, or how well-appointed they are. Each time you step outside, the space should make you feel totally at home, totally at ease, and totally pampered.

Think about how you'd like to use the yard. If you often work at home, an outdoor office is a practical and enjoyable addition. A special dining area makes alfresco entertaining easy and elegant. Everyday needs for daytime shade, nighttime lighting, or warmth on cool evenings all have creative solutions.

This may seem like a tall order for soil, water, plants, and paving. Indeed, it may seem like a tall order for those short on cash, time, space, experience, or all of the above. Some do-it-yourselfers tackle their yard projects all at one time. Still others work on their goals one flowerpot, one meandering path, one shade tree, one canvas canopy, one fire pit, one flagstone patio, and one planting bed at a time.

This is where picking the brains of HGTV designers and those who have lots of experience comes in handy. Good ideas should be shared. The voices of experience and the calloused hands of people who enjoy getting dirty and learn from mistakes are invaluable. Creating your own comfortable, convenient, cozy environment may take time as you work out details and tackle them as time and budget allow.

LOUNGING ON THE PATIO, MERE STEPS FROM THE BACK DOOR, CAN FEEL LIKE BEING AT A POSH RESORT, WITH THE ACCESSORIES YOU SELECT FOR YOUR LANDSCAPE.

COMFORT & CONVENIENCE

needs and wants
your preferences, whether for parties or privacy, should set the tone of your outdoor rooms

Rethinking spaces may be in order if all you have is a small back porch or small slab of concrete. You probably need to think bigger, as in expansion. Most designers agree that a patio that adjoins the house should be about the same size of the room that has visual and physical access to it. Otherwise, the outdoor room overwhelms the inner space.

If you enlarge your porch or an inadequate size patio slab, designers say that using material similar to the original hard surface blends in the addition without making it look newly added. Wood, brick, concrete, and

A PAINTED FLOWERPOT BECOMES A PERSONALIZED END TABLE WITH THE ADDITION OF A GLASS TOP (ABOVE). STORE MAGAZINES, TEA TOWELS, OR OTHER SMALL ITEMS INSIDE.

stone can be used in various combinations. There are so many choices in design and color of masonry and concrete pavers that deciding which to choose could be the most difficult part of the project. A medium-color paving material will reduce glare and radiant heat.

Knowing your patio's purpose or function will help you decide its size. Do you want it to be a private space that accommodates an outdoor office or intimate dinner party, or a space that's open to views and spacious enough for large gatherings? With this information, you can decide on either a low-growing shrub border or planting beds on berms that enclose the space.

A typical 10×20-foot patio will comfortably accommodate a table and four chairs, a barbecue unit, and maybe a lounge chair. Ignore the temptation to add more furniture. Consider how guests will be able to navigate the maze, a matter of safety and aesthetics. If you need more seating, consider an alternate area in the garden, farther from the back door. An intimate space under a canopy of tree branches, canvas, or light-filtering fabric provides just the right getaway. Attach lights for a go-to ambience.

Consider a sunken dining table in a corner of the yard. If colorful and comfortable, it will be a destination whether you are eating alone or with family and friends. If you are one who likes to hold gatherings of 15 and more people, you may need adequate lawn space for extra tables and chairs. If your lawn area is large and it feels as if people are lost in space, you can cozy it up by defining the space using pots

of shrubbery and maybe some portable screens and plants.

For safety's sake, keep the additions to the deck or patio on the same level. If they must be different levels, make sure the transition or landing from one level to another is wide and at a comfortable height. Install a handrail if necessary.

If patio furniture is going to be placed on the hard surface, leave sufficient room for people to get in and out of the dining chairs without tipping them over.

Designers recommend allowing a 3×3-foot space for each chair. Table sizes vary widely, but most patio tabletops are 3 feet in diameter, 4 feet square, or 5-foot rectangles. Some come with extensions. The more guests you can fit at the table, the merrier the dinner party.

A POTTING BENCH AND STORAGE UNIT OUTFITTED TO CONVENIENTLY HOLD TOOLS AND SUPPLIES MAKE PLANTING CHORES EASIER (BELOW LEFT). AN ATTRACTIVE HOSE HANGER HELPS ORGANIZE THE EFFICIENT AND PLEASANT SPACE.

RELAX IN LUXURY IN AN OUTDOOR BEDROOM UNDER THE TREES (BELOW CENTER).

A FAMILY MARSHMALLOW ROAST IS FESTIVE AROUND AN IN-DECK FIRE PIT (ABOVE).

LET THE KIDS RINSE OFF CHLORINE FROM THE POOL OR DIRT AND GRIME AT AN OUTDOOR SHOWER (LEFT).

climate control

Sunshine and breezes.

What's overhead may determine how much time you spend in your outdoor room. However, you can make the decisions on where the sun shines, where breezes blow, and where shade and shadows fall.

Think scale. The absence of a roof makes a space feel bigger. A patio may only need partial shade. An arbor with a retractable canopy gives you control over the amount of shade and light, and the sense of spaciousness. A simple wood or iron frame could support a colorful canopy of canvas, acrylic sun-resistant fabric, or

something more romantic, such as silky or gauzy material that lets the stars and moon shine on you.

Or it could be you want canopies of leafy trees. If you rely on trees to provide shade, locate them so they cast their shadows on your favorite areas when the sun is directly overhead. Deciduous trees give you shade in summer and sun in winter, when they are leafless. Selecting the right kind of tree, one that is not too messy and offers dappled shade, is the ticket. If you want to sit in the shade of a tree, select an open, spreading, or vase shape. Mature trees should enhance

your landscape without overpowering the house. They should be selected with the scale of the house in mind.

If winds frequently break up your outdoor parties, consider planting windbreaks in the form of trees and tall shrubbery. The most effective windbreaks filter the wind, slowing it down. When it's hot, you want air to circulate. A dense windbreak slows wind speed the most but over a shorter distance than a looser windbreak, which slows it less but for a longer distance. If using shrubbery, plant the material in a bed that is at least half as wide as it is tall. Staggering rows offers

A PAIR OF TRELLISES FRAME A SWING AND CANOPY (ABOVE) TO CREATE A COZY SPOT AND PROTECT YOU FROM THE SUN.

A WINGED CANOPY (RIGHT) OFFERS PROTECTION FROM SUN OR FALLING LEAVES. GAUZE SLIPCOVERS GIVE ORDINARY GARDEN CHAIRS AN ETHEREAL PRESENCE, WHILE A BRIGHT TABLECLOTH BRINGS A SPLASH OF COLOR TO AN INTIMATE DINING AREA.

more visual interest and at the same time deflects wind more effectively than a flat-topped dense hedge. To avoid a closed-in feeling, you may want to consider looser rather than denser plantings.

Built windbreaks are solid structures such as fences or baffles and they can be as colorful or subtle as you like. If you want a screen that's unique for your neighborhood, think about a pair of old French doors set in a frame. The see-through doors allow, or even enhance, views by framing them. Knowing the patterns of sun, shade, and wind in your yard helps you decide on effective placement.

Bugs on the run. Flying insects are the annoying uninvited guests at outdoor gatherings. Yet there are simple decorative ways to help keep these pests reasonably under control.

First, eliminate stagnant water and increase the air circulation in your yard. Keep water flowing in water features with submersible pumps, and treat ponds with Mosquito Dunks. Install ceiling fans on the underside of your patio cover or in the arbor, or place pedestal fans in appropriate spots around the yard. If you live in an area with lots of biting insects, screen the deck or patio.

Other suggestions include buying commercial bug zappers, lighting citronella candles and torches, and using blue light bulbs in the garden away from people areas. Flying insects are attracted to blue lights and may leave your guests alone.

EXTENDING THE ROOF ON A CARPORT CREATES SHADE FOR A DINING SPOT (BELOW).

MICROCLIMATES, protected pockets that differ in temperature from the rest of the yard, are good sites for trying plants that aren't usually hardy in your area. Check near windbreaks, south slopes, wall niches, or even boulders, for spots for new plantings.

SUSPENDING A CEILING FAN OVER A PATIO SEATING AREA (FAR LEFT) ENHANCES AIRFLOW AND CHARM.

SALVAGED WINDOWS SPIFFED UP WITH PAINT BECOME A CLEVER WINDBREAK FOR A PORCH (LEFT). A VALANCE HELPS CONTROL SUNLIGHT.

light up the night

Light a fire. With the sun, the wind, and the flying insects tamed, what more do you need to get the most out of your yard? Have you ever thought about building a fire in your own backyard?

Outdoor fireplaces, those built on the exterior walls of houses, and those freestanding portable units that you buy at home improvement centers

and online, are finding their way into outdoor rooms. Just as they do for the inside, the dancing flames spell coziness and comfort. They take the chill off spring and fall evenings and, in some climates, provide outdoor drama on winter nights.

A chiminea is an example of a portable fireplace. Usually made of kiln-dried ceramic with a tapered chimney, it resembles a potbelly stove and is for decorative warmth only. Check local regulations; their use is not permitted in some cities.

Freestanding fire pits that are fueled by gas and wood add ambience and can be used for cooking. Invite the neighbors over for s'mores and roasted marshmallows.

Building fire pits in the yard is a fairly simple do-it-yourself project. Whether made of brick or stone, a fire pit should be built in a safe place with adequate space between the fire and anything flammable. Build it where people have enough room to sit a safe distance from the pit.

Fire pits are usually lined with firebrick surrounded by a wide fire-resistant coping such as stone or brick. Check local regulations; there may be an ordinance that requires using spark arrestors; or there may be a burning ban because of pollution.

If you can't go the campfire route, votive candles floated in water, luminaries, lanterns, torches, or outdoor candelabras mimic the ambience of fire. Common sense candle precautions include placing candelabra on stable surfaces, or hanging dripless candles to avoid accidents with hot wax.

Illuminate your life. Garden lighting stretches the hours of outdoor living and makes you feel comfortable, cozy, and safe. Thoughtful lighting adds a sense of artistry to your landscape. Backlighting plants and structures creates dramatic effects. Uplights give a glow to leaves. Low-voltage lighting mimics the moon, giving a shadow effect that's pleasant whether you're outside in the garden or inside looking out. Seeing the garden at night from the inside eliminates the black-window effect and allows your yard to shine all year-round.

LIGHTING THE WAY UP THE STAIRS WITH LANTERNS IN A STYLE THAT COMPLEMENTS THE DECK RAILINGS PROVIDES STYLISH SAFETY (ABOVE).

A FIRE PIT IN A PATIO KEEPS THE FIRE A SAFE DISTANCE FROM FLAMMABLE OBJECTS (TOP LEFT).

A STURDY COVER (LEFT) THAT IS LEVEL WITH THE PATIO'S SURFACE FREES THE SPACE FOR OTHER USES ONCE THE FIRE IS OUT.

If you have an umbrella or canopy outside, dress it with tiny lights. Wind lights around trunks of trees and among the vines trailing along a stair rail. Add punch to a garden party by weaving Japanese paper lanterns with strings of lights. Floating candles in birdbaths or tea lights in glass holders hanging on shepherds' hooks are fun. Lights in trees should be hung 10 feet high, above guests' heads yet allowing access when bulbs need to be changed.

Fixtures among plants should be hidden; only the light should be seen. Path lights should project downward on the path for safety. Use low-voltage lights rather than brighter lights, which can create a blinding glare.

Now that you have light effects, it is time for action. Accept the invitation for a well-deserved night out in your own backyard. It has all the warmth and comfort of home.

VOTIVE CANDLES AND HURRICANE LAMPS CLUSTERED ON A DINING TABLE (ABOVE) CREATE A ROMANTIC SCENE. LOW-VOLTAGE LIGHTS AMONG THE PLANTS PROVIDE A SOFT GLOW.

DIFFUSE LIGHTING FROM DISCREETLY HIDDEN LANDSCAPE FIXTURES AND PILLAR CANDLES IN HURRICANE SHADES ON A SIDE TABLE (LEFT) SET A CASUAL MOOD.

SIMPLE CHIMNEY CAPS (BELOW LEFT), PAINTED AND DECORATED, ARE A TERRIFIC WAY TO SHIELD CANDLES FROM GUSTS OF WIND.

convenience

The work in progress that is your home is always improving. Tweaking things here and there, changing plants as you become aware of new ones, updating lighting, painting patio furniture a fresh color, installing a water feature, creating more shade, or drawing up a design for a low-maintenance yard means that your comfort zone is evolving.

There will always be new surfacing material, new plant hybrids, new barbecue units, new outdoor fabrics, and new ways of doing things that you introduce to your outdoor spaces to see if they work. And, as you add new gadgets, new toys, and new dimension to your spaces, it may mean that you will garden and entertain differently.

Consider the possibilities. Until a few years ago, most people thought outdoor kitchens were only for the rich. Now there are ready-made outdoor kitchen units, complete with tiled eating bars, at home improvement stores. They can be delivered and installed in half a day.

What's more, people are building their own backyard cooking stations. A barbecue grill that held enough hamburger patties to feed a family of five used to be considered adequate. Today, patios boast gas units with multiple grills, burners, spits, and smokers where multicourse meals can be prepared for multiple guests.

If you have looked at outdoor furniture recently, you know that besides garden chairs, there are recliner-rocking chairs, cushiony settees, and patio swings along with traditional chaises to make your outdoor rooms comfortable.

AN OUTDOOR KITCHEN

Placement is key, says landscape designer Dan Berger.

■ **Avoid overhanging tree** branches or nearby plants that could pose a fire hazard.

■ **Choose a clear,** level site for your cooking units.

■ **Check local fire codes** to learn the clearance requirements of an open flame from combustible surfaces and structures.

LOW-HANGING BASKETS (ABOVE) EASE GARDENING FOR THE ELDERLY, DISABLED, OR ANYONE WHO DISLIKES KNEELING. AN AUTOMATIC DRIP IRRIGATION SYSTEM DOES THE WATERING FOR YOU.

LIGHTWEIGHT PLASTIC FENCING (ABOVE RIGHT, RIGHT) HAS A TRADITIONAL APPEARANCE BUT IS DESIGNED SO THAT PANELS CAN BE REMOVED TO ELIMINATE TRIMMING AFTER MOWING.

A BAMBOO GUTTER WITH A
RAIN CHAIN (FAR LEFT) TURNS
A UTILITARIAN ITEM INTO A
WATER FEATURE. THE CHAIN
DIRECTS WATER IN A GENTLE
FLOW TO A DRAIN.

MULTIFUNCTION OUTDOOR
STORAGE HIDES CUSHIONS
(LEFT) AND WORKS AS A
POTTING BENCH (BELOW).

nightlighting
points of light give your yard security, safe passage, and mood

Outdoor lighting once meant having a fixture or two outside your front door, maybe a post lantern at the entry to your driveway, and a floodlight behind the house aimed at the patio for parties. Now you can find about any type of lighting plan imaginable, whether it's designed to improve security, safety, or ambience. The best systems do a good job of contributing to all three categories.

Having so many choices can be daunting when it comes to deciding which type of system to choose and how to set it up. Randall Whitehead, lighting designer, offers advice and shows how he did it at his home.

Installing landscape lighting should start with an inventory of your yard. You need to assess safety and identify features you'd like to highlight. If you haven't taken a good look at your outdoor lighting for a while, set aside

some time to tour the premises. Here's what to look for.

Safety. Whether you're stepping outside for fresh air or hosting a party for dozens, you need to be able to see the landscape well enough to avoid potential injuries.

Look for blind spots, uneven walkways, protruding walls, and areas that are obstructed from view. Walk from the street to your entry. Go up and down stairways. Check the grounds for abrupt dropoffs and objects that could cause stumbles.

Use low-voltage fixtures such as path lights and riser lights to

illuminate sidewalks and stairs. Be sure to light any change in grade where people travel. You'll find that landscape lighting comes in handy in directing people to where you would like them to be. They will stay out of the dark areas and congregate in spots that are lit.

Security. A well-lit yard discourages burglars, who prefer the protection of darkness. Make sure the perimeter of your house is well illuminated. You can accomplish this with well-shielded lighting that won't disturb the neighbors. Powerful floodlights attached to the side of your house or

DAZZLING EFFECTS DEVELOP (RIGHT) WHEN UPLIGHTS SET THE STAGE AND SIDELIGHTS DEFINE THE ENTRY AND STAIRS. UMBRELLA LIGHTS AND CANDLES SET A FESTIVE SCENE (FAR RIGHT).

BEFORE

AS EVENING SHADOWS FALL, THE DINING AREA (ABOVE) IS DREARY WITHOUT LIGHT.

Check out more ideas from HGTV.com
For more on landscape lighting techniques, see
■ www.hgtv.com/landscapemakeoversbook

nightlighting
(continued)

under the eaves can have motion sensors, or you can switch them on manually as needed.

Consider motion detectors at key entry points—even at the beginning of the driveway, so the minute you arrive after dark, the approach to your garage is flooded with light. Plan similar illumintion for the pedestrian path approaching your front door.

If your backyard is especially large, strategically place shielded fixtures at spots that are too far away for illumination by lights on the house. Plan the same security lighting for areas around sheds or tall plantings.

Mood lighting. Your goal for mood lighting is twofold: Extend the use of your backyard into the nighttime hours and give it a magical ambience that pleases and relaxes family and friends. Mood lighting can be more than accent; it, too, can fill safety needs.

Begin by standing inside a window and looking at your backyard—patio, deck, stairways, play area, fireplace, conversation pit, footbridge, planting areas, garden trails, and statues. Pick out favorite elements that you want to highlight as focal points, such as pieces of yard art or a particularly spectacular tree. Use accent lighting to single them out from their surroundings, then fill in around the focal points with a layer of softer lighting that completes the overall scene and gives depth and dimension to the surrounding areas.

A good soft-lighting scheme doesn't call attention to itself; rather, it mimics the effect of a beautiful moonlit night. As you plan the lighting, have a friend aim a portable fixture toward the area while you play director to achieve the effect you want. There are three main types of accent lighting—uplighting, downlighting, and sidelighting.

Uplighting. With this technique, the light fixture is at the base of an object with the beam directed upward. The light can be in front of the object or behind it for different effects. Uplighting shows off forms and works

DOWNLIGHTING A TIKI FIGURE AND A WATER FOUNTAIN MAKES A SEATING AREA TUCKED AMONG THE YUCCAS INTO A POLYNESIAN-STYLE PARADISE (BELOW).

AN ENTRANCE (RIGHT) SEEMS TO BE LIT BY MOONLIGHT. IN REALITY, IT'S A LOW-VOLTAGE LIGHT HIGH IN A TREE. FERN FRONDS, CANDLES AND A LIGHTED MORAVIAN STAR CAST INTERESTING SHADOWS ON THE TEXTURED WALL.

well for highlighting trees and other plants with a sculptural form. It's ideal for accenting large ferns, with their frond patterns casting artistic shadows.

Downlighting. More like natural light, downlighting highlights a single object from overhead. Use it to accent a statue or specimen plant, or to create the shadowing effect of moonlight.

Sidelighting. Use spotlights that cut in laterally, focusing on a point of interest. Two lights—one on each side of a plant or object—will almost completely illuminate the object. Or you can aim a single fixture toward a plant or other object near a wall, creating a shadow effect.

The nighttime effects that can be produced with accent lighting are virtually countless. Just remember to hide the fixtures so they will do their work subtly, rather then stick out as annoying sources of glare.

Some styles of low-level lights used to line walkways can cause hot spots that call too much attention to themselves because they are designed to throw the light in all directions. This type of fixture may

OUTDOOR LIGHTING FIXTURES INCLUDE (FROM LEFT) UPLIGHT, DOWNLIGHT, AND SIDELIGHT.

nightlighting

(continued)

need to be replaced by one with a conical head that projects light downward and is less noticeable.

Fixture choices. The simplest and most economical systems, available at home improvement centers across the country, usually consist of a small transformer that you plug into an outdoor receptacle, a roll of underground cable, and a set of six to 10 spiked fixtures that you attach to the wiring and poke into the ground. These sets work fine as low-level lighting along driveways and paths.

However, if you want to install fixtures that can direct a beam of light toward a target higher off the ground, you'll need to shop for more expensive alternatives. The styles shown on these pages are just a sampling of what's available. For example, there's a special tree-mount fixture called a shielded directional light, which comes with an adjustable strap; you position the light, wrap the strap around a tree limb, and tighten the two strap ends together. Most tree-mounted fixtures are either black, bronze, or green, so they'll blend in well with their leafy surroundings. (Avoid mounting lights more than 10 feet above the ground unless you don't mind climbing higher to change bulbs.)

CUSTOM PARTY LIGHTING

Once you install a basic lighting system, you have the perfect backdrop for the special effects you can add temporarily for parties and other festive activities. Some of them need electricity, while others depend on candles.

- **String lights.** Several types of these inexpensive accessories are available. Christmas or fairy lights are the most familiar. Wind them around tree trunks. Tuck them among the stems on a vine-covered railing or fence to create a twinkling-star effect as breezes stir the leaves. You can also find globe lights like those used at car lots for about $5 a foot at electrical supply stores. Use these for a real party atmosphere or to light paper lanterns.

- **Umbrella lights.** One of the most effective ways to light a party is to install a pair of special lights inside a canvas table umbrella. These small dishes direct the illumination up through the top of the fabric, filtering a dramatic glow throughout the area. These expensive fixtures are waterproof, so you can install them permanently. If you opt for a temporary treatment, substitute low-cost clip lights; remove them after the party is over, because they aren't weather-resistant and could short out.

- **Japanese paper lanterns.** Rice-paper covers diffuse light and create a festive mood. Use them in combination with globe lights or fairy lights. Attach one bulb inside each lantern and hang a row of them along the upper reaches of the perimeter. You can buy paper lanterns at home and party stores.

- **Hanging glass lanterns.** You can use these mood-setters without bothering with wiring. Insert a metal support into the ground for each one and hang a lantern on each hook. Lift up the globe and light the candle.

- **Candle lanterns.** Arrange groupings of two or three translucent candle lanterns on tables interspersed throughout the area and enjoy their cozy ambience.

- **Mix and match.** You'll have fun experimenting with the number and placement of the many devices you have to work with. Each lighting plan produces a different mood. For example, the simple combination of Japanese lanterns and strings of Italian lights is surprisingly dramatic. And the uplit umbrella shares its glow beautifully with the nearby groupings of candle lanterns. Stretch your imagination and creativity.

globe lights

umbrella lights

candlelight and glass lanterns

install low-voltage lighting

tools & materials

- Low-voltage lighting kit (or transformer, light fixtures, cable and wiring, timer)
- Zip ties or soft nylon straps (for tree-mounted lights)
- Wire nuts

Simplicity itself The simplest systems come with easy, complete instructions. You just plug the waterproof transformer in to a 120-volt circuit, run the underground cable along the lighting path, fasten the fixtures to the cable, and stick the spikes on the fixtures into the ground. You don't have to make any complicated buying decisions.

Other options If you go with a more complex system, there are some decisions. Determine which transformer is right for your job. A transformer converts household power of 120 volts to 12 volts—the same as a car battery—so you can avoid working with dangerous voltage. When selecting the transformer, you need to know the number of fixtures and the distance to the most remote fixture from the transformer. The salesperson at the electrical supply house or home improvement center can recommend a transformer with the right capacity.

1 | install transformer

Transformers come in various sizes and shapes; for some, you attach the cable wires to the transformer wires with wire nuts, while in others you slip the cable wiring into slots.

Whatever the hookup, wait to plug the transformer in to your household current until after you've completed the wiring. Some transformers come with timers and still others offer a multitap option, which means that you can choose voltage, usually from 11 to 14 volts. Higher voltages are for longer cable runs. Mount the transformer near an outlet and attach the cable.

2 | bury cable

String the cable according to your lighting plan. If installing path lights, dig a shallow trench along the lighting path, run the cable, then replace the sod or soil.

For fixtures anchored in the soil, take care when spiking stakes into the ground that you avoid the cable run.

For tree-mounted fixtures, run the cable up the trunk and across the tree limb, securing the cable with zip ties or nylon straps.

3 | connect fixture

Wire fixtures in place (or attach tree mounted units to tree limbs) following the manufacturer's instructions.

After dark, aim the fixtures for maximum effect. It often helps to have an assistant give you directions from a vantage point several feet away.

DESIGN PLANS

goal Install low-voltage lighting that illuminates landscape focal points.

cost Varies depending on number of fixtures.

time 1 weekend.

difficulty scale Even more complex systems are relatively easy to install.
◓○○○○

skill scale Digging a shallow trench for cable is the most difficult task.
◓○○○○

BUILDING

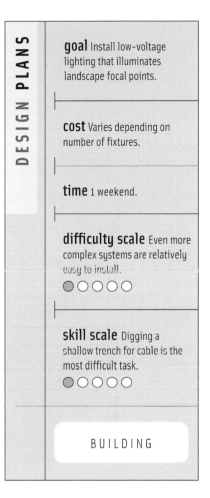

solar-powered lights
use sunshine for powering lamps that bring a soft firefly glow to areas far from an outlet

If you're mainly concerned with lighting pathways, solar-powered light fixtures are an attractive option, especially if the site is a long way from the nearest source of electricity. Solar fixtures convert the sun's rays to electricity, store it in batteries, then power the lights at night. If your site offers plenty of direct sun, the lights should serve you well. Trimming branches that shade the lamps helps keep the batteries energized, as does occasionally wiping the solar panel with window cleaner.

You can buy solar lights in kits or individually. Shop around because there are many different shapes, styles, and colors available. Some of the less expensive fixtures come with short spikes attached to the bottom so you just stick them in the ground and let them work their magic. Others are attached to longer rods that raise the lights so they can illuminate larger areas. And a few are equipped with flanges that allow you to mount the fixtures on your own posts. This latter type is the basis for this simple project from Duncan McIntosh.

AS THEY ABSORB ENERGY FOR NIGHTTIME SERVICE, ARTS AND CRAFTS-STYLE SOLAR LAMPS MARCH ALONG FENCE POSTS (BELOW).

AFTER DARK, THEY GLOW LIKE FIREFLIES, DEFINING THE EDGE OF THE PATHWAY (RIGHT).

solar lights

tools & materials

SPECIAL TOOLS: Circular saw

- Low-voltage post lights
- Landscaper's paint
- Pressure-treated 4×4s
- Pressure-treated 2×4 rails

Use daylight as a power source for nighttime lighting by placing solar-powered lights on a rail fence for a soft glow after sunset. An advantage of solar lights is the easy installation with no electrical work. Each light has a built-in solar panel that collects sunlight during the day to power the light at night. Another plus is the ability to quickly replace lamps, as this homeowner did to accommodate a change in design from basic bollard lamps to Arts and Crafts-style.

1 | mark the site Measure the distance between fixtures and mark locations with landscaper's paint. Using the circular saw, cut 4-foot-long posts for the lamps from pressure-treated 4×4s.

2 | dig postholes Dig holes 8 inches square and 2 feet deep.

3 | level and backfill Set each post in a hole, then have a friend hold the post in position, keeping it plumb and level. Fill in around the post with dirt. Tamp the dirt firmly around it.

If you're concerned about stability, expand the postholes to a 12-inch diameter and pour concrete around the posts; let the concrete set overnight before you continue.

4 | mount the fixtures Stand a light on top of each post and screw through the flanges into the post.

5 | attach rail Screw rail to posts. Paint or stain fencing to suit your landscape style.

simple landscaping might include low-growing fragrant evergreen shrubs that fit under the fence rail.

BEFORE

DESIGN PLANS

goal Create a solar-powered lighting feature.

cost Varies depending on number of fixtures.

time 1 weekend.

difficulty scale Digging post holes is the most strenuous part.

● ○ ○ ○ ○

skill scale Solar lights require no electrical work.

● ○ ○ ○ ○

BUILDING

hanging bottle candles
beautiful wind-proof outdoor candleholders give bottle recycling a decorative twist

Flickering like Tinker Bell inside a Neverland glass greenhouse, these hanging tea lights make a bewitchingly festive display.

They're practical as well. Glass bottles once destined for the trash bin are put to use as delightfully decorative lighting features. Green glass fades into the leafy canopy, making the tiny flame seem as if it's bobbing on the breeze. Frosted glass shimmers with light. Designs you etch onto the glass, along with artistic wire curlicues, glass beads, and weather-resistant clear glue, make these candles unique extensions of your personality.

Long-necked bottles with their bases removed make wind-proof chimneys that keep the flicker from snuffing out in a puff of air. Chains do double duty, suspending the lights from tree branches and making it easy to replace the candles.

CANDLES SWAY AMONG TREE BRANCHES (RIGHT), FLICKERING LIKE TWINKLING STARS. THEIR FLAMES ARE PROTECTED FROM THE BREEZE, INSIDE CANDLEHOLDERS MADE FROM RECYCLED BOTTLES.

Check out more ideas from HGTV.com
For many other crafty ideas, see
- www.hgtv.com/landscapemakeoversbook

MORE IDEAS FOR BOTTLE-CANDLE CREATIONS

Additional decorative options include gluing on crafts materials and wire curlicues to create designs. Use clear glass paints for stained-glass effects.
- **Salvage bottles** with less than perfect cuts by wrapping sandpaper on a dowel and using it to safely smooth sharp edges. Glue decorative glass baubles along scalloped edges to create new looks.
- **The bottom halves of bottles** with extra tea lights become tabletop candles when you smooth cut-glass edges and decorate glass bases in coordinating or complementary designs.

creating hanging lights

tools & materials

SPECIAL TOOLS: Bottle cutter, wire cutter

- Glass long-necked bottles
- Newspaper
- Light machine oil
- Sandpaper; coarse and fine
- Disposable pan with low sides
- Etching cream and stencils
- Decorative glass craft jewels
- Jeweler's wire, various colors
- Clear waterproof adhesive
- Metal chain, #16 zinc
- Galvanized wire, 20 gauge
- Metal washers 1-inch diameter
- Tea-light candles in metal holders

Prep work Clean and dry bottles, removing labels and neck rings. Cover a wide area of work surface with several sheets of newspaper; tiny shards of glass can land a long way from the cutting blade. Wear eye protection while cutting.

1 | cut glass Remove bottle bottoms with a bottle cutter. Lubricate the blade before each cut.

Masking tape around the bottle helps prevent cracking.

2 | sand edges Cut coarse sandpaper to fit inside a disposable pan. Fill pan with water to cover the sandpaper. Smooth cut bottle edges by gently twisting on wet sandpaper. Repeat with fine sandpaper.

3 | etch Apply etching stencils to dry bottle. Thickly dab etching cream on stencil, let sit for one to five minutes (according to package directions) then wash off. Decorate bottle with craft jewels and jeweler's wire, attaching items with waterproof adhesive.

4 | attach chain Cut a length of chain at least twice the height of the bottle. Insert chain into bottle's neck until it's 3 inches from the bottom. Mark the link closest to inside bottom of the bottleneck. Loop a washer on a short wire and attach to marked link. This keeps the chain from sliding out.

5 | attach candle Thread chain out the bottom of the bottle. Bend a 4-inch length of wire into a "U" shape; turn in one end ⅓ inch. Insert the wire end into candle wax by puncturing the thin metal holder. Thread wire through bottom link on chain, and repeat bend and puncture on opposite side, securing the tea light. Light candle. Pull chain back inside bottle until washer stops at neck.

DESIGN PLANS

goal Make windproof outdoor candleholders.

cost Bottle cutter runs $30.

time 1 weekend.

difficulty scale Using the bottle cutter takes practice.
⬤⬤⬤○○

skill scale Have fun with mistakes; turn them into creative opportunities.
⬤⬤○○○

DECORATING

a movable canopy
a clever arbor has a sliding cover

The typical arbor gives you some shade, some of the time. It works well on sites where you need occasional relief from the full effect of the sun, but it falls short of giving you 100 percent protection. At the other extreme, solid roofing keeps out the direct sun, but you miss the option of inviting in some of those wonderful rays when you want them. A happy medium—full protection some of the time, full sun the rest of the time—is this movable canopy designed by Peter Parker.

Some movable covers—whether they slide, fold, or roll up—are awkward.

IT'S A SUNSHINY DAY BUT COOL SHADOWS PLAY UNDER THE FULLY EXTENDED OVERHEAD CANOPY THAT SHADES A PATIO SEATING AREA (BELOW).

STRIPES IN COLORS THAT REFLECT THE TONES AND SHADOWS OF TERRA-COTTA ROOFING TILES BLEND WITH THE HOUSE'S ARCHITECTURE (RIGHT). HEAT-LOVING PLANTS ADD BRIGHT ACCENTS.

But the simple system designed for this family works smoothly and looks great, thanks to the attractive arbor unit that supports it.

It evolved out of the family's desire to create a relaxing area behind their Spanish-style home where they could escape the almost constant sun but still be able to enjoy the beauty of a nearby citrus orchard. Peter Parker suggested an arbor with minimal posts to avoid interfering with the view and with widely spaced crosspieces on top to continue the light and airy feeling. Then when the sun hits the area with full force, a sliding canopy provides instant relief.

The overall unit is about 12×14 feet—big enough to do its job, but not so massive that it dominates the landscape. The four main beams are 2×10s. The eight crosspieces are 2×8s. For posts, the designer used 6×6s that were custom milled to match

A WAND PULLS THE CANOPY INTO POSITION (ABOVE) TO SHADE THE PATIO.

A SUN-DRENCHED PATIO AREA (ABOVE) WAS OFTEN TOO HOT FOR COMFORTABLE USE.

a movable canopy
(continued)

the architecture of the house. A second-level balcony already existed, so the two posts supporting it took on the extra role of holding up one end of the arbor. If you want to build a similar unit and lack two existing posts attached to the house, you'll be putting up four posts, rather than the two needed by this family. Be sure to sink all four in concrete to below the frost line because you will need the additional stability.

USING JUST A FEW POSTS KEEPS THE FANTASTIC VIEW CLEAR (RIGHT). A WATER FEATURE GURGLES QUIETLY, PROVIDING THE REFRESHING SOUND OF NATURE.

CITRUS TREES COMMAND ATTENTION AS THEY GROW RIGHT TO THE EDGE OF THE SHELTERED BRICK PATIO OFF THE BACK OF THE HOUSE (BELOW).

construct the frame

tools & materials

SPECIAL TOOLS: Circular saw, jigsaw, ⅝-inch auger bit (9 inches long)

- 4 – 6×6s, 12 feet long
- 1 – 6×6, 8 feet long
- 4 – 2×10s, 16 feet long
- 8 – 2×8s, 16 feet long
- 8 – ⅝-inch hex bolts, 9 inches long
- 8 eyebolts, ¼-inch diameter, 8 inches long
- Steel cable, ¼-inch diameter, 50 feet long
- 36 snap hooks
- Deck screws
- Custom-made acrylic canopy
- Concrete mix

An arbor to support a retractable canopy allows you the choice of soaking up rays or staying protected under the sun-screening fabric. The crew on this project constructed a low wall to frame the area and incorporated into its design two large concrete footings for the new posts.

1 | put in the posts

Use posts long enough to extend about 9 feet 5 inches above the ground; this will result in 8 feet of clearance between the floor of the arbor area and the bottom of the lowest beam. The owner had his posts custom milled to match the architecture of his home. Square posts also work, and you might consider adding decorative details to your post as well.

Dig four postholes to the proper depth for your area. (You could attach the arbor to your home, in which case, only two postholes are needed.) The postholes should be about 11 feet 8 inches apart, center to center, side to side.

Add 2 inches of gravel to the bottom of each hole. Set a 6×6 post atop the gravel. Stabilize the post with braces fastened to stakes in the ground, making sure it is plumb. Fill the holes with concrete and let it dry. Wait at least 24 hours before removing the braces and beginning work on the framework.

2 | decorate beams

Cut a decorative curve on the ends of four 16-foot 2×10s. From the top corner on one end, measure down and mark the top point of the curve on the edge of the board. Draw a 45-degree angle across the bottom corner of the board from that point. Then, make a string compass with a pencil and a piece of string that is the same length as the

AFTER

curve's top point. Holding the string end at the bottom corner of the board and the pencil at the top point of the 45-degree-angle line, draw a curve, ending at the bottom point of the line.

3 | cut design

Cut out the curve with a jigsaw. Sand the edges.

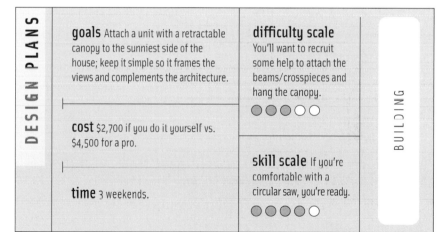

DESIGN PLANS

goals Attach a unit with a retractable canopy to the sunniest side of the house; keep it simple so it frames the views and complements the architecture.

cost $2,700 if you do it yourself vs. $4,500 for a pro.

time 3 weekends.

difficulty scale You'll want to recruit some help to attach the beams/crosspieces and hang the canopy.

●●●○○

skill scale If you're comfortable with a circular saw, you're ready.

●●●●○

BUILDING

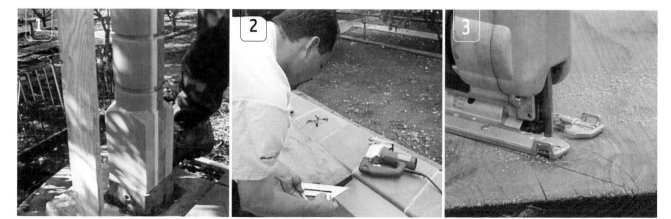

construct the frame
(continued)

4 | attach main beams Sandwich the posts with the beams, allowing 7¼ inches of each post to extend above the top of the beam and the ends of the beam to extend past each post by about a foot. Temporarily nail the beam to both posts. Repeat with the other two beams at the other two posts.

5 | drill for bolts Using the long auger bit, drill holes through the beams on both sides of the post.

6 | add hex bolts Pound ⅝-inch bolts—two per post—into the holes to secure the beams to the posts.

7 | add spacers To keep the top of this arbor open and airy, you will install four pairs of 2×8 crosspieces 4 feet apart. Begin by cutting four

17-inch-long chunks from 6×6s to use as spacers and points of attachment for the crosspieces. The 6×6×17 spacers will stand vertically inside the beam "sandwiches" and extend upward, two in each sandwich. Slip them into position between the front and rear posts, evenly spaced at 4-foot intervals.

Make sure the bottom end of each spacer is flush with the bottom edges of the beams and that the top end extends 7¼ inches above the top edges of the beams. Attach the spacers by screwing through the beams and into the spacers.

8 | curve ends and install crosspieces Give the end of each crosspiece the same decorative curve as you used for the beams.

Install the 2×8 crosspieces in pairs,

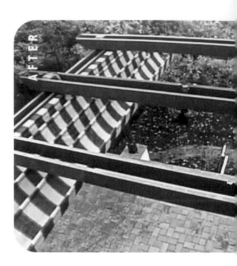

with the ends of each pair flanking a spacer. Let the decorative ends of the 2×8 pairs extend beyond the beams about 16 inches. Using deck screws, screw the crosspieces to the 6×6 spacer extensions. This completes

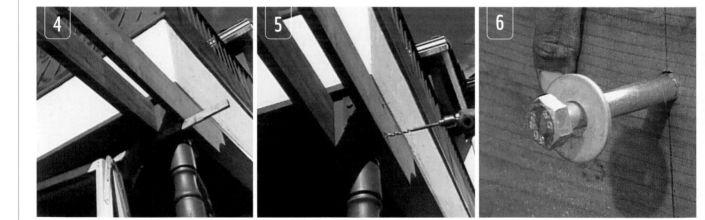

CUSTOM CANOPY FABRIC

The custom-made canopy the family chose is made from sturdy, mildew-resistant acrylic. A canvas fabricator or awning shop can make yours. To duplicate the one pictured, you probably have to spend upwards of $2,000. You can save about $500 by doing the installation yourself.

construction of the arbor, now you're ready to install the canopy.

9 | run cable To begin installing the canopy, run a steel cable inside the length of each of the four crosspiece sandwiches.

10 | attach eyebolts The cable is attached to eyebolts, which are fastened to each of the vertical spacers at the front and back of the structure.

11 | snap hooks The canopy should be made from canvas with metal rods sewn into it every 4 feet to match the beams. Thirty-two heavy-duty snap hooks are then sewn to the rods, lined up in rows across the canopy.

Call in a couple of helpers to help you hang all the hooks from the steel cable. Choose which end of the canopy you want to be stationary, then anchor it to the eyebolts at that end. Snap on the rest of the hooks to the cable, starting from the free end of the canopy and continuing until all are attached.

12 | open canopy In about two hours you should have the canopy hung. Grab the wand that guides the movable end and easily slide the cover open and closed.

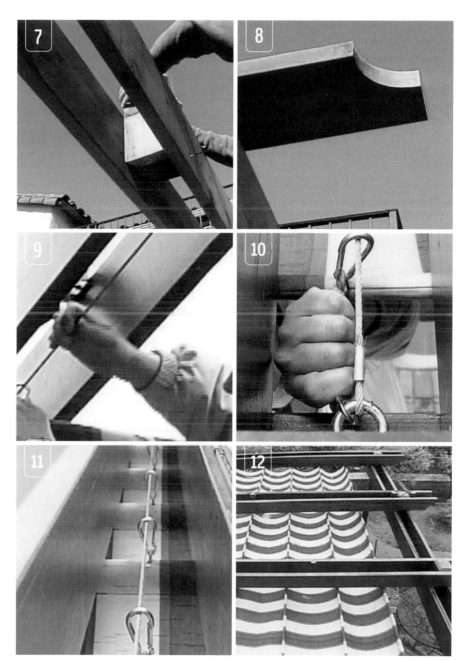

ARBOR PROPORTIONS should be pleasing to the eye, says Peter Parker, who designed the structure with heavy pieces at the base and lighter pieces with decorative ends at the top.

outdoor office
going to work means just a short trek outside

If you've ever looked out the window of your home office and wished you could be outside, this project may appeal to you.

It's an outdoor office—headquartered on the deck, just a few feet from sliding glass doors. It features a fold-down desk, waterproof connections for electricity and a phone, and a handy storage unit to shelter filing cabinets, a chair, and other office practicalities. Topping it off is an attractive arbor roof that defines the area and provides partial shade.

When the desk is folded away and the doors of the storage space are closed, the entire area is available for the usual deck activities that take place at your house. It's a great way to mix business with pleasure, especially if you live in an area where you enjoy a moderate climate year-round.

THIS LOVELY SPACE CONSTANTLY BECKONED THE OWNERS TO COME OUT RATHER THAN WORK IN THE HOME OFFICE. NOW THEY CAN DO BOTH.

The storage unit makes good sense if you use the office often and don't want to cart out your supplies every time you work outside. If you only need a few materials and don't mind bringing them with you each time, you could forgo the storage unit and save a few hundred dollars. You could also save time and money by eliminating the 4×12-foot arbor, although you'd need to devise some other way to waterproof the wiring and electrical hookups. If you're game to take on the entire project, the combination of coordinated elements will make a big hit as a practical and attractive addition to your backyard environment.

Dan Berger, designer of this project worked with existing components—in this case, a two-story exterior wall, a deck, and a pair of sliding glass doors leading to an interior home office. The new arbor and folding desk extend 8 feet up the house wall. To keep water from the wiring behind the desk, flashing was installed where the arbor meets the house .

For a one-story ranch with an existing overhang, tucking the arbor under the overhang might work. But before building it there, make sure you'll have enough headroom once the arbor is in. You might need to lower the deck to make way for the arbor. Every installation will be different and you will need to alter some of the procedures and materials used in this example as you adapt the ideas to your own site.

Check out more ideas from HGTV.com
For many great tips on outdoor living, see
- www.hgtv.com/landscapemakeoversbook

ALMOST TOO TRANQUIL FOR WORK (RIGHT), THIS OUTDOOR HOME OFFICE OFFERS VIEWS OF A KOI POND AND LUSH PLANTS.

THE CLOCK SAYS IT'S TIME TO
GET BUSY ON THE LAPTOP
COMPUTER THAT CONNECTS
EASILY TO A WATERPROOF
POWER SOURCE (TOP).

OFFICE SUPPLIES ARE AT HAND
ON A SMALL BUT EFFICIENT
DESK THAT FOLDS AWAY WHEN
NOT IN USE (ABOVE).

build the arbor

tools & materials

SPECIAL TOOLS: Jigsaw, circular saw, table saw, compound miter saw

- 5 – 4×6s, 10 feet long
- 4 – 2×8s, 14 feet long
- 2 – 2×6s, 12 feet long
- 9 – 2×6s, 12 feet long
- Concrete mix
- 5 metal post anchors
- 5 carriage bolts
- 11 feet of 16-inch aluminum flashing
- Exterior caulk
- Deck screws

DESIGN PLANS

goals Add a backyard office; include amenities that make it practical; devise a way of hiding every component when not in use and when area is needed for entertaining; use materials that complement the architecture.

cost $1,600 if you do it yourself vs. $6,000 for a pro.

time 5 weekends.

difficulty scale Several steps require additional help; setting the posts and building the arbor can be hard work.

●●●●○

skill scale The whole project requires good carpentry skills; you'll be doing lots of measuring and remeasuring; it's essential that you plan carefully.

●●●●●

BUILDING

The first step in creating an outdoor office is building an arbor that lets in light and air but also protects electrical wiring from rain. This arbor extends slightly past the house so that a storage closet can be added on. Depending on your situation, you may be able to build it all on the house.

1 | install posts This arbor requires five 10-foot-long 4×6 posts, three at the back and two in front. Two of the back posts stand against the wall of the house on either side of the sliding glass doors. The third post is placed 5½ feet beyond the corner of the house in line with the two posts on the deck.

The front two posts are four feet from the house and 12 feet apart. The four posts on the deck line up with each other.

Pour concrete piers for the posts and embed metal post anchors in them. (You can also sink the posts, pouring concrete around their bases. In that case, buy longer posts and dig the holes deep enough to satisfy local building codes.)

Before installing the posts, cut a 7¼-inch-long by 1½-inch-deep notch in three of the posts 16 inches below the post tops (or 8 feet above the deck) for the arbor beams. Stand each post inside its anchor.

2 | drill for bolts Drill through the post, then install a carriage bolt to secure the post to the anchor.

3 | position notches Install the three notched beams next to the house with the notches pointing toward the wall.

4 | install back support beams These consist of two 14-foot-long 2×8s, sandwiching the three back posts. Before installing them, cut a decorative design on both ends of each beam with the jigsaw.

Slide one 2×8 beam through the notches on all three back posts. The beam will overlap the end posts by a foot. Drive deck screws on angle through the edges of the post into the beam.

Sandwich the posts with the second beam, attaching it to the front face of the post. Screw directly through the beam into the face of each post.

5 | install front support beams Mount the remaining two 2×8 beams to the front two posts, flanking the posts as you did at the rear and extending past each post by a foot.

6 | make spacers Fill in the top and bottom of the back beam sandwich with 2×6 spacers. This will

help prevent water from getting into the wiring and electrical hookups.

Measure the distance between the two end posts at the back of the structure. Cut the two 12-foot 2×6s with the circular saw to that measurement. Use a table saw to rip them to a 4-inch width.

Insert one spacer in the top space between the parallel beams and the other in the bottom space; nail them flush with upper and lower edges of the 2×8 beams.

7 | prepare flashing

Bend a 1-inch lip along one long edge of the aluminum flashing. Measure 7 inches in from this bend and make a second bend in the flashing. You'll end up with a 16-inch long U-shaped piece that has one short lip and one long leg.

8 | install flashing

Cover the rear beam sandwich with the folded flashing. Place it so that the short lip overhangs the front beam and the longer leg slips down behind the rear beam, snugly fitting against the wall of the house. Run a bead of long-lasting exterior caulk along the intersection of the flashing and the house.

Resist the temptation to nail the flashing in place. Piercing flashing damages its effectiveness at waterproofing. The crosspieces will hold the flashing in place.

9 | install rafters

Make the crosspieces, or rafters, from 2×6s. There are 16 rafters in this arbor, each 5½-feet long. For your installation, measure the distance from the house and rear beams to the front beams and add 16 or 18 inches for overlap.

Using the table saw, cut eight 2×6s to length. From the remaining 2×6, cut twelve 10-inch-long spacers.

Next, cut the same decorative design at one end of each rafter as you used on the 2×6 beams with a jigsaw. The decorative ends face the front; the back ends will be flush against the house.

Install the rafters working from one side to the other. Rest the first rafter on the front and back beams against the outside edge of the end posts. Angle screw the rafter to the beams without piercing the flashing.

Sandwich the post with the second rafter, attaching it as before. At the rear of the structure, stand a 10-inch spacer on edge on the flashing and screw it on an angle into the side of the rafter. Alternate rafters and spacers until you get to the opposite end of the arbor.

10 | finish rafters

When you get to the opposite end of the arbor, build another sandwich that flanks the posts. Screw the front ends of the rafters to the tops of the paired 2×8s supporting them.

build the shed

tools & materials

SPECIAL TOOLS: Jigsaw, circular saw, table saw, compound miter saw

- 3 – 4×4s, 8 feet long
- 3 – 2×6s, 8 feet long
- 2 – 2×6s, 10 feet long
- 3 – 2×6s, 8 feet long
- 6 – 2×4s, 8 feet long
- 2 – 1×4s, 8 feet long
- 3 – 4×8 sheets, ¾-inch exterior-grade plywood
- 1 – 4×8 sheet, ⅝-inch plywood sheathing
- 1 – 4×8 sheet, coated, exterior-grade plywood siding
- Concrete mix
- Metal post anchor
- Deck screws, 2½-inches long
- 6 joist hangers
- 10 linear feet roofing paper
- 12 feet metal drip edge
- Shingles to cover 16 square feet
- Roofing caulk
- Exterior paint to match house color
- 4 – 4-inch door hinges

Storage space. The arbor extends past the house far enough to frame in a shed recessed behind the deck. Use the shed for office supplies and for stashing the desk legs when the desk is folded away.

1 | install posts

You already installed one front post for the shed when you built the arbor, the one that is farthest from the house. Now install the second front post. Use a 4×4. Locate it in line with the rear arbor posts, 16 inches from the corner of the house. It's side that is closest to the house should be 4 feet from the outside face of the first post. If decking is already in place, cut it out to accommodate the post.

Trim the post to fit tightly between the anchor and the beam. Pour a concrete footing with embedded post anchors. Let the concrete dry, then install the post. Screw the post to the underside of the beam.

Pour concrete footings with concrete anchors for the rear posts, in line with and 3 feet behind the front posts. Cut these posts to 7½ feet long. Since the front posts are 8 feet tall, this shorter length allows the roof to slant so that it sheds rain and snow.

install the floor

First, attach a 2×6 support to the horizontal frame of the deck. Before installing it, measure the thickness of the flooring you will be installing. Measure down the distance from the top of the deck and attach the support with deck screws. When installed, the distance from the top of the support to the top of the deck should be the same as the thickness of the floor.

AFTER

Next, frame the floor area with 2×6s. The 2×6s should be installed at the same height as the floor support. Screw them to the inside faces of the posts, making sure they are level first.

Attach joist hangers to the frame perpendicular to the house. Evenly space them across the floor area, staring at the rear of the shed. Screw the 2×6s to the hangers; nail the flooring to the joists.

2 | frame shed

Install a top plate of 2×4s on three sides of the shed. This top plate rests on the rear posts. Angle screw the top plate to the front posts and nail it to the rear

posts, making sure everything is level first. Set a second layer of 2×4s on the top plate, driving screws at angles to secure them to the first.

At the rear of the shed, attach a 2×4 between the floor and the top plate to help support the siding. Center this 2×4 between the two back posts.

3 | roof shed

Cut four 4-foot-long rafters from 2×4s. You may want to experiment first with scrap lumber so that you cut the correct angles on the ends that attach to the arbor beam. Notch the rear ends of the rafter to fit around the top plate. At the rear of the shed, the rafters

should extend about 6 inches past the top plate.

Before installing the rafters, cut the arbor flashing at the edge of the roof closest to the house. Temporarily bend the flashing up out of the way. Screw the upper end of each rafter to the back of the arbor beam, and at the rear, screw them to the top plate.

Nail or screw a piece of ⅝-inch plywood sheathing to the rafters, allowing it to extend a couple of inches beyond the rafters at the rear. Cover the plywood with a layer of tar-impregnated roofing paper, also called roofing felt. Install metal drip edges, then shingle the roof.

Bend the flap of arbor flashing down against the shingles. Nail through it and through the shingles into the sheathing. Caulk the nailheads to ensure watertightness.

4 | attach siding

Choose siding that blends with the exterior of your house or nearby buildings. The crew building this project used coated, exterior-grade plywood siding that comes in 4×8 sheets. Cut the material to size and nail or screw it to the framing.

5 | install doors

Cut two doors from ¾-inch exterior-grade plywood. Size them to fit inside the opening between the front posts as well as between the underside of the arbor beam and the deck floor. Apply two coats of exterior paint to match the house.

Screw one 1×4 to the front face of each door, running vertically, flush with one edge of the plywood. Mount exterior hinges to the 1×4s. Hang doors in the opening by screwing the free halves of the hinges to the front surfaces of the posts.

Finishing touches.

It's up to you how your new shed can be used best. Install shelving for supplies. Save enough space for holding a patio-table umbrella or other paraphernalia, as well as stashing the desk's removable legs when office hours are over and it's time for entertaining on the deck.

A GARDEN FOR THE OFFICE

Landscape architect Dan Berger chose low-maintenance plants to fill in around the garden office, selecting varieties that offer plenty of color, fragrance and texture. Featured plants:

- **Double mockorange** (*Philadelphus virginalis* 'Minnesota Snowflake'), Zones 5–8
- **Cranesbill** (*Geranium cinereum* 'Ballerina'), Zones 5–9
- **Peony** (*Paeonia lactiflora*), Zones 4–8
- **Giant timber bamboo** (*Bambusa oldhamii*), Zones 7–11

build the desk

tools & materials

SPECIAL TOOLS: Jigsaw, circular saw, table saw

- 2 – 2×4s, 8 feet long
- 2 – 4×8 sheets, ¾-inch exterior-grade plywood
- 3 – 2×2, 8 feet long
- 1 – 1×4, 10 feet long
- Coated deck screws
- Exterior caulk
- 40 square foot sheet, 16-gauge galvanized steel
- Exterior paint
- Exterior-grade glue
- 2 – 4-inch door hinges
- 1 roll, translucent board cover

Desk set A foldaway desk lets you easily convert the outdoor office back into a deck.

1 | frame the L-shaped desk pocket The first step is to put in the 2×4 framing that will hold the fold-down desk. Using the circular saw, cut a 2×4 crosspiece to fit horizontally between the center arbor post and the end post. This crosspiece is where the hinge for the desk will be attached.

2 | attach crosspiece Measure 31 inches from the deck and install the crosspiece, making sure it is level. You may need to tap the crosspiece to wedge it into place; use a piece of scrap wood between the hammer and the 2×4 so you don't gouge it. Drive deck screws on an angle through the 2×4s into both posts to hold the crosspiece in place.

3 | add center brace Attach a vertical 2x4 between the deck and the crosspiece at the midway point.

4 | make backboard Cut a backboard from ¾-inch exterior-grade plywood. This backboard covers the exterior wall of the house and spans the entire space between the posts. This unit is 4×5½ feet, but adapt the dimensions for your own situation. Paint the backboard to match your house.

Use a table saw to rip 1-inch-wide mounting strips from a 1×4. Cut two strips the same length as the sides of the backing piece and two the width of the top. Attach these mounting strips to the backboard.

5 | attach backboard Screw through the mounting strips to attach the backboard to the wall.

6 | caulk frame Caulk around the frame to ensure it's watertight.

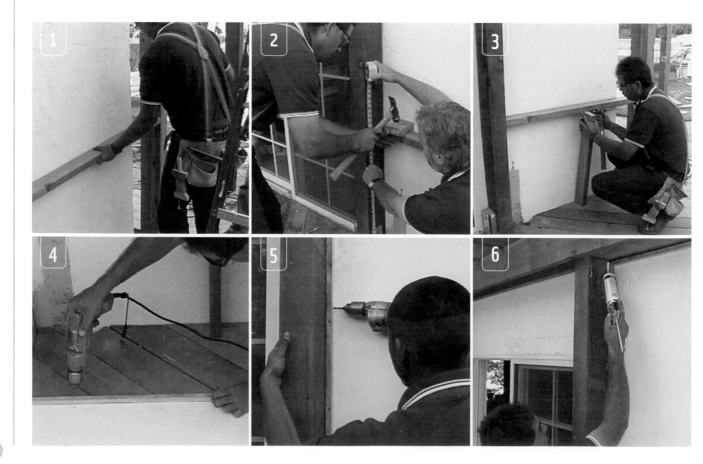

7 | fit metal facing Have a metal shop cut a piece of 16-gauge galvanized steel to size to face the backboard and an L-shaped piece for the top of the desk. Hold the wall facing against the plywood, inside the mounting strips.

8 | attach facing Predrill holes, then attach the metal facing, screwing the metal to the backing. Add a bead of caulk around the edge of the metal.

9 | finish the "L" framing Rip a 2×4 to a width of 2¾ inches and cut it into two pieces—one 4 feet long and the other 2 feet long. Notch one end of the 4-footer so it fits around the mounting strip. Attach it vertically to the metal facing. Notch the other

AFTER

build the desk
(continued)

and attach it horizontally to form a rectangular frame.

10 | insert spacer Rip a 2×2 to 1¼ inches wide. Place it over the fastening strip running along the top of the pocket, screwing it to the bottom of the beam. When the desk is folded up, this spacer will keep it flush with the framing.

make desktop Cut an L-shaped piece of ¾-inch exterior-grade plywood to fit inside the L-shaped frame. Paint the underside to match your house.

11 | attach edging Cut redwood edging pieces from 2×2s with a table saw. Attach them to the edges of the plywood with glue and screws. The edging should extend beyond the top surface of the plywood ¹⁄₁₆ inch.

12 | add hinges Screw two 4-inch, heavy-duty exterior hinges to the pivoting end of the desk top.

13 | install desk top Ask a couple of helpers to hold the top in position while you screw the other half of each hinge to the 2×4 crosspiece. Drill holes in the 2×4 for the telephone and electrical wires. Temporarily prop up the other end of the desk.

14 | install metal surface Position the metal top on the desk. Drill holes and screw the metal to the plywood.

15 | heat-proof top To keep arms from getting burned on hot metal, apply a translucent board cover from a drafting supply outlet.

16 | cut to fit Smooth the cover over the metal desk top and trim off the excess for a snug fit.

A METAL SURFACE makes good sense if you live in a windy area. It allows you to use flat magnets to keep papers from blowing away.

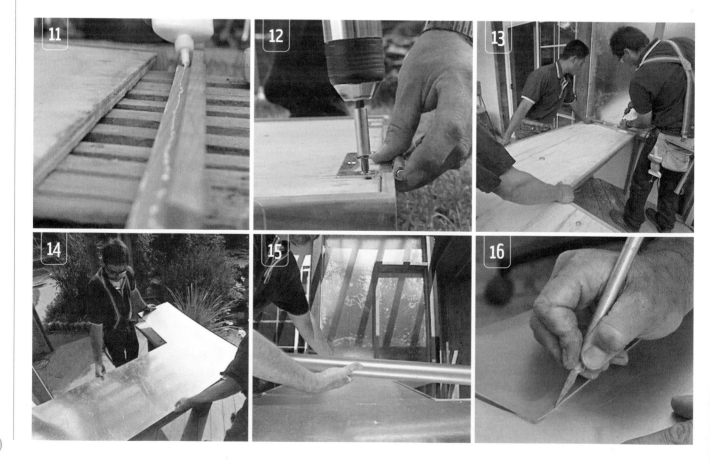

wiring and finishing

tools & materials

SPECIAL TOOLS: Circular saw, table saw, compound miter saw

- 1 – 4×8 sheet, ½-inch exterior-grade plywood
- 1 – 6×6, 8 feet long, redwood or pressure-treated
- 220 linear feet, grape stakes or similar wood strips
- Wiring, boxes, outlets
- 4 feet, ½-inch rebar
- Epoxy glue
- 1 barrel bolt
- 2 cane bolts

1 | run the wiring You may want to hire an electrician or wiring specialist to help with this part of the job. Pull wires from the house into the space directly beneath the desk top. Feed the wiring through the house wall into the void beneath the desk, then continue up through holes in the 2x4 crosspiece that supports the desk hinges.

2 | service boxes Install boxes for each service, and wire the appropriate devices.

3 | dress up the area Cut sheets of ½-inch exterior grade plywood to cover voids below and to the right of the desk pocket. Paint the plywood to match the house and screw the sheets to the framing. Fold the desk top into its pocket so that all of the plywood surfaces, including the doors on the storage shed, are in one continuous plane.

Decorate the wall. This homeowner used a fencing material called grape stakes, but you can substitute another material to your liking. The important point is to choose a material that works well with the style of your home.

4 | make desk legs Because the deck needs to be uncluttered when

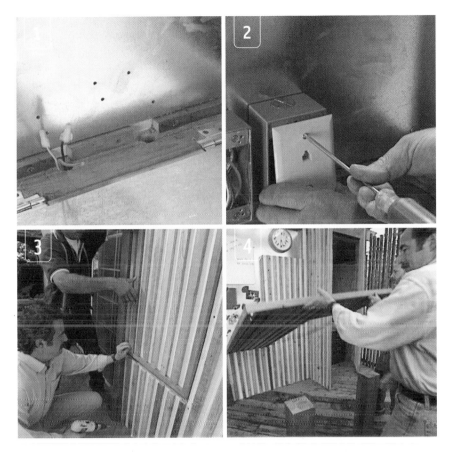

the office is put away, the legs must be easily removable. Have someone hold the desk in the open position while you measure the distance from the deck to the grape stakes on the bottom of the table. Then cut two 6×6s to that length.

Cut eight 5-inch-long pieces of ½-inch rebar. Attach four of the pieces to the bottom of each of the two 6×6 posts. To do this, drill four ½-inch-diameter holes 3 inches deep, in a rectangular pattern in the bottom of each leg. Then line the sides of the holes with epoxy glue and hammer each rebar into a hole.

Stand the leg on the deck where it needs to go to hold the desk, and, by putting your weight on the top of the leg, make an impression of each rebar in the decking. Take care to position the legs so the rebar doesn't

fall in one of the spaces between the deck boards. Drill holes through the decking for the rebar.

After you fold away the desk top, pull up the legs and stash them in the storage shed.

To keep the desk top closed, fasten a barrel bolt to the underside of the deck and drill a hole in the bottom of the arbor beam to accept the end of the sliding bolt.

At the bottom of each storage door, attach a cane bolt vertically, so its barrel engages a hole in the deck board. Alternatively, plan the spacing of the wood strips so one of them overlaps the junction where the doors meet. That way, you need only use one cane bolt on the door that contains the overlapping wood strip; the strip holds the opposite door closed.

al fresco dining
a cozy corner with a recessed table embraces the outdoors and is as comfortable as being indoors

As product design improves, patio furniture is becoming more attractive and more comfortable. Whether you use it mostly as a place to relax or as your outdoor dining spot, there's a style and color to please everyone. But you'll be hard-pressed to find anything that offers the charm and intimacy of this eating area, tucked into a secluded corner of a yard and surrounded with a graceful fence

and a dramatic flagstone border.

The homeowners asked landscape designer Dan Berger to suggest some ideas for a dining area—something distinctive—that could handle four to six people comfortably. Dan came up with a combination of several complementary elements.

First, he designed a slightly raised area in the back of the yard, stabilizing it with a dry-stacked stone wall. Then he created a patio in this space and built a pedestal table topped with a design-it-yourself mosaic surface. The table takes its inspiration from Japanese restaurants where the diners sit on the floor with their feet in a pit. Here, the seats are made from large

flagstones covering the ground around the table. The nice thing is that the sunken table takes up less space than a purchased table would.

The finished project, embellished with colorful pillows and coordinated plantings, is not only a comfortable and beautiful addition to the backyard, but assures the family's dining pleasure for decades.

A FLAGSTONE BORDER CREATES BENCH SEATING FOR THE SUNKEN TABLE (OPPOSITE).

CUSHIONS MAKE THE OUTDOOR DINING AREA A COMFORTABLE PLACE FOR THE FAMILY TO GATHER (BELOW).

A MOSAIC MADE FROM BROKEN DINNER PLATES CREATES A UNIQUE WEATHER-RESISTANT SURFACE FOR THE DINING TABLE (ABOVE).

BEFORE

"STAY INDOORS," THIS PATCH OF YARD SEEMED TO SAY (ABOVE).

make the table

tools & materials

SPECIAL TOOLS: Hand grinder with diamond blade, steel finishing trowel, notched trowel, grout float

- Landscaper's paint
- Medium-size boulders
- Native stones
- 2-inch-thick flagstones, large and medium-size
- 3-inch PVC pipe, 90-degree elbow, drain flange & cover
- PVC cleaner/primer and glue
- 3½-inch bender board, 100 linear feet
- Wood screws
- Small decorative pebbles
- 1 – 10-inch-diameter, cylindrical concrete form, 4 feet long
- ¾-inch decorative rock
- 1 – 4×8 sheet (4×4 if available), ¾-inch exterior-grade plywood
- 1 – 3×5 sheet, ½-inch cement backer board
- Plates, tile pieces, colored stones
- Ceramic-tile mortar and grout
- 4 concrete anchors

Site selection. Pick a secluded corner, preferably near a fence or wall, maximizing privacy and minimizing the amount of retaining wall you'll need to build. If you don't have a fence, you might want to select a site that you can surround with plantings for privacy.

1 | prepare the site Clear the site to the bare ground, then mark the location of the table. To do this, pound a stake into the ground at the center of the spot where the table will go. Tie a 5-foot-long string to the stake, then pivot around the stake and mark the circle with landscaper's paint. (Or have a helper hold the end of a measuring tape at the center point while you draw the circle.)

2 | mark location of wall Lay out the path of the curving stone wall, keeping it at least 5 feet from the pit. Dig a trench 2 inches deep and a foot wide to hold the rock wall.

3 | build two steps The raised area will be 20 inches higher than the yard, so steps will be needed. Lay the foundation for the first step by placing a flat medium-size boulder in the trench. The boulder should be tall enough to extend 8 inches above the top of the trench. Fill in around the boulder with medium-size stones.

DESIGN PLANS

goals Create a distinctive and intimate dining area in the backyard; place it in a private setting; make sure it complements and enhances the ambience of its surroundings.

cost $1,000 if you do it yourself vs. $4,800 for a pro.

time 4 weekends.

difficulty scale You'll move lots of dirt, dig trenches, and carry heavy stones. Bender board fabrication and mosaic work can become tedious.
●●●○○

skill scale Cutting the big flagstones with the hand grinder requires practice and dexterity.
●●●○○

BUILDING

attach a short piece of pipe to the elbow as an extension so that the drain will sit at ground level when the patio is completed. Cover the ends of the pipe with a cap or a piece of cloth, then backfill the trench with dirt.

Start building the retaining wall by dry laying stones and boulders in the trench and filling in behind them with dirt up to their tops. Continue building the wall, dry-stacking and backfilling as you go, until the wall and the patio area are 18 to 20 inches high. Roughly level the backfill soil when finished.

8 | begin pit liner Build a light-weight liner for the pit by forming a cylinder from bender board. Bender board is a lightweight, quarter-inch-thick, flexible product used in building forms for concrete projects. It may be composed of wood or composite. It is available in widths ranging from 3½ to 6 inches. (Check home improvement centers and the Internet for resources.)

To make the liner, you will form five rings from the 3½-inch-size bender board and join them together. For each ring, roll one 188-inch length of bender board into a 5-foot-diameter circle and join the ends with an 18-inch-long bender board splice.

9 | form rings To do this, place the splice on the ground. Lay the longer bender board piece on top of the splice, overlapping half of the splice about ½ inch below its top edge. Fasten the two pieces together with wood screws.

Curl the longer piece into a circle. Holding its loose end to the secured end, screw it to the splice, again ½ inch below the top edge. This lip makes it easier to stack the rings and keeps the stack stable.

4 | level course Use a level to help you place the stones so their tops are at the same height as the boulder. The first step will rest on top of both the boulder and the smaller stones.

5 | fill with dirt Shovel fill dirt behind and on top of the boulder and stones. Level the soil so that it is flush with their tops. Then, firm it with the back of a shovel.

6 | set step Place a 2-inch-thick slab of flagstone on the dirt-and-stone base. The top of the step will be about 10 inches above ground level and should overhang the base slightly. Check that it is level, filling in behind the step with dirt as needed.

Set narrow flagstone strips at the rear of the step, forming an 8-inch-high riser for the next step. Backfill,

to the top of the riser, tamp the soil as before, then lay the second step into place. It too should overhang the front of the riser and be level.

7 | install drain To prevent water from filling the pit, add a drain line. It should run from the pit to a location far enough away from the area that the water will run out and not flow back into the pit. Mark a spot 18 inches from the center of the pit in the direction you want the water to drain. Dig a trench from that spot to the discharge point. Near the pit, the trench should be about 12 inches deep. Moving away from the pit, it should slope steadily downward toward the discharge point.

Lay a 3-inch PVC pipe in the trench. At the pit end, glue a 90-degree elbow to the pipe, then

make the table

(continued)

10 | stack pieces Make the other four rings in the same manner, then stack them one on top of the other.

Cut eight more pieces of bender board, each 17 inches long, to use as vertical braces. Have someone steady the stack while you screw the braces to the outside of the rings to form a cylinder.

11 | excavate the pit Roughly mark the perimeter of the dining table pit. Dig a 5-foot-diameter 17½-inch- deep hole. You should be at or near the original ground level when you finish.

Place the pit liner inside the hole and backfill around the outside of it, smoothing out the dirt so it's level and flush with the top of the liner.

12 | lay the seating area For the seats, use six 2-inch-thick flagstone pieces that are large enough to allow people to be able to walk around the table without disturbing anyone who may be sitting at the table.

Set the six flagstones on the ground around the pit, spacing them evenly apart and overlapping the edge of the pit. Fill in the spaces between the seats with smaller pieces of flagstone, chipping off any protrusions with a hammer. Wear eye protection when breaking stone.

To ensure the seats are comfortable without the flagstone poking into the back of you legs, cut the front of the seats flush with the pit. To do this clearly mark the curve of the liner on the stones.

13 | score lines Using a hand grinder with a diamond blade; score along the marks. Then tap on the stone with a hammer to knock off the overhang.

Finish the joints between the stones by pouring decorative pebbles into the spaces. Also, fill the space between the seat closest to the stairs and the top step with a piece of flagstone matching the seats.

Complete the drain by cutting off the pipe extension so that it is flush with the bottom of the pit at the

original ground level. Glue a drain flange that has a grate on top of it onto the pipe. Re-cover the drain with a cloth while you make the table.

14 | set table base Dig a circular hole, 16 inches in diameter and 18 inches deep, in the center of the pit. Cut a 4-foot-long column from a 10-inch-diameter fiber form used for concrete piers. Stand it in the center of the hole. The top of the form should extend 9 or 10 inches above the flagstone seats.

15 | pour table base Pour concrete mix into the form. Trowel the top surface smooth. Make sure that the column is plumb and the top is level, then let the concrete set for 24 hours before cutting off the form.

Mix another batch of concrete. Fill the hole at the base of the column so that the table is extra sturdy.

After the concrete has set up, remove the cloth from the drain. Fill the bottom of the pit with 3 inches of ¾-inch decorative pebbles. The pebbles will keep the floor of the pit

clean. Because it is larger than the openings in the floor grate, it won't clog the drain.

16 | make tabletop Using a jigsaw, cut a 42-inch circle from a sheet of ¾-inch exterior-grade plywood. Then cut pieces of cement backer board (also called tile backer or fiber-cement underlayment) large enough to cover the plywood. Tightly screw the backer board to the plywood, then cut off any overhang with a jigsaw. The tile backer should mirror the plywood. This backer board forms the base for the mosaic.

17 | prepare plates Choose plates without a lot of curvature or ridges and bumps. They can be old, new, or already broken. Grind off the foot of each plate with a hand grinder. One at a time, set a plate upside down on a piece of plywood. Cover it with a towel and gently break it into pieces with a hammer. Have a friend help you carefully turn over the plywood while firmly holding the towel against the pieces to preserve the shape of the plate.

18 | assemble mosaic With the broken plates and other materials ready, spread a ¼-inch-thick layer of tile mortar over a small section of the backer board with a notched trowel. Reassemble one plate, setting the pieces in the mortar. Continue mortaring small sections and reassembling plates. When you have put all the plates back together, fill the gaps around them with the other mosaic materials you've chosen.

19 | trim edge Smear mortar on the table edge, then place trim tiles all around the edge.

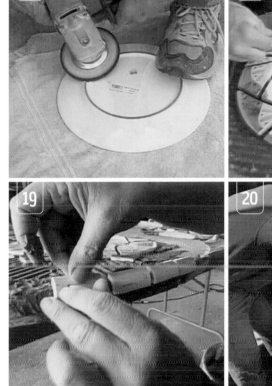

Allow the mosaic to set up overnight. The next day, fill the joints with a tile grout, spreading it on with a grout float. Let the grout dry for about 15 minutes, then carefully wipe off the excess with a damp sponge.

20 | make flange To attach the tabletop to the column, cut a 20-inch diameter disk from a piece of the ¾-inch plywood. Using four concrete anchors, screw it to the top of the concrete column.

21 | complete the table Center the mosaic tabletop on the disk and secure it in place by driving screws from underneath through the disk and into the plywood bottom.

fire pit
add sizzle to your evenings with a backyard fireplace that lights up a yard

Your barbeque grill, as useful as it is, pales before the enjoyment and ambience this flagstone-faced fire pit offers. It's an attractive addition to any landscaping scheme, serving as a graceful gathering point for many evenings of food and fun. For a few hundred dollars more than a grill, you can build a version of this entertainment center just a few steps from your back door.

Designer Nancy Driscoll came up with this design for her own home. It is built low enough that children can easily roast marshmallows and hot dogs, and the flat shelf around it can serve both as seating and as a table surface for food, plates, and accessories. Its style and convenience will also increase the resale value of your property.

Site the fire pit in a spot that's safe—away from outbuildings, overhanging branches, or flammable plantings. If you're concerned that sparks could spread to dry areas, install a hood to serve as a spark arrestor.

The design of this particular unit is simple and straightforward. You'll be working with just two main materials—volcanic rock for the inner liner and flagstone for the veneer

THE MORNING FOG DRIFTS OVER AN EMPTY PATIO (ABOVE).

construct the fire pit

tools & materials

SPECIAL TOOLS: Mason's line, brick trowel, steel finishing trowel, joint striker, masonry hammer

- 2 rebars, ½-inch×14 feet
- Concrete mix
- Volcanic rocks
- Small and medium-size flagstones, 1 to 1½ inches thick
- Extra-large flagstone slabs, 2 inches thick
- 2 metal barbecue grates, 36-inch diameter
- Masonry mortar
- Powdered mortar coloring (optional)
- Liquid concrete bonding adhesive

Building a fire. This rustic 5-foot-diameter fire pit is built from volcanic rock and flagstone in shades of rose, buff, and gray. Volcanic rock is used because it is less expensive than firebrick and doesn't crack like other masonry materials. The pit will have a bottom grate for the charcoal that sits about 6 inches off the ground, and an upper grate 8 to 10 inches above it. Both grates are removable for cleaning. It's important that the upper and lower grates are fairly close together so that the charcoal heats the food.

1 | lay out perimeter Drive a metal stake into the center of the area in which you plan to build the fire pit. Tie one end of a length of mason's line or strong twine to the stake and use the stake as a pivot point as you mark three concentric circles on the lawn.

For the first circle, measure 18 inches from the stake. Draw the circle on the grass with landscaper's paint. This circle is the inside wall of the fire pit.

2 | mark the other circles Next measure and mark 30 inches from the stake for the second circle, which is the outside wall for the fire pit, and 48 inches from the stake for the last circle. This third circle is the outside boundary of

THE SCULPTURAL PRESENCE OF THE FLAGSTONE PIT MAKES IT A FOCAL POINT (ABOVE).

EVENING SHADOWS MEAN IT'S TIME TO FIRE UP THE FIRE PIT (FAR LEFT).

AT NIGHTFALL A WELCOMING FIRE PROMISES WARMTH, CONVERSATION, AND FUN ROASTING HOT DOGS OR MARSHMALLOWS (LEFT).

DESIGN PLANS

goals Create a backyard fire pit and surrounding elements to serve as an inviting and relaxing entertainment area; keep the design casual to complement the informal architecture of the adjoining ranch-style house.

cost $800 if you do it yourself vs. $2,000 for a pro.

time 4 weekends.

difficulty scale
Plan on lots of heavy work, and assemble a crew of friends to help you.

●●●●○

skill scale
Good masonry work requires lots of practice and a knack for troweling mortar.

●●●●○

construct the fire pit

(continued)

an 18-inch-wide flagstone floor that encircles the outside base of the fire pit.

Remove the sod between the first and second circles, then dig it out to form a 6-inch-deep trench for the wall's concrete footing. Also remove the turf at four evenly spaced spots around the inner edge of the footing.

3 | bend rebar Bend each ½-inch rebar into a circle, overlapping the ends by 2 feet. Both circles should be large enough to fit inside the trench, but one should be 4 inches larger in diameter than the other.

4–5 | wire the ring Wire the ends of the rebar together to form a ring. Position the two rings inside the trench. These rings reinforce and strengthen the concrete footing.

6 | pour wall footing Mix a batch of concrete, then pour it into the trench. Smooth the poured concrete with a steel finishing trowel.

7 | place volcanic rock Before the concrete sets up, place a volcanic rock at each spot where you removed sod in the inner ring. The rocks should protrude a couple of inches into the fire pit area. They will support the bottom barbecue grill grate. Make sure these four rocks are level in relation to one another.

8 | lay first course After the concrete dries for 24 hours, set the grate in place and begin laying the first course (row) of volcanic rock around it. Fill the joints between the rocks with masonry mortar, applying it on the sides that will face the outer

wall, which will be hidden by the veneer course.

9 | add supports Eight to 10 inches above the lower grill, set four more volcanic rocks to protrude into the fire pit enough to support the top grate, evenly spacing them around the fire pit. Depending on the size of volcanic rocks you're using, you may need to add a second course before installing these supports. Set the upper grate on the rocks. Finish that course and top it with a final course.

10 | dig trench After the mortar has set up overnight and before you begin adding the flagstone veneer, dig out the space between the outer edge of the fire pit wall and the last paint line—a circle about 18 inches wide and about 3 inches deep.

11 | arrange veneer Lay some pieces of plywood on the ground around the fire pit and prearrange the veneer flagstone on it. You'll find having the pieces at hand and visible will save time and effort as you look for pieces to fit between pieces.

12 | tint mortar Mix mortar, tinting it with powdered coloring to complement the flagstone. Add liquid concrete bonding adhesive to it to improve the bond between the flagstone and the volcanic rock. This adhesive is available at masonry retailers and home supply stores.

Beginning with the bottom course, coat the backs of the flagstone pieces with an inch of mortar. Stack them vertically against the volcanic rock wall. Fill the spaces between the pieces with mortar as you go. If you need to reshape any of the stones, use a masonry hammer to chip off excess chunks. Plan ahead as you proceed upward, so that the uppermost course will be even with the top of the wall.

Top the wall with flat flagstones, adjusting mortar thicknesses to maintain a level plane.

13 | clean up About half an hour after finishing the mortaring, carefully remove the excess from around the joints with a joint striker tool and sponge off the stones. Finally, fill the trench around the fire pit with concrete. Trowel it smooth and let it set up for at least 24 hours.

14 | set flagstone surround Mix a batch of stiff mortar (1 part portland cement to 3 parts sand). Spread it on small sections of the concrete surround. Set flat flagstones in the mortar, tapping them to bed them. Fit as you go, leaving gaps no larger than ½ to ¾ inch between stones. Fill between stones with mortar. Along the wall, fit the stones snugly against the veneer. When finished, remove excess mortar and sponge off the faces of the flagstones with a wet sponge.

15 | lay outside flagstones Surround the fire pit with extra-large flagstone slabs a few feet from the fire pit, experimenting with their placement.

16 | remove sod Once satisfied with the arrangement, slice around the perimeter of each slab with a shovel. Move the slab out of the way, and remove the sod and soil so the cavity is about 1 inch deeper than the slab thickness. Pour an inch of builder's sand into the cavity. Smooth it, then replace the slab, shifting it back and forth to seat it properly.

safe planting ideas Designer Nancy Driscoll has landscaped her fire pit by setting terra-cotta containers of herbs, such as rosemary, thyme, chamomile, cilantro, and parsley, on the large outer stones. She also edges the patio with bedding plants and more container plants to unify the two areas. Driscoll reminds you to keep the plants away from the heat.

index

Note: Page references in **boldface type** refer to building instructions; references in *italic type* indicate photographs or illustrations. Plants are listed by their common names.

A

Accents
    for children's gardens, 150–151, 156, 158
    as focal points, 84
    garden art, *8*, 62, *149, 150,* **155,** 185
    on gates, *12, 64*
    for Italian gardens, 26–28
    mirror mosaic, 104, *104,* **108–109**
Access
    address numbers, 7, *8–9*
    assessing site, 58–59
    front walk, *56,* 58–59
    for gates, *59, 60, 61*
    safety concerns, 55, 56, 58, 178
    side yards, 58, *59*
    tips for enhancing, 8
    See also Lighting; Pathways and walkways
Adam's needle *(Yucca filamentosa),* 91
Address numbers, 7, *8–9*
Air circulation, 38, 40
Air-conditioners, screening, 80, 100, **101**
Algae, controlling, 70
Allium, 148, 127
Anacharis *(Egeria densa),* 76
Angel's trumpet *(Datura),* 159
Annuals
    for children's gardens, 154
    for cottage gardens, 20
    design role, 12
    for dry, windy sites, 135
    maintenance requirements, 12
    for shade gardens, 133
    See also specific annuals
Arbors
    for cottage gardens, 18, *18–19,* 20
    to enhance access, *57, 61, 58,* 58–59, *65, 69*
    and faux gate, 136, **138–141**
    for outdoor office, 194–195, 196–197 *198–199,* **200–201**
    for patios, 172, 188, *188,* **191**
    for privacy, 35
    rebar, 67
    with retractable canopy, 190, **191–193**
    for small yards, 136–137
    trellised bench, 19, 20, **22–25**
    See also Trellises

Arborvitae, 44
Artemisia. *See* Wormwood *(Artemisia)*
Asphodel *(Asphodelus albus),* 28
Aster, 18, 97
Astilbe, 125
Azalea *(Rhododendron),* 133

B

Baby's tears, 58
Bacopa *(Sutera), 96, 96*
Balcony gardens, 30, 35
Bald cypress *(Taxodium distichum),* 76
Balloon flower *(Platycodon grandiflorus),* 97, 156
Bamboo
    building with, tips for, 42
    for children's gardens, 148
    fun facts, 42
    living, tips for growing, 40
Bamboo, heavenly *(Nandina domestica),* 44
Bamboo fences, 40-41, **43**
Bamboo fountains, *38, 46,* **46–47**
Bamboo gutters, *177*
Bamboo wind chimes, 50, **51**
Baptisia. *See* False indigo
Barberry 'Crimson Pigmy' *(Berberis thunbergii),* 14, 125, 135
Barren strawberry *(Waldsteinia ternata),* 68
Barrenwort, red *(Epimedium × rubrum),* 91
Basket-of-gold *(Aurinia saxatilis* 'Gold Ball'), 97, *97*
Bee balm *(Monarda),* 127
Begonia, wax *(Begonia semperflorens-cultorum* hybrids), 133
Benches. *See* Chairs and benches
Bergenia, heart-leaf *(Bergenia cordifolia),* 133
Berger, Dan, 59, 62, 128, 150, 194, 199, 204
Berms
    plants for, 44, 46, 170
    for small yards, 44, 122
    tips for creating, 44–46, **48**
Berries, for seasonal color, 8
Bethlehem sage *(Pulmonaria* 'Sissinghurst White'), 90
Birdbath, 175
Black-eyed Susan *(Rudbeckia),* 28
Blanketflower *(Gaillardia),* 28
Bleeding heart *(Dicentra)*
    D. spectabilis, 133
    fringed *(D. formosa* 'Luxuriant'), 90–91

Blue-eyed grass *(Sisyrinchium angustifolium),* 133
Blue flowers, 97
Blue star creeper *(Laurentia fluviatilis),* 58, 68, *68*
Bluestem, 46
Bog plants, 76
Borders, for paths, *58,* 60, 62, *62,* 63, *63*
Bottles
    hanging candles, 186, *186,* **187**
    ideas for using, 186
Bougainvillea, 126
Boxwood, 36, 39
Bridges, *70–72,* **74–75,** *76*
    design role, 58, *59, 60,* 70
    site selection, 70
Buri (dried palm leaf) screens, 84
Bush violet *(Browallia speciosa),* 133
Butterfly bush *(Buddleia),* 127
Buttonbush *(Cephalanthus occidentalis),* 76

C

Caladium, 125, 159
Calendula, 16, 28
Callaway, Laurie, 26, 27
Camellia 'Setsugekka,' 40
Candles
    bottle, hanging, 186, *186,* **187**
    for decks and patios, 172, *173,* 174, *175, 175,* 178, *178, 181,185,* 186
    for outdoor dining, 172, 173, *179,* 182, *182*
Candytuft *(Iberis)*
    globe *(I. umbellata),* 28
    evergreen *(I. semperflorens-cultorum* 'Little Gem'), 97
Canopies, 170, *172*
    fabric for, 192
    retractable, 188–190, **191–193**
Cardinal flower *(Lobelia cardinalis),* 76, 159
Carnations, 148
Castor bean, 159
Cat mint *(Nepeta),* 121, 127
Cedar, 125
    flammability, 126
Chairs and benches
    on bridges, 58
    as focal points, 8
    stone benches, 26
    trellised bench, **22–25**
Cherry *(Prunus)*
    purple-leaf sand *(P. × cistena* 'Big Cis'), 134
    weeping *(P. serrulata),* 44

USDA plant hardiness zone map

This map of climate zones helps you select plants for your garden that will survive a typical winter in your region. The United States Department of Agriculture (USDA) developed the map, basing the zones on the lowest recorded temperatures across North America. Zone I is the coldest area and Zone II is the warmest. Plants are classified by the coldest temperature and zone they can endure. For example, plants hardy to Zone 6 survive where winter temperatures drop to −10° F. Those hardy to Zone 8 die long before it's that cold. These plants may grow in colder regions but must be replaced each year. Plants rated for a range of hardiness zones can usually survive winter in the coldest region as well as tolerate the summer heat of the warmest one. To find your hardiness zone, note the approximate location of your community on the map, then match the color band marking that area to the key.

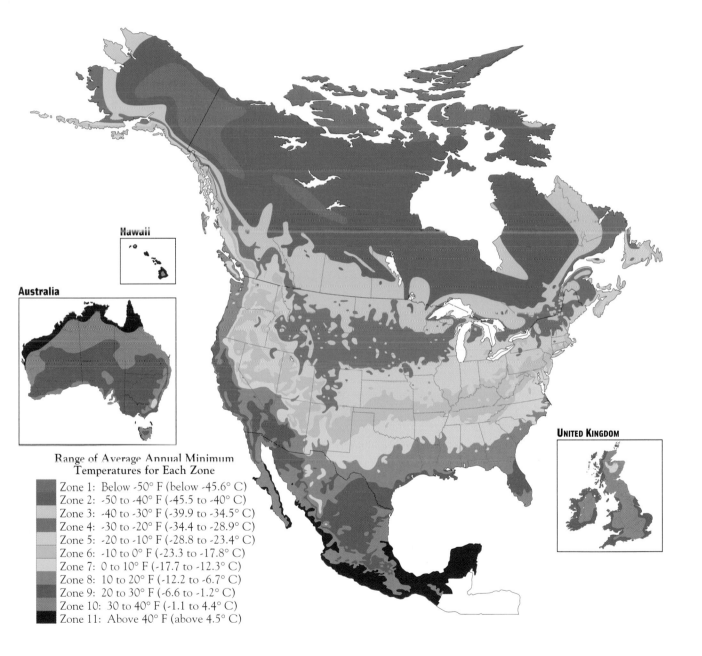

Range of Average Annual Minimum Temperatures for Each Zone

Zone 1: Below -50° F (below -45.6° C)
Zone 2: -50 to -40° F (-45.5 to -40° C)
Zone 3: -40 to -30° F (-39.9 to -34.5° C)
Zone 4: -30 to -20° F (-34.4 to -28.9° C)
Zone 5: -20 to -10° F (-28.8 to -23.4° C)
Zone 6: -10 to 0° F (-23.3 to -17.8° C)
Zone 7: 0 to 10° F (-17.7 to -12.3° C)
Zone 8: 10 to 20° F (-12.2 to -6.7° C)
Zone 9: 20 to 30° F (-6.6 to -1.2° C)
Zone 10: 30 to 40° F (-1.1 to 4.4° C)
Zone 11: Above 40° F (above 4.5° C)

Hawaii

Australia

United Kingdom

designers

Dan Berger
LandPlans Landscaping Inc.
P.O. Box 58
Pleasanton, CA 94566
925/846-1989
www.landplanlandscaping.com

Laurie Callaway
Callaway Garden Design
1524 Dana Ave.
Palo Alto, CA 94303
650/325-1790
Lauriercallaway@aol.com

Jeff Castro
Castro & Associates
37 Terrace Dr.
Concord, CA 94518
925/691-4042

Michelle Derviss
Michelle Derviss Landscapes Designed
1408 Park Avenue
Novato, CA 94945
415/892-3121

Nancy L. Driscoll
Landscape Design-LandArt
Glen Ellen, CA

Cynthia Egger
Landscape Design, Inc.
1928 Fifth Avenue
San Rafael, CA 94901
415/460-0858
www.eggerlandscape.com

Michael Guttman
Mike Guttman Design and Construction
1070 E. Magnolia Blvd.
Burbank, CA 91501
818/842-6642

Bruce Holliday
Pike Family Nursery
4020 Steve Reynolds Blvd.
Norcross, GA 30093
770/921-1022

Kim Kocher
Stonewater Landscapes
110 Railroad Ave., Suite E
Suisun City, CA 94585
707/427-1423

Yoshi Kuraishi
Kuraishi Design
El Cerrito, CA

Louise Leff
Louise Leff Landscape Architecture
504 Webster St.
Petaluma, CA 94952
707/789-0150
www.lefflandscapearchitecture.com

Duncan McIntosh
McIntosh Design
6321 Church St.
Los Angeles, CA 90042
323/254-8762

Peter Parker
Peter Parker Design
1220 Country Club Dr.
Ben Lomond, CA 95005
831/336-2581

Dave Phelps
Gardens & Gables
8 Mabry Way
San Rafael, CA 94903
415/499-0331

Scott Soden
Artscapes
603 Alameda de Las Pulgas
Belmont, CA 94002
650/591-1222

Marguerite Stamos
Defining Spaces Landscape
1078 Point View St.
Los Angeles, CA 90035
323/939-1718

Isis & David Schwartz
Isis and David Schwartz & Associates
219 Shoreline Blvd.
Mill Valley, CA 94941
415/388-5263

Andy Simms
Andy Simms Custom Construction
674 Mariano Court
Sonoma, CA 95476
707/996-6957
www.simmsconstruction.com

LIGHTING DESIGNERS

Randall Whitehead
Randall Whitehead Lighting Inc.
1246 – 18th Street
San Francisco, CA 94107
415/626-1277
www.randallwhitehead.com

credits

HGTV® Landscape Makeovers
Editor: Marilyn Rogers
Writers: Kathy Barberich, David Haupert, Jan Riggenbach
Contributing Assistant Editor: Diane A. Witosky
Senior Associate Design Director: John Eric Seid
Contributing Graphic Designer: Theresa Cowan
Contributing Prop Stylist: Susan Strelecki
Copy Chief: Terri Fredrickson
Copy and Production Editor: Victoria Forlini
Editorial Operations Manager: Karen Schirm
Managers, Book Production: Pam Kvitne, Marjorie J. Schenkelberg, Rick von Holdt, Mark Weaver
Contributing Copy Editor: Sharon E. McHaney
Contributing Proofreaders: Mary Duerson, Fran Gardner, Holly Gilliland, Sara Henderson, Margaret Smith
Indexer: Ellen Davenport
Contributing Researcher: Rosemary Kautzky
Editorial and Design Assistants: Mary Lee Gavin, Karen McFadden, Kathleen Stevens

Meredith® Books
Editor in Chief: Linda Raglan Cunningham
Design Director: Matt Strelecki
Executive Editor, Home Improvement and Gardening: Benjamin W. Allen
Executive Editor, Gardening: Michael McKinley

Publisher: James D. Blume
Executive Director, Marketing: Jeffrey Myers
Executive Director, New Business Development: Todd M. Davis
Executive Director, Sales: Ken Zagor
Director, Operations: George A. Susral
Director, Production: Douglas M. Johnston
Business Director: Jim Leonard

Vice President and General Manager: Douglas J. Guendel

Meredith Publishing Group
President, Publishing Group: Stephen M. Lacy
Vice President-Publishing Director: Bob Mate

Meredith Corporation
Chairman and Chief Executive Officer: William T. Kerr

In Memoriam: E. T. Meredith III (1933-2003)

All of us at **Meredith® Books** are dedicated to providing you with information and ideas to enhance your home and garden. We welcome your comments and suggestions. Write to us at: **Meredith Books, Garden Editorial Department, 1716 Locust St., Des Moines, IA 50309-3023**.

If you would like to purchase any of our gardening, cooking, crafts, home improvement, or home decorating and design books, check wherever quality books are sold. Or visit us at: **meredithbooks.com**.

For more information on the topics included in this book as well as additional projects, visit **HGTV.com** or **HGTV.com/landscapemakeoversbook**.

All location photography is by Rob Cardillo, Rob Cardillo Photography, assisted by Tim Teahan

Photographers: (Photographers credited retain copyright © to the listed photographs.) L = Left, R = Right, C = Center, B = Bottom, T = Top

Mark Bolton/Garden Picture Library: 60BL
Densey Clyne/Garden Picture Library: 80R
R. Todd Davis: 122T, 125R
Catriona Tudor Erler: 80L, 123BR, 175T
Derek Fell: 156L, 159C
John Glover: 39L (Design: Alan Titchmarsh), 40R, 146L, 148C (Design: Sarah Eberle), 149BR
John Glover/Garden Picture Library: 30
Harry Haralambou/Positive Images: 97TL
Jerry Harpur: 149TR
Marcus Harpur: 133BR, 157
Jerry Howard/Positive Images: 44BR
Saxon Holt: 4, 51C, 97TR, 120, 125L, 126-127, 156C, 158R
Rosemary Kautzky: 57B, 60TL, 60BR, 81R
Donna Krischan: 106B
Dwight Kuhn: 81TL
Andrew Lawson: 91C, 127L (Designer: Naila Green), 148L (Burton Agnes Hall), 149I, 159R
Janet Loughrey: 2R, 45BR, 168-169
Charles Mann: 134-135
Keeyla Meadows/Positive Images: 5TL, 83
Clive Nichols: 32B (Designer: Penny Smith); 56BR (Designer: Jill Billington); 147B, 158L (Clare Matthews); 159L; 175C (Joe Swift)
Mayer/LeScanff/Garden Picture Library: 37TR
Jerry Pavia: 56TR, 58L, 91L, 156R
Ben Phillips/Positive Images: 133TR, 135BR
Richard Shiell: 45BL, 97TC, 122B, 134L, 134R
Pam Spaulding/Positive Images: 38T, 127R
Michael Thompson: 133TL, 174L
Mark Turner: 171L
Deidra Walpole: 135BL
Justyn Willsmore: 91R, 97B, 124L, 132-133, 148R

Special thanks to: Janet Anderson, Staci Bailey, Tonya Hall

Cover Photograph: Rob Cardillo.

Note to the Readers: Due to differing conditions, tools, and individual skills, Meredith Corporation assumes no responsibility for any damages, injuries suffered, or losses incurred as a result of following the information published in this book. Before beginning any project, review the instructions carefully, and if any doubts or questions remain, consult local experts or authorities. Because codes and regulations vary greatly, you always should check with authorities to ensure that your project complies with all applicable local codes and regulations. Always read and observe all of the safety precautions provided by manufacturers of any tools, equipment, or supplies, and follow all accepted safety procedures.

HOME & GARDEN TELEVISION

metric conversions

U.S. UNITS TO METRIC EQUIVALENTS

To Convert From	Multiply By	To Get
Inches	25.4	Millimeters
Inches	2.54	Centimeters
Feet	30.48	Centimeters
Feet	0.3048	Meters
Yards	0.9144	Meters
Square inches	6.4516	Square centimeters
Square feet	0.0929	Square meters
Square yards	0.8361	Square meters
Acres	0.4047	Hectares
Cubic inches	16.387	Cubic centimeters
Cubic feet	0.0283	Cubic meters
Cubic feet	28.316	Liters
Cubic yards	0.7646	Cubic meters
Cubic yards	764.55	Liters

To convert from degrees Fahrenheit (F) to degrees Celsius (C), first subtract 32, then multiply by $5/9$.

METRIC UNITS TO U.S. EQUIVALENTS

To Convert From	Multiply By	To Get
Millimeters	0.0394	Inches
Centimeters	0.3937	Inches
Centimeters	0.0328	Feet
Meters	3.2808	Feet
Meters	1.0936	Yards
Square centimeters	0.1550	Square inches
Square meters	10.764	Square feet
Square meters	1.1960	Square yards
Hectares	2.4711	Acres
Cubic centimeters	0.0610	Cubic inches
Cubic meters	35.315	Cubic feet
Liters	0.0353	Cubic feet
Cubic meters	1.308	Cubic yards
Liters	0.0013	Cubic yards

To convert from degrees Celsius to degrees Fahrenheit, multiply by $9/5$, then add 32.